IMPERIAL WARRIOR

By the same author

*The Golden Warrior: the life and legend
of Lawrence of Arabia*

*The Iron Duke: a military biography
of the Duke of Wellington*

IMPERIAL WARRIOR

The Life and Times of
FIELD-MARSHAL
VISCOUNT ALLENBY
1861–1936

LAWRENCE JAMES

Weidenfeld and Nicolson
London

Copyright © 1993 by Lawrence James
First published in Great Britain by
George Weidenfeld and Nicolson Limited
The Orion Publishing Group
5 Upper St Martin's Lane
London WC2H 9EA

British Library Cataloguing in Publication Data is available

ISBN 0 297 81152 5

Photoset by Deltatype Ltd, Ellesmere Port, Cheshire
Printed in Great Britain by
Butler & Tanner Ltd, Frome and London

CONTENTS

ILLUSTRATIONS

With King Albert of the Belgians, near Arras, spring 1917 (*Imperial War Museum*)

British infantry move up to the front for the Arras offensive, April 1917 (*Imperial War Museum*)

A British tank, Arras, April 1917 (*Imperial War Museum*)

British cavalry, Arras, April 1917 (*Imperial War Museum*)

Turkish riflemen and machine-gun crew at Beersheba, 1917 (*Imperial War Museum*)

Australian light horsemen charging at Beersheba, 31 October 1917 (*Australian War Memorial*)

The mayor of Jerusalem surrenders his city (*Imperial War Museum*)

'The Last Crusade' – Bernard Partridge's *Punch* cartoon (*Punch*)

Australian Flying Corps machines in Palestine, 1918 (*Australian War Memorial*)

A Lewis-gun section of British infantry, Palestine, 1918 (*Imperial War Museum*)

T. E. Lawrence, 1928 (Photo: Fl.-Lt. Smetham; *National Portrait Gallery*)

Allenby during the advance on Damascus, September 1918 (*Liddell Hart*)

Australian Light Horse following the road to Aleppo, October 1918 (*Australian War Memorial*)

Allenby and his wife in Cairo, 1922 (*Liddell Hart*)

Lord and Lady Allenby in the Residency Gardens, Cairo, with his pet Maribou stork (*Liddell Hart*)

Allenby is driven through the streets of Cairo at the time of the riots (*Liddell Hart*)

'The Strong Man and the Diplomat' – Bernard Partridge's 1922 *Punch* cartoon of Allenby and Lord Curzon (*Punch*)

The author and publishers wish to thank the above copyright owners for permission to reproduce the pictures.

MAPS

Drawn by John Gilkes

INTRODUCTION

ON 10 December 1917 an official camera crew filmed General Sir Edmund Allenby as he walked through Jerusalem, the city that had surrendered to his army the day before. It was an historic moment, which would soon be seen in cinemas in every Allied country, and the tall, sturdily built British general held the centre of the stage. Among the supporting actors, the throng of officers who marched in his train, was Major Thomas Edward Lawrence. Over forty years later the two men again appeared on the screen together, but this time the roles were reversed. In the epic *Lawrence of Arabia*, the major had moved to the centre of attention while his commander was reduced to a supporting character. If Allenby has any place in our consciousness today, it is as the bluff, amiable general played by Jack Hawkins who gives Lawrence and the Arabs encouragement and the wherewithal to wage a modern war.

And yet it had been Allenby, who on his return to England in the autumn of 1919, had been hailed as a hero as he was driven through London. He had in the course of eighteen months defeated the Turks in two major battles, conquered Palestine, Syria and the Lebanon, delivered the blow which finally ended 400 years of Ottoman supremacy in the Middle East, and had just crushed an insurrection in Egypt. These were considerable achievements by any standards. Comparisons were drawn between Allenby's campaigns in the Holy Land and the Crusades, 800 years before, and his success was compared with the noble failure of Richard the Lionheart.

But a romantic war required a romantic hero. Allenby was temperamentally unfitted for such a role, for he looked and sounded too much like that breed of generals which had presided over the mass slaughter of the Western Front. It was Lawrence, a far younger, more glamorous figure, who caught the imagination of a public which, after the war, came to mistrust and deride the professional officer caste from which Allenby came. At its bitterest this mood was expressed by Lawrence's biographer, Robert Graves, whose regiment had been part of Allenby's command in France during 1916. 'We used to wonder in the trenches whether the real dirt about our bugbears, the generals and the politicians, would ever come out while we were still alive,' he wrote in a review of Leon Wolff's *Flanders Fields* (*Observer*, 1 March 1959).

My own interest in Allenby was aroused when writing a biography of Lawrence. Lawrence's admiration for his superior was sincere and he always treated him with respectful deference, which was unusual. For these reasons, a few percipient remarks apart, Allenby remains something of a cipher in Lawrence's writings. I have tried to make amends by telling Allenby's story, looking at the ideas and forces that shaped his life and thought and offering a revaluation of the man and the general.

It has not been an easy task, for Allenby was an intensely private man. His diaries were lost shortly after his death and his letters seldom reveal anything of the inner man. He never engaged in those post-war campaigns of vindication and vilification waged by his fellow commanders in their memoirs. He thought the business unseemly, had no taste for factional intrigue, and was usually circumspect in his judgements of others. I have therefore relied heavily on the recollections and observations of those who knew and served with him, in particular the not always favourable reminiscences gathered by his first biographer, Field-Marshal Lord Wavell.

Wavell subtitled his life of Allenby the soldier 'A Study in Greatness' and, out of affection for a profoundly admired comrade and kindness towards his widow, repressed much hostile material, largely concerning Allenby's conduct and performance in France. I have included this, and related evidence which sheds much light on the pressures and tensions within the British High Command and on the slow and often painful way in which Allenby and his fellow generals learned the techniques of modern warfare.

In truth, Allenby was not a 'modern' general, although he assimilated what he needed to know about the new technology of warfare and how to use it. He was in essence an 'imperial' general who flourished fighting the traditional wars of empire. He fought these as a young man in South Africa, and in middle age his victories won Britain a new dependency,

Palestine, and over twenty years of supremacy in the Middle East. Artillery, aeroplanes, armoured cars and wireless played their part, perhaps the most important, but Allenby the cavalryman believed, as did many others, that horsemen had been the key to his success. Most of his horsemen were Australians and New Zealanders, for Allenby commanded an imperial army with contingents from India and the West Indies besides the British and Anzac troops.

The imperial general's career ended on a note of paradox. A man noted for firmness, and feared for the ferocious temper which gave him the nickname 'the Bull', became the High Commissioner who was willing to accommodate Egyptian nationalism. Rigid Imperialists believed he had shown a dangerous failure of nerve. But Allenby was always inconsistent. In private he was a congenial, intelligent and widely read conversationalist at a time when such accomplishments were uncommon among senior officers, and an able naturalist. By contrast, the official man was often a short-tempered and minatorial martinet who frightened his subordinates. In this form he appears as the fictional general 'The Buffalo' in C. S. Forester's excellent study of First World War command, *The General*, which was published in 1936, the year of Allenby's death.

I have included this flaw in Allenby's character, as well as his virtues, in what I hope is a measured assessment of a long, sometimes controversial and hitherto neglected life. I hope as a result Allenby may, as he did in Jerusalem in 1917, take his place in the foreground of history.

Lawrence James
St Andrews, July 1992

ACKNOWLEDGEMENTS

I WISH to thank the following for their kind assistance and advice: Dr Allen Bell, Dr Ian Bradley, Dr Gerard de Groot, Hilary Laurie, Rosemary Legge, Andrew Lownie, Jane and Nicholas Roe, Kate and Brian Waldy, Andrew Williams, Vivian Williams, and many others who have given their time and help. Special thanks are due to my wife, Mary and sons, Edward and Henry. I am also indebted to Patricia Methven, Kate O'Brien and Marie Stuart of the Liddell Hart Centre for their patience, good humour and invaluable assistance; also the staff of the Bodleian Library, Oxford, St Andrews University Library, the National Library of Scotland, and the Public Record Office, all of whom have been extremely patient and accommodating.

I am grateful to the Trustees of the Liddell Hart Centre for Military Archives for permission to use and quote from the papers of Lord Allenby, Sir Basil Liddell Hart and Brigadier-General Sir James Edmonds, and to the Meinertzhagen Trustees for passages from Colonel Richard Meinertzhagen's Diary. Quotations from Crown Copyright records in the Public Record Office appear by permission of the Controller of Her Majesty's Stationary Office.

PART 1

IMPERIAL WARRIOR

1861–1902

CHAPTER 1

A VICTORIAN UPBRINGING

1861–1882

EDMUND Henry Hynman Allenby was born on 23 April 1861, St George's Day, the second child and eldest son of Hynman Allenby, a Norfolk landowner. Squire Allenby was a gentlemen of good pedigree who lived comfortably from his rents and was free to indulge his tastes as he chose. He had purchased estates at West Walton, Outwell and West Bilney, in the western parts of Norfolk, during the mid-Victorian years of 'high farming' when agriculture prospered; in 1871 his annual income was £1,500. He owned two houses, one at Felixstowe, then a small fishing village where his family spent the summer, and another at West Bilney where they stayed through the winter.

This choice of homes was dictated by Squire Allenby's passions. At Felixstowe he sailed and at West Bilney he rode, shot and fished, the traditional pursuits of the country gentleman. His family roots lay in neighbouring Lincolnshire, where the Allenbys had been people of some account for over 200 years. His wife came from similar stock; Catherine Anne Cane was the daughter of a Nottinghamshire squarson who preached the gospel, bred livestock, fished and dispensed justice from the bench. It was at his house at Brackenhurst that Edmund Allenby was born.

The novelist Anthony Trollope, who knew and wrote about such families, would have described Squire Allenby as 'the first man in his parish', that is, a substantial landowner whose influence never reached beyond the boundaries of his own property. Hynman Allenby had no ambition to cut a figure in county society, nor did he seek those public offices and responsibilities that were usually undertaken by men of his birth. As a young man he had studied at Cambridge, left without a degree and then dallied with medicine. Once in possession of his fortune, his easy nature took over and he was content to live the life of a backwoodsman, dedicated to sharing with his family the delights of boats and country living.

Mrs Allenby, who died in 1922 aged ninety-one, was a more practical creature. She ran the affairs of the household and appears to have had a considerable influence over her son who, throughout his life, wrote her accounts of his activities. Like her husband she was a devout Christian, and in later years Edmund attributed his achievements to a text he had learned from her, 'Whatsoever thy hand findeth to do, do it with thy might' (Ecclesiastes, 9:10). A straightforward Puritan saw, and one fitting for a man who could claim a very distant kinship with Oliver Cromwell and his son-in-law, Henry Ireton. Like these generals, Allenby regularly read the Bible, but unlike them and his contemporary Douglas Haig (later Field-Marshal Earl Haig) he never went as far as to believe himself an instrument of Divine Providence. Allenby was, however, profoundly affected by the ideal of adherence to duty and the virtue of hard work implicit in his mother's guiding precept. Many years later there were echoes of simple truths learned in the nursery in his advice to a junior officer, 'Always do something. You may be right, if you do nothing you cannot be.'[1]

Allenby was not given to self-analysis or speculation about the validity of the values he had absorbed as he grew up. In 1900, he gave away a little of his inner self in a letter to his wife on the upbringing of their only son Michael, then aged two. Memories of parrot-like recitals of prayers may have prompted him to caution her against making the boy pray until he was old enough to understand the meaning of the words he was using. He also observed, revealing much of what he had accepted in his own youth, that his son should be brought up in that 'cheerful obedience that is itself really *religion*'. He concluded, perhaps again remembering his own childhood, 'I think a child's parents should stand to him as an ideal.'[2]

His obviously were, and he had a happy, carefree boyhood which was one outcome of using 'cheerful obedience' as a rough guide to how he should behave. His parents fostered an interest in the natural world which lasted throughout his life and gave him a pleasurable distraction from often tedious duties. Whenever the opportunity occurred he would go in search of plants and birds; during a short break from campaigning in

South Africa in 1901 he told his wife, 'I walked about the kloofs [valleys] looking at dicky birds and insects'. Another letter home, this time from the Western Front in 1915, included details of nightingales' nests in a wood close by the trenches.[3] This interest in botany and ornithology must have appeared incongruous in a general notorious for his hectoring and acerbic manner.

Young Allenby also learned how to shoot, ride, sail and swim, shared his father's musical interests (years later there were concerts at his HQ in France), and developed into a competent draughtsman. His early education followed no pattern, and was largely received from his parents and local clergymen who satisfied the curiosity and awakened the enthusiasms of a lively and intelligent boy.

There was no need for Edmund Allenby to acquire more knowledge than was necessary for a gentleman to hold the respect of his equals or pursue any one of the scientific or antiquarian diversions then so popular among the rural gentry. Nevertheless, in 1875, Hynman Allenby decided to follow a comparatively new fashion and send his son to public school. He himself had been educated by private tutors and for generations men like him had despatched their sons to country grammar schools, a practice that was fast dying out. Instead the gentry, and for that matter the growing professional and commercial classes, were turning to public schools. Hynman Allenby chose Haileybury in south Hertfordshire, a former training school for East India Company administrators and officers that had been resuscitated in 1862. When Allenby arrived at Bartle Frere House (named after the proconsul whose management of Natal's affairs would shortly lead to the Zulu War) the school's laundry and bakehouse had just been built and work on the mock-Gothic main school, chapel and fives court, was in its final stages.

Not only the buildings at Haileybury were new. Allenby's headmaster, the Reverend Edward Bradby, like his equivalents at similar schools, was an apostle of the new philosophy of education created forty years earlier by Dr Thomas Arnold of Rugby. The principles applied by Arnold and broadcast by schoolmasters who had served under him had come to dominate the entire public-school system by the 1870s. The importance of Arnoldian doctrines extended far beyond school bounds and permeated every area of British public life well into the twentieth century. In particular, they left an indelible stamp on the thinking of generations of men who, like Allenby, occupied the highest positions in the state. Nowhere was this more obvious than in the Army where, throughout the First World War, British troops were commanded by generals imbued with Arnoldian attitudes. The patterns of thought of Allenby (Haileybury,

1870s), Haig (Clifton, 1870s), Sir Henry Wilson (Marlborough, 1880s), Sir Horace Smith-Dorrien (Harrow, 1870s), Sir Archibald Murray (Cheltenham, 1870s), Sir Henry Rawlinson, Sir Julian Byng, Sir Herbert Plumer and Sir Hubert Gough (Eton, 1870s and 1880s) all owed much to what they had heard in schoolroom and chapel and, above all, experienced on the playing field.

This was exactly what Arnold and his missionaries had intended. All believed that it was their highest duty to instil into their pupils a code of conduct and morals that would transform them into strong, healthy Christian gentlemen who would serve their country. This process was designed to mould 'character', an abstraction whose ingredients were courage, fortitude, integrity, selflessness, continence and, most importantly, a manly Christian faith.

Many, perhaps the majority of the young men who underwent this preparation for life came from backgrounds like Allenby's, where the right to rule others had always been taken for granted. Historically, gentlemen were expected to devote some at least of their leisure to public service, and they and their offspring had always directed the nation's government, made and enforced the law, and commanded armies and navies. By the mid-nineteenth century this pattern was changing; during the lifetime of Allenby's father (he had been born in 1822) the landed class's monopoly of power had been challenged and Britain was edging slowly towards democracy. Rather than lose all their powers, the traditional ruling elite opened their ranks and thereby agreed to share authority with the expanding middle classes who drew their wealth from commerce and the professions. In turn, this alliance gave way to pressure from below and, by 1885, most working men had been given the vote. At the same time the middle classes were getting control over the machinery of government which had hitherto been operated exclusively by men with landed connections. When Allenby joined the Army in 1880, nearly every senior officer had paid for his commission, a practice that had only been abolished ten years earlier.

Against this background, Arnold and his acolytes devised educational theories designed to produce a new breed of leaders whose authority derived from the virtue of their 'character' rather than birth and ancestry. For this reason schools like Haileybury attracted thousands of middle-class boys whose fathers were anxious for them to become assimilated into the world of gentlemen. In effect, Arnold and his disciples had given a new lease of life to the old social order at the same time as giving young men from the upper and middle classes a set of common values.

So, in 1875, Allenby found himself in a school where every activity was dedicated to the development of his character along lines that assumed he would eventually occupy some position of authority. Pure ambition was discouraged since, according to the Arnoldian creed, the opportunity to undertake a duty and its fulfilment were the highest rewards a man could expect. This selfless example was set by Allenby's own headmaster, who retired in mid-career and afterwards devoted himself to the regeneration of the slum-dwellers of London's East End.

Lessons of altruism and devotion to higher causes were taught in the chapel and on the playing field. The sermon's message was expounded on the rugger pitch or cricket square, where young men learned that what mattered most was playing the game for its own sake, rather than winning. What drove the player to the limits of skill and endurance was loyalty to his captain, team-mates, house and school. Moral stamina was more vital then physical, since learning how to 'play the game' involved perseverance, the suppression of individual will and its replacement by team spirit, and keeping up an outward jauntiness in the face of injury and defeat. There were plenty of lessons in 'cheerful obedience' for Allenby on Haileybury's playing fields and he learned them, although his heart was never in team games; selected for house teams, he never reached the Olympian heights of the First XV or First XI.

Self-control was necessary before one could control others. The public school prefectorial system, which lay at the heart of Arnold's ideals, prepared a boy for the responsibilities of manhood. Despite never getting beyond his house team, Allenby showed enough inner resources to be chosen by his headmaster as a prefect. Over sixty years later, a junior boy recalled that Allenby 'had no difficulties with discipline, which he exercised without harshness'. Another remembered that he 'could be rough and almost fierce, but he was always noble and fair'. A third wrote that Allenby did not create much impression on 'us small fry', but added 'I just dimly remember him as a big fellow leaning up against the mantelpiece of the fire at the end of the Dormitory'.[4] His large size and sturdy frame were assets, since they gave him protection from the bully, a pest that survived in all public schools despite the Arnoldian Revolution. Indeed, there were some who saw bullying as a positive aid to character-building, a view that was offered to boys at his old school by General Sir Charles Warren, Allenby's commander in Bechuanaland. 'You must have a rough time. I got badly bullied for a short time . . . and I thank heaven that it occurred,' he told his audience, who probably excused this twaddle on the grounds of the speaker's senility. He was ninety-two.[5]

This was an extreme statement of the prevalent belief that character was enhanced by suffering knocks, preferably on the playing field. This and much else within the Arnoldian philosophy inevitably led to boys leaving school with dulled sensibilities, limited critical faculties and a hearty philistinism. Imagination and creativity were frowned on and intelligence only encouraged when it could be channelled into the study of moribund languages. Even Latin and Greek were pushed into second place by sporting prowess; as a fictional Rugbeian exclaimed in Thomas Hughes's *Tom Brown's Schooldays*, 'I know I'd sooner win two School-house matches running than get a Balliol scholarship any day.'

How did Allenby fare in this world? He played but never relished team games and, while strong, was not an outstanding athlete. His con-temporaries recalled an agreeable boy with a sense of humour and an 'ironic' smile, who was intelligent and happiest when reading.[6] He won none of the many prizes for Classics, but his schoolmasters thought him bright enough to attempt the rigorous examination for the Indian Civil Service.

The need to earn a living in one of the professions then considered fitting for a gentleman had been forced on Allenby by the death of his father in February 1878. He died at the beginning of an extended agricultural depression so his Norfolk estates were sold at a loss, leaving his widow and children in marginally reduced circumstances. The house in Felixstowe was retained and Edmund, while he had a small private income, had no choice but to find an occupation.

Despite the intensive efforts at two crammers, he failed the 1879 and 1880 Indian Civil Service examinations, although he did well the second time round in the face of formidable competition. Disheartened, he followed a friend's advice and sought an Army commission. It was a natural choice for a young man of his talents, and had been taken by over a quarter of the boys who had come up to Haileybury with him in 1875. The examination for the Royal Military College at Sandhurst was widely known not to be taxing; indeed, thirty years later one candidate remarked that it was common knowledge that 'no one fails Sandhurst'.[7] In 1880 Allenby, clearly well above the average ability of Sandhurst aspirants, passed fifth into the college.

The progression from public school to officer cadet was a conventional one for young men of Allenby's background and cast of mind. In most respects Sandhurst was an extension of schools such as Haileybury, since the ethos of the Arnoldian public school was universally recognised as an ideal one for the potential officer, giving him the physical toughness and moral qualities needed for leadership. 'Public school spirit and public spirit are almost synonymous expressions' observed a Guards officer in 1911 and, for this reason, the Army welcomed droves of public-schoolmen. He added, revealingly, that while Continental officers were better taught and were masters of their profession, they 'cannot compare with our own dash, initiative and commonsense'.[8]

Champions of the public-school officer always emphasised character as the key to his achievements and underplayed, even sniffed at, intelligence. In 1892 an officer wrote that the dull man could often show astonishing courage and presence of mind on the battlefield, and that experience as a school prefect meant that the new officer understood perfectly how to treat the rank and file, who were just like junior schoolboys. Just as small boys looked up to the heroes of the playing field, so rankers admired sporting officers.[9] Another officer praised the 'eminently manly and healthy pastimes of polo, cricket and shooting', which were vital 'to develop qualities of mind and body that are priceless in war'. Such exercises were 'as good a training for a campaign as much poring over textbooks of strategy'.[10]

Such views were held at all levels. In his autobiography, General Sir Hubert ('Goughie') Gough devoted more words to his hunting exploits at Sandhurst than to what he learned there, which was little. Not that this mattered greatly, for a few years later he discovered that the commandant at Aldershot, General Sir Evelyn Wood (who had won a VC in the Crimea), cherished 'sporting' officers above all others.[11] An alumnus of the theoretically more professional college at Woolwich, where Gunner officers learned their craft, dismissed what he studied there with the remark, 'An officer needs to know how to use a gun, not make one.'[12]

All this made much sense, at least to the officers of Allenby's generation for whom war meant Imperial campaigns of conquest and pacification waged against native armies whose reckless bravery, stamina and fieldcraft never wholly compensated for their outdated weapons. During the Zulu War of 1879, a young officer wrote from the front that the campaign was 'like a shooting expedition, with just the spice of danger thrown in to make it really interesting'.[13] When danger threatened in the form of a charging Zulu impi or a Pathan ambush on the North-West Frontier, then the devil-may-care gallantry of the sporting officer could inspire his men and save the day. Moreover, the fit, muscular officer was always at an advantage during long marches and rides across rough country on thin rations.

Allenby was never completely in the grip of the sporting mania although he rode frequently, but with more enthusiasm than skill. Lieutenant-General Sir William Furse, who watched him ride at Staff College in 1896–7, was reminded of a remark he had once heard from a Woolwich riding-master, 'Fat arse and big thighs never assist horsemanship.'[14] Despite these physical drawbacks, Allenby persisted with polo until 1889, when a bad fall injured his shoulder, and both before and after the accident he regularly competed in regimental races. He hunted in England and Ireland until 1905, when the pressure of meeting his son's school fees forced him to give up.

In many respects Allenby was ideally suited for the late-Victorian Army. His birth and upbringing made it easy for him to exist within the society of gentlemen and his education had extolled loyalty, service to others, conformity and the comradeship of the team. These were the ingredients of character, and those who knew Allenby later agreed that he possessed this quality to a high degree. He also possessed considerable native intelligence and, soon after he was commissioned, he struck a brother-officer as far better read and informed than others in his mess. That these accomplishments were unusual says much about the institutions that shaped Allenby's youth and his own strength of character, since nether Haileybury nor Sandhurst strove to promote intellectual curiosity.

The ideal to which Allenby's generation aspired was set down by Sir Henry Newbolt in his 'Vitaï Lampada', a poem the first two verses of which likened the cricket square at Clifton College to the killing ground of the Sudanese desert.

> There's a breathless hush in the Close to-night—
> Ten to make and the match to win—
> A bumping pitch and a blinding light,
> An hour to play and the last man in.
> And it's not for the sake of a ribboned coat,
> Or the selfish hope of a season's fame,
> But his Captain's hand on his shoulder smote—
> 'Play up! play up! and play the game!'
>
> The sand of the desert is sodden red,—
> Red with the wreck of a square that broke;—
> The Gatling's jammed and the Colonel dead,
> And the regiment blind with dust and smoke.
> The river of death has brimmed his banks,
> And England's far, and Honour a name,
> But the voice of a schoolboy rallies the ranks:
> 'Play up! play up! and play the game!'

In time that schoolboy, and many like him, would be promoted. Middle-aged generals in 1914, they would find themselves, as Allenby did, in command of mass armies fighting a modern war against adversaries equipped with sophisticated weaponry. How these generals, the subalterns of the 1870s and 1880s, reacted to this task was largely conditioned by codes of behaviour and habits of mind cultivated at their public schools, at Sandhurst, and in their regimental messes.

Allenby entered the closed world of the regiment in May 1882 when he was commissioned as a subaltern in the 6th (Inniskilling) Dragoons, which were then stationed in South Africa. Six months earlier he had passed out twelfth from Sandhurst, where he had struck his fellow cadets as a taciturn, thoughtful fellow whose temperament was reflected in his favourite pastime, fishing. He found no difficulty in joining in the relaxed, sport-dominated society of his brother dragoon officers where, in the words of one, all thoughts 'centred mainly on polo and racing' and it was commonly assumed 'that the army was maintained chiefly for the amusement of junior officers'.[15]

CHAPTER 2

A SOLDIER OF THE QUEEN

1882–1896

IN July 1882, the newly commissioned Allenby collected a handful of Inniskilling recruits from the cavalry depot at Canterbury and took ship for Durban, where for the past fourteen months his regiment had formed part of the Natal garrison. The Inniskillings were a cavalry regiment and therefore enjoyed social prestige and glamour, but they were not considered 'smart'. So Allenby, with limited private means, would not find himself discountenanced by having to keep up with the ostentatious living that was *de rigueur* for a young officer in a more fashionable regiment, nor would he have to maintain an over-large stable. In fact, on arrival in South Africa he prudently distanced himself from the hard-drinking set in his mess, although then and later he relished food and drink and smoked cigarettes heavily.[1]

Colonial garrison duty in temperate Natal was a very satisfactory form of service for a young officer, allowing him considerable spare time in which to ride, hunt, shoot or follow whatever indulgence took his fancy. Allenby fitted well into the social life of his mess, carried out his routine duties efficiently, was a firm but just disciplinarian, and was regarded by his colleagues as a pleasant fellow with a good sense of humour.

South Africa offered not only an agreeable way of life, it presented opportunities for professional advancement. If the colony's history during the past eighty years was anything to go by, Allenby could expect some active service during his regiment's tour of duty. The ladder of promotion was most swiftly climbed by officers who had proved their courage and resourcefulness fighting the small wars of empire, and these had been plentiful in southern Africa. Lord Roberts, Sir Garnet Wolseley, Evelyn Wood, and Redvers Buller, all coming men in the Army of the 1880s, had served their apprenticeships-at-arms in colonial wars in India and Africa where they had gained experience and public recognition. This was the age of the war correspondent whose front-line reports, conveyed by telegraph, satisfied a growing newspaper readership which relished the vicarious excitement of Imperial campaigns and idolised victorious generals. Officers were, however, uneasy about reporters who could publicise blunders as well as gallant deeds, but they could not ignore or muzzle them. When one commander refused information to a journalist during a frontier campaign in the 1890s, he was bluntly told, 'Remember I can make or mar you.'[2]

Southern Africa was an ideal place for Allenby to learn practical soldiering, and he could also, like other ambitious young officers, earn coveted campaign medals. Their iconography provides a fascinating insight into Victorian Imperialism; those awarded for South African service in 1853 and 1877–9 show a prowling lion; the same beast, roused to fury, tramples on native shields and assegais on the Rhodesian War Medal of 1896.

There had been little rest for the British lion since 1806, when Cape Colony had been annexed. The region was a boiling pot of political and racial antagonisms which created conditions of chronic instability and intermittent wars. The indigenous Afrikaner colonists – the Boers – wanted independence from the British colonial government, which in turn was unwilling to allow them a free hand with natives or to let them settle wherever they liked. By 1850, substantial numbers of Boers had withdrawn from the Cape and the recently established Natal Colony and set up the inland republics of the Orange Free State and the Transvaal. There was also continual friction between the authorities and the black population. The white man's land-hunger and demand for cheap labour eroded tribal lands and disrupted traditional patterns of life. Clashes of interest between the races led to a prolonged series of bush wars. British forces, backed by locally recruited volunteers, black and white, always kept the upper hand, but tensions between the authorities, natives and Afrikaners remained.

In 1877, five years before Allenby's arrival, the region exploded again with a spate of native rebellions. There were uprisings of Xhosas, Gcalekas, Ngquikas and Mpondoes in the eastern Cape; a Griqua revolt in the north, close to the new Kimberley diamond fields; and in the

Transvaal Afrikaner dominance was challenged by the Bapedi and Basotho. For a time the fragile and penniless Boer state seemed on the verge of collapse – one of its kommandos (a force of volunteer, mounted riflemen) had been beaten by the Bapedi in 1876. To forestall the Transvaal's disintegration, it was annexed and occupied by a small British contingent the following year.

The struggle to restore order was also one to enforce European supremacy throughout the region. Sir Bartle Frere, the new Governor of Cape Colony, was convinced that this would never be assured until the most powerful local black state, the Zulu kingdom, had been disarmed and dismantled. By January 1879 he had contrived a war with its ruler, Cetewayo, on the pretext that his army, whose strength he exaggerated in reports to London, was a threat to regional stability. The Zulu War started badly when the misjudgement of the local commander, Lord Chelmsford, caused the destruction of a column of over a thousand British, Natal and native troops at Isandlwana. This was a salutary blow to British prestige and served as a warning never to underestimate the determination, bravery and skill of native adversaries.

Chelmsford was sacked for his blunder and replaced by Wolseley, whose methodical professionalism earned him W. S. Gilbert's half-mocking accolade, 'the very model of a modern Major-General'. He reached Zululand in time to hear that Chelmsford's second invasion had ended triumphantly with a decisive victory (massacre would have been a more fitting description) at Ulundi. Mopping-up operations in Zululand and other disaffected regions dragged on until the end of the year, by when it was clear that white paramountcy had been restored everywhere.

Under Wolseley's supervision, the Zulu kingdom was split into petty states which, by the time Allenby arrived in Natal, were locked in internecine war. In 1883 the nervous Cape government brought back Cetewayo in the hope that he might unite his people. His return was marked by a show of force by his sponsors, and Allenby was sent with a detachment of the Inniskillings to the frontier fort at Eshowe. They failed to overawe the Zulus and not long after the cavalrymen had to rescue Cetewayo and his family from rebels. His death in February 1884 gave the Transvaal Boers a chance to infiltrate Zululand by lending support to his son, Dinizulu, who was proclaimed king in May. Inniskilling reinforcements were rushed to Eshowe, and during the summer Allenby led his horsemen in a series of patrols across the Zulu reserves as a reminder to their inhabitants that the British were more to be feared than the Boers.

Boer meddling in the affairs of the Zulus and the consequent cavalcade of Imperial power were signs that the old conflict between Afrikanerdom and the British government had been reopened. The extinction of native resistance in 1880 had removed the need for British garrisons in the Transvaal, at least in Boer minds. Suspicious of Colonial Office schemes to unite the Cape, Natal, the Orange Free State and the Transvaal in a British-dominated federation, the Transvaal Boers rebelled at the end of 1880.

The scattered garrisons soon caved in and, early in the new year, Transvaal kommandos penetrated northern Natal. A bungled attempt to dislodge them led to the battle of Majuba Hill on 27 February 1881, in which a British detachment was thrown back in disorder under heavy rifle fire. For the Boers Majuba was as intoxicating as Bunker Hill had been for the Americans just over a hundred years earlier. In religious terms, which mattered profoundly to the devout Calvinist Boers, their victory was a mark of Divine favour; in political, it proved that they could beat the British Army.

The Inniskillings had originally been ordered to Natal as part of the reinforcements sent to pursue the war and restore British prestige. In the event they were not needed: Gladstone's Liberal government, elected in 1880 on an anti-Imperialist platform, halted operations and opened negotiations with the Boers, who were allowed to keep their independence. Majuba Hill, unlike Isandlwana, remained unavenged, and many officers felt that the Army had been humiliated by faraway politicians who placed expediency before national honour. By and large Army officers, including Allenby, were conservative by instinct and Conservative in their political opinions.[3] Deep-rooted tradition dictated that soldiers always put their private views on one side when called upon to implement public policy, but during the years that led up to the outbreak of the second Boer War in 1899 the memory of the government's sell-out after Majuba rankled.

Within three years of Majuba the British government faced another collision with the forces of Afrikaner nationalism, this time over the ownership of Bechuanaland. Government policy was more resolute than it had been in 1880 and, on 19 November 1884, the Cabinet, in the absence of Gladstone, who always mistrusted Imperial adventures, approved the formation of the Bechuanaland Field Force. Its commander Colonel Charles Warren was ordered to enter Bechuanaland, expel all European intruders and assert British sovereignty. Among the small army which mustered at Barkly West in northern Cape Colony were the Inniskillings; Allenby was about to have his first taste of active service.

What was at stake in the forthcoming campaign was possession of a vast area north of the Cape Colony and the Transvaal which, despite its Tswana inhabitants, was considered 'open' territory and ready for white occupation and colonisation. Whoever dominated this region gained control over the 'missionaries' road', the main route northwards into Zambesia where, according to a prevalent but mistaken belief, there were extensive gold deposits.

During the early 1880s parties of armed pioneers, mostly Boers, had established settlements in the Tswana country which had coalesced into the two republics of Stellaland and Goschen. Both were seen by the British as satellites of the Transvaal and by 1884 it was estimated that they contained at least 1,000 settlers or 'filibusters'. Their appearance had alarmed the Tswana chiefs, who turned to their missionaries for guidance and advice. In turn the missionaries' spokesman, the Reverend John Mackenzie, appealed to the influential humanitarian lobby in London on the grounds that, if unchecked, the influx of settlers would lead to the loss of tribal lands and the reduction of the Tswana to helotry. Only the immediate declaration of a British protectorate over Bechuanaland would save its people from exploitation.

Another voice, that of the Cape politician Cecil Rhodes, was also clamouring for the extensionof British rule over Bechuanaland, but for very different reasons. Rhodes was thirty-two in 1885, a diamond millionaire and an Imperial visionary who had dedicated himself and his cheque-book to the enlargement of British territory and influence in southern Africa. His arguments counted most with the Europeans of the Cape, who wanted to absorb Bechuanaland into the colony.

In the end the British government was swayed not by the canvassing of Mackenzie and Rhodes but by developments outside Bechuanaland. In 1883 German colonists had settled at Angra Pequeña on the coast of Namibia, and showed every sign that they would soon extend their embryo colony inland. This raised the possibility that at some time in the future Boers moving westwards would meet Germans moving eastwards. The result would be a barrier against the northwards expansion of British influence, and a Boer-German block of territory might menace the vital naval base at Simon's Bay, near Cape Town. As so often with British Imperial policy, the principal reason for acquisition of a territory was to make sure that no other power would get it.

Warren, a peppery and autocratic officer, had been chosen to command the field force because of his previous experience of South African campaigning and his assumed ability in handling local irregulars. When he received his instructions from London, he had no way of knowing whether or not the Stellaland and Goschen pioneers would resist eviction. Intelligence as to how many there were was vague; at the onset of his march Warren believed that there were between 1,000 and 1,500. Ignorance of the numbers and attitude of the Stellalanders and

Goschenites, and memories of Isandlwana and Majuba, made him extremely cautious.[4]

He calculated that for safety he would need 800 British infantrymen, 360 cavalry (the Inniskillings), an artillery battery, and 3,000–4,000 locally recruited mounted infantrymen, a type of soldier he had commended before and categorised as either good or 'frightful'. Firepower was essential if he was to overcome settlers armed with modern weaponry, and so his artillery included four five-barrelled ·45 Gardner machine-guns, the latest military technology imported from the United States.

Methodical staffwork was crucial to the success of Warren's enterprise, and Allenby was able to observe for the first time how an operation was planned. Warren followed the lines of careful management which had been laid down by Wolseley for his campaign against the Asante in 1874 and the invasion of Egypt eight years later. Remembering how vulnerable scarlet-coated infantrymen had been on the bare slopes of Majuba, Warren insisted that as many as possible of his regulars wore khaki.[5] The extremes of heat dictated corduroy or cotton, and Warren preferred the broad-brimmed cowboy-type hat worn by settlers to the regulation pith helmet, a choice that Allenby would take many years later when he was campaigning on the veldt of the eastern Transvaal.

Light clothing helped preserve the health of men marching across an arid, hot landscape. The chances of sickness were further reduced by a ban on alcohol, the burning of all camp refuse, proper latrines ('Every endeavour should be made to induce the natives to make and use separate latrines'), and, when water was in short supply, all soldiers were to keep themselves clean by 'rubbing the body smartly with a dry towel'. Woollen and flannel shirts were recommended by Warren, who added that when they became sweaty they should 'be hung up in the sun and when thoroughly dry, beaten and brushed'.[6] This rigmarole, like other procedures detailed by Warren and his staff, was designed to conserve water; the Field Force was crossing an area where it was scarce, and knowledge of its whereabouts hazy. A detachment of specialist engineers with drilling gear, pipes and pumps accompanied the column.

As they proceeded, the soldiers were ordered to offer no provocation to anyone they encountered. Political discussions were forbidden, and Warren insisted that 'The white colonists of all races are to be treated with the courtesy due them, and ill-treatment of natives will be punished.'[7]

Warren's plan of campaign was simple. Supplies would be carried by train from Cape Town to the Oranjerivier railhead and then 30-odd miles overland to his main base at Barkly West. Lines of communication, which would stretch nearly 200 miles by the time the column reached its ultimate objective, Rooigrand, the capital of Goschen, were guarded by the colonial mounted infantry. Forward detachments maintained links with the main force by heliograph (some natives imagined that its flashing mirrors were the white man speaking to his god), and engineers in the rear set up a telegraph which linked Warren with Cape Town, from where messages could be transmitted to London by the recently laid submarine cable.[8] The days when the government could exercise little or no control over its front-line commanders in remote lands were passing away, which was reassuring for ministers, if not generals.

The advance northwards began on 22 January 1885. Having considered 'the excited state of feeling among the farmers of the [Cape] colony' and 'the entire unreliability of the Transvaal government', Warren decided 'to take precautions, as though in an enemy territory'.[9] For Allenby and the Inniskillings this meant routine outpost and reconnaissance duties. On occasions when it was necessary to impress settlers and natives, Warren was accompanied by a squadron of dragoons.

On 25 January Allenby took command of the troop which escorted Warren and Rhodes, who had been appointed Deputy Commissioner for Bechuanaland, for a conference with the recently elected president of the Transvaal, Paul Kruger, at Fourteen Streams. Allenby was an eyewitness to a sullen exchange in which, according to Warren, Kruger attempted to persuade him to halt his advance, but then gave way and pledged himself to make a declaration expelling the 'filibusters' from Bechuanaland. Kruger, whose guiding principle was that 'God's Word should be my rule in the conduct of politics', recalled only that he agreed to co-operate in the delineation of the Transvaal–Bechuanaland border.[10] In fact Kruger dared not risk a war and had already conceded the British occupation of Bechuanaland during negotiations in London the previous year, when he had been warned to keep off the missionaries' road. Having assured himself of Kruger's malevolent neutrality, Warren felt free to push forward, although he warned his officers not to infringe the Transvaal's borders.[11]

Once it was clear that the Transvaal would offer them no support, Stellaland and Goschen fell apart. News of their disintegration came from Rhodes, who had visited the region in 1875 and 1883–4, and had made contacts who, presumably, sent him intelligence which he passed on to Warren. As the column's vanguard neared Stellaland's capital, Vryburg, there were reports that the area was 'in great disorder, and fast drifting into anarchy'.[12] Abandoned camps and cannon indicated that the settlers had no will to fight. On 5 March the advance guard of the Inniskillings, some mounted riflemen, artillery and machine-gun batteries rode into Vryburg unopposed. The next day there were rumours that the Boers might seize Mafeking, but on 10 March that town was occupied without resistance.

Allenby's first campaign had been bloodless. In retrospect it appears as a cavalcade of British might against an enemy who had no stomach for a war, although at the time Warren and those under him expected some kind of opposition. Allenby, while he saw no action, had to follow all the routines and procedures expected of a cavalry subaltern on active service. He learned how to conduct intelligence-gathering patrols ahead of the column, and to mount outlying pickets. He also had to rough it, and to sleep in the open during the cold African night; once he shared a blanket with Rhodes, who revealed a true empire-builder's instinct by getting it all for himself.[13] There were some compensations for such discomforts, however, and Allenby spent some off-duty hours shooting wildebeest.

Once the main part of his mission had been accomplished. Warren visited local tribal chiefs and explained to them how their affairs would be managed under British protection. The Queen's new subjects were given demonstrations of their ruler's power in the shape of parades in which the Inniskillings were prominent. The climax of these shows was the ascent of an observation balloon, a novelty that had been attached to the Field Force. The Tswana's amazement at this sight prompted the *Graphic's* correspondent to write smugly, 'It is most satisfactory to see what a profound impression of England's greatness these practical and scientific exhibitions have made on the wondering native mind.'

By October 1885 the Inniskillings were back in Natal, and Allenby returned to the humdrum round of regimental duties. In the summer of 1886 he returned to England for a regulation two-year stint at the Canterbury cavalry depot and two seasons of fox-hunting. He returned to Natal two years later, now a captain, with some hounds with which he hunted jackal and deer. He reached South Africa too late to join the Inniskillings in Zululand, where they were part of a force putting down a half-hearted uprising led by Dinizulu.

In his absence, the course of South African history had changed dramatically. Four months after his meeting with Warren, Kruger heard how enormous gold deposits had been discovered on the Witswatersrand, deposits that were capable of supplying a quarter of the world's demand. Within ten years the Transvaal's annual gold revenues were £8.6 million, making it the richest state in Africa. In the meantime, Rhodes, having secured Bechuanaland as a base, was forming his British South Africa Company in order to run a private-enterprise colony in Zambesia. The first pioneer column, bristling with cannon and machine-guns, headed north in 1889 towards a region that, in seven years' time, would be given the name Rhodesia.

Some of Allenby's brother officers were keen to play a part in these events, which offered the enticements of manly adventure and private profit. Three transferred to the Bechuanaland Police and one of these, Raleigh Grey, commanded the detachment that participated in the 1895–6 Jameson Raid. This attempt to overthrow Kruger masterminded by Rhodes, failed; Grey lost his commission and received a prison sentence, imposed in London, for making war on a friendly country. The outbreak of the Boer War three years later brought him redemption and he died a respected colonial administrator and a knight.

An expanding empire had always offered opportunities for ambitious Army officers, and the prospect of advancement lured several more from the Inniskillings into the British South Africa Company's gendarmerie. Allenby was briefly infected with the restless mood; he contemplated throwing in his lot with Rhodes and, in 1890, planned an expedition to Nyasaland, where missionaries were fighting a miniature war against Arab slavers.[14] In the end he plumped for a more conventional military career, and returned to England with his regiment when it was recalled in the autumn of 1890.

Although noted for his casual diffidence, Allenby was determined to work for promotion and, in 1894, he presented himself as a candidate for the Army's Staff College at Camberley. He failed the entrance examination but succeeded at the second try and, in January 1896, began his studies of the higher abstractions of war and command.

CHAPTER 3

THE ART OF WAR

1896–1899

THE Staff College at Camberley had been opened in 1859. It had been created in the response to the early calamities of the Crimean War which had been blamed, not altogether fairly, on the absence of a trained staff. Throughout its first thirty or so years Camberley was a controversial institution, widely criticised by conservative senior officers. Wellingtonian orthodoxy, which still carried some weight, decreed that any able and experienced regimental officer could take on staff work, and that this had been proved during the Peninsular War. Furthermore, if the despised Continental staff colleges were anything to go by, Camberley would turn out a breed of conceited know-all officers.

In the Army, as in contemporary public schools, character counted more than brains, and in many messes it was considered bad form to discuss military business, while gentlemen amateurs frowned on colleagues who appeared to take their profession too seriously. Such prejudice disappeared, but slowly, thanks in no small part to the obscurantism of the Commander-in-Chief, the Duke of Cambridge. This stout, pop-eyed and purple-faced grandson of George III showed his disapproval of the methods of modern soldiering when he visited the Staff College in 1894. His reaction was observed by one of the instructors, Colonel Henderson: 'The old hero of many banquets grunted ferociously at the pile of schemes, maps, etc. and then darted off to revel in pork chops and other delicacies, giving us to understand that we were very dull dogs.'[1]

But the 'dull dogs' were taking over. A year before Allenby entered Camberley, the ageing Duke had been replaced as Commander-in-Chief by Wolseley, a soldier in the new mould and a national hero, who had once accused his predecessor of knowing 'as much of modern warfare – or indeed of any warfare, as my top-boot'.[2] The personal jealousies and sneering, behind-the-hand denigration which characterised so many relationships between senior officers during and after the First World War were very much a tradition of Army life.

Wolseley's ascendancy raised the status of the Staff College. He set a high store by its graduates and declared it to be 'the surest avenue to advancement' for the ambitious officer.[3] For Allenby and the rest of the class of 1896–7 their attendance at Camberley was an indication of a professional commitment, one that now counted something in an army which was shedding its old amateurism; it was, of course, also an advantage in terms of promotion.

Two 1896 entrants, Allenby and Captain Douglas Haig of the 7th Hussars, went further than all their classmates and became Field-Marshals. In later years, the less successful were encouraged to dig into their memories to recall the characteristics of the two men who had risen so spectacularly. As a result of their reminiscences, collected but not always used by Allenby's former staff officer and biographer, General Sir Archibald ('Weevil') Wavell (later Field-Marshal Earl Wavell of Cyrenaica), Allenby the man comes clearly into focus for the first time. Major-General Sir George ('Hooky') Forestier-Walker, who later became a close colleague, recalled that he possessed 'a great sense of humour, of a fine rapier-like quality' and was better read than his brother officers. Another future colleague and friend, General Sir George Barrow, noticed that Allenby was uninterested in learning the routines of administration; did not seek advice, but never minded it when it was offered; and could bear contradiction.[4]

The most detailed but least sympathetic account of Allenby at this time came from Brigadier-General Sir James ('Archimedes') Edmonds who, as his nickname suggests, was an outstandingly clever engineer, and who had been first in the Staff College entrance examination. A waspish intellectual, addicted to gossip, his career did not flourish as he might have wished; after a lectureship at Sandhurst he served on the General Staff during the Boer War and again in the First World War. Having stayed on the fringes of power, although taking some part in operational planning, Edmonds was appointed editor of the Official History of the war which appeared in instalments during the 1920s, 30s and 40s. He occupied a position of power and, through access to secret official information and the confidential observations of senior participants, built up an unparalleled knowledge of men and events during the war. Basil Liddell Hart, a post-war friend and confidant, thought he idealised war too much.[5]

Then and earlier, Edmonds had little time for Allenby, something which in a large part stemmed from his knowledge of the latter's bouts of brutish ill-temper in France. At Camberley, Edmonds recalled him as resembling 'a typical young English fox-hunting squire', at times withdrawn and always 'rather out of his depth in the very medium company of 1896–7'.[6] Allenby's appearance was certainly striking; he was 6 foot 2 inches tall, burly and with a powerful chest (in 1915 he required an overcoat with a 44-inch chest), which was not surprising since Edmonds had been struck by his 'splendid appetite for food and drink'.[7] This hearty giant was, as Edmonds admitted, popular with his brother officers, who elected him to the prestigious office of Master of the Drag Hounds for the 1896–7 season.

Personality rather than horsemanship recommended Allenby for the post, since the rival candidate, Haig, was an accomplished rider. Stand-offish and self-assured, Haig made no friends. His announcement, at the start of the course, that he was taking a few days' leave to join a shooting party with the Prince of Wales struck less well-connected officers as arrogance. Their hostility was revealed before lectures, when the last seat to be taken was always next to Haig's.[8] He was probably not perturbed, for he was at Camberley solely to absorb knowledge, which he never found easy, and to further his career. Haig was not a malevolent man, but he was pugnacious and a ruthless manipulator whenever his own interests of advancement were involved. His ambition was unlimited and, whether or not his inner sensibilities had been bruised by Allenby's election to the mastership of the college hunt, he simply regarded him as a competitor in the race for promotion. Allenby did not see things in this way and imagined that Haig's animosity was personal. In later years he repeatedly complained, 'Haig was always so infernally jealous of me'.[9]

Edmonds and, later, Wavell were fascinated by the contrasts between the two officers. Both had drifted into the Army after other careers had been closed to them through an inability to pass examinations. Both respected and aspired to professional excellence, but Haig pursued this goal and promotion with an obsessive single-mindedness that to some extent compensated for his intellectual weakness. Moreover, and here the contrast with Allenby was strongest, Haig showed little tolerance for the opinions of others and disdained advice. This did not reflect self-confidence, rather the opposite, since he was a poor debater. He meticulously kept a diary that was filled with sometimes Pooteresque self-justification. Allenby lacked Haig's drive and dedication; his mind and conversation were eclectic and he was happy to diffuse his energies in non-military pastimes and interests, diversions which Haig did not, and possibly could not afford to, follow.[10] When together, the pair were visibly uncomfortable, to the point where each became tongue-tied and reduced to silence.

At Camberley both concentrated in their differing ways on the acquisition of military wisdom and passing a final examination. Examinations were distrusted by the Commandant, Colonel Hilyard, who favoured progressive assessment, no doubt because it would end the universal habit by which officers stuffed themselves with often undigested facts just before the examination. Cramming for professional examinations was a part of the Victorian educational system (Allenby had crammed for the Indian Civil Service, Sandhurst and Staff College), and while it helped many to jump hurdles that might otherwise have proved insurmountable, it also allowed into the Army and other professions men with shallow knowledge and limited understanding.

There was much in the Staff College curriculum that made cramming unavoidable, particularly the course on strategy and tactics delivered by Colonel Henderson, which relied on memorising chunks of military history. Henderson exerted an extraordinary influence and his theories made a deep impression on Haig and, to a lesser extent, Allenby, both of whom relied on them when they held high command twenty years later. When they arrived at Camberley, the class of 1896 followed public-school tradition and gave their instructors nicknames, which they extracted from Kipling's recently published *Jungle Book*; Henderson was called 'Baloo', a compliment to his wisdom.[11]

It was 'Baloo' Henderson's task to acquaint his pupils with the new forms of warfare which had evolved over the pasty thirty years. While his lectures ranged back to the Napoleonic period (one of his assessment papers asked a student to 'discuss Wellington's dispositions up to the time he left Brussels on 16 June 1815' i.e. two days before Waterloo), Henderson concentrated on the American Civil War of 1861–5, the Franco-Prussian War of 1870–1, and the Russo-Turkish War of 1877–8. All were landmarks during an age in which warfare was being transformed by technical innovation. Railways enabled large numbers of soldiers to be moved quickly, concentrated for battle, and fed and equipped as they campaigned, without cumbersome, slow-moving convoys of supply wagons. Breech-loading rifles and rifled cannon with extended ranges and explosive shells had dramatically increased the firepower of armies and forced generals to rethink strategy and tactics.

Henderson's lectures distilled the new thinking, or at least that part of it which had been applied to warfare during the 1860s and 1870s. He was convinced that what had occurred on the battlefields of the United States and eastern France held the key to the future conduct of war. Later developments, particularly the magazine rifle (first issued in the British Army in 1889), the highly efficient Maxim machine-gun (first used in West Africa in 1887), and lyddite explosive shells (introduced in the 1890s) were discounted by Henderson.[12] While not fully aware that new weapons were providing an intensity of firepower far greater than that available in 1870, Henderson understood that the armaments revolution had given the infantry formidable superiority; on the modern battlefield, rifle fire could now create a killing-zone that extended for at least 900 yards in front of a defended position, an area over which an advance would be suicidal.

How then did strategists react to such innovations? Henderson contended that decisive victory could only be achieved when a commander co-ordinated all three arms, infantry, artillery and cavalry, in such a way as to make possible an irresistible offensive. 'The attainment of superiority of fire and the breaching of a defender's line were unquestionably the decisive factors in war,' he insisted. None of these conditions were obtainable without what Henderson called 'the doctrine of unhesitating obedience', and he warmly approved of its adoption by General Ulysses S. Grant when he took command of the Army of the Potomac in 1864. Then, wrote Henderson, 'Brigadiers and colonels forbore to intrude their ideas upon the general commanding.' 'Insubordination', he claimed, 'is the most contagious of diseases' and 'no respecter of persons'.[13] Allenby, already a disciple of 'cheerful obedience', took this lesson to heart, but he never swallowed Henderson's strictures about a general's immunity from subordinate advice.

In developing his theories of the decisive offensive, Henderson paid much attention to the morale factor. If, as he argued, a victorious army was one that always imposed its will on its opponents, then morale was vital. His digressions on this subject were of special interest to Allenby, for they touched directly upon the contemporary debate about the future of cavalry. Increased firepower meant that horsemen could no longer charge infantry, fracture their line and harry the fleeing survivors. This was how battles had been won a hundred years ago when massed horsemen could still deliver a decisive hammer-blow. But were such spectacular gallops with sabre and lance any longer possible against massed rifles with ranges of a thousand yards or more? Some strategists said they were not, and that cavalry had become an anachronism on the battlefield, although still useful for the less dashing duties of reconnaissance and screening an army from enemy patrols.

Henderson disagreed. The cavalryman was still, he claimed, 'the soldier of the charge and mêlée', although he added, no doubt conscious of the terrible losses suffered by charging horsemen during the Franco-Prussian War, that in a future war the mounted soldier would have to show a spirit of 'self-sacrifice'. He also warned that rifle-armed infantry with high morale and confidence in their weapons might not panic when charged. Nevertheless, and after some astonishing mental acrobatics, he maintained that in the right circumstances a cavalry charge pushed home with determination could prove as decisive as it had in the past.[14] He also distanced himself from those contemporary strategists who contended that horsemen might be valuable on a modern battlefield if they exchanged their bladed weapons for rifles and fought as mounted infantry.

Cavalrymen like Haig regarded as wormwood any suggestion that they were redundant. Many of their arguments were emotional; the cavalry charge was the essence of war's glory, if such a thing existed, and the horse-soldier, impelled by the reckless, aggressive cavalry spirit, could still ride down infantrymen paralysed with fear.

There was more to the cavalry controversy than disagreements about what, if any, part the horseman would play in tomorrow's war. Following antique tradition, the cavalry was the most glamorous wing of the late-Victorian army, elegantly uniformed and mounted and led by aristocratic officers whose pedigrees were matched by their cavalier gallantry. They were conservative, well-connected and, like Haig, fierce in justifying their existence. Often they simply refused to accept the awesome potential of firepower. Colonel Philip Chetwode (later Field-Marshal Lord Chetwode) of the 19th Hussars, who commanded a cavalry brigade under Allenby in August 1914, wrote two years earlier that the cavalry still retained 'its power of pushing home the mounted attack' against terrified infantrymen. Its morale effect was as great as ever, he claimed, since the modern infantry was filled with 'men rendered ten times more "jumpy" by education and the enervating effects of modern industrial life than the old-time soldier who scarcely knew what imagination meant.'[15] In other words, men recruited from the industrial slums would flinch before the spectacle of charging horsemen and be too frightened to raise, let alone fire, their rifles.

Allenby, for all his passionate attachment to horses, was flexible in his attitude towards how cavalry ought to be used. Boer War experience taught him not to despise the mounted infantryman, and what he saw during the first six months of the First World War convinced him – much to Haig's disgust – that conventional cavalry warfare was obsolete.[16]

In reaching this conclusion, Allenby displayed the 'practical common sense' which distinguished him in the eyes of his tutors. In their final assessment of his progress, they noted how his 'sufficiently good abilities' enabled him to cope with familiar situations, although he was easily flummoxed by the unexpected. Still, there was praise in his end-of-term report: Allenby was 'a clear thinker and writer' with 'energy, good judgement and rapid decision'. He passed twenty-first out of a class of sixty-four, in the summer of 1897 with middling marks in Mathematics, Military History, Fortification, Administration and Military Law.[17]

His best performance was in French, but this was not surprising since he had toured in Belgium, Germany, and Switzerland during 1879 and stayed at Saumur, home of the French Army's cavalry school, during the winter of 1880–1. And yet those who heard his French said it was spoken 'with determination rather than great accuracy' and, in 1914–15, he thought it prudent to employ an interpreter, Arthur Capel, who had lived in Paris and was serving on Allenby's staff as an Intelligence Officer. This was a wise precaution: some years later, when Allenby and his wife were giving luncheon to a 'distinguished Frenchman' at the High Commission in Cairo, the following conversation was overheard, just before the cigars and cigarettes were produced:

Allenby: '*Etes vous un foumart* [polecat or ferret]?'
Lady Allenby: '*Il veut dire, êtes vous un fumeux* [dunghill]?'

The Frenchman was convulsed with laughter.[18]

If, as Edmonds suspected, Allenby was out of his depth at Staff College, he had not drowned. He had understood something of the nature of the routine staff work that was essential to move, feed and equip armies in the field, although it was a subject that did not interest him greatly. He had also learned about grand strategy and how the decisive offensive could be achieved on the modern battlefield. And yet, unlike his German counterparts at the Kriegsakademie, his training had not been a preparation for a career as a maker of strategy.[19] British doctrine ruled out an élite of specially qualified staff officers who created battle plans. Instead, a British officer remained a subordinate who followed unquestioningly the will of his commander-in-chief who alone decided how a battle would be fought. This practice owed everything to the peculiarly British experience of Continental wars. Twice military geniuses in the form of Marlborough and Wellington had emerged from the Army and achieved spectacular successes. It was assumed that somehow a general of equal stature would emerge from the officer corps when he was needed. If, like Allenby, this commander was a graduate of Camberley, his mind would be filled with ideas about an 'offensive spirit' which could sustain morale and drive an army to victory.

During the first half of his year at Staff College, Allenby had been paying court to Miss Mabel Chapman, whom he had encountered at a shooting party in Scotland. She was a strikingly handsome young woman with a warm, engaging personality, and she shared Allenby's love of field sports and natural history. Her father, Horace Chapman, was a country squire whose seat, Donhead Hall, lay in south Wiltshire close to the border with Dorset. He had misgivings about his daughter's suitor, for while Allenby's background was acceptable, his prospects were not great and his private income was insubstantial. Squire Chapman relented, however, and the couple were married at Donhead St Mary on 30 December 1896; after their honeymoon they settled near Camberley.

The Allenbys enjoyed a stable marriage. The bonds between them were always close, and his letters to his wife from South Africa reveal the depth of an emotional and physical attachment that was clearly reciprocated. Their only child Horace Michael (he was always known by the second name) was born in 1898. After Allenby's return to England in 1902, Michael became the focus of his father's life; he was a bright, highly intelligent boy and a good games player. In 1911 he entered Wellington School, and shortly afterwards began to prepare for an Army career.

The Allenbys were a close-knit family, and he always managed to keep his private world entirely separate from his public. When he relaxed he did so with his wife and son, and occasionally on his father-in-law's yacht. It was perhaps felicitous that the three Allenbys enjoyed common pursuits, and that his strong-willed mother was on cordial terms with his wife. Money was always a problem: when his son first went to school Allenby had to forgo polo to meet the fees, although he continued to indulge his other pleasures, shooting and fishing.

There were plenty of opportunities for these after Allenby was posted as Brigade-Major to the 3rd Cavalry Division in Ireland in 1897. It was an ideal appointment for a sportsman-officer and his similarly inclined wife; the duties were not onerous and there were ample opportunities to hunt, shoot and fish. Allenby turned his attention from wild flowers to cultivated ones and began work in earnest on the garden of his Dublin house. Strangely for one of his tastes and background he had no time for dogs, and never kept one.

This agreeable life was interrupted on 23 October 1899 when the Inniskillings were ordered to take ship for South Africa. Since the spring the British and Boer governments had been on a collision course and by September, when it was clear that further negotiations would be pointless, the Transvaal and the Orange Free State began mobilisation. On 2 October they issued an ultimatum, and ten days later kommandos invaded Cape Colony and Natal. The already swollen British garrison in South Africa was found to be insufficient and extra forces, including the Inniskillings, were hurriedly summoned from Britain.

CHAPTER 4

FIGHTING BROTHER BOER

1899–1902

ALLENBY believed that 'Kruger and his gang' were 'totally responsible for this war'.[1] This explanation of the Boer War was a simplification, although one accepted unquestioningly by Conservatives like Allenby and millions of Imperialist jingoes at home, who took their opinions from the pro-government newspapers' interpretation of the events that had led to the war. For them, blame lay with Kruger, who had refused to extend political rights to thousands of uitlanders (foreigners) who had settled in the Transvaal to run its gold-mines and railways. But, as Kruger realised, concessions to these immigrants would have overturned the traditional Afrikaner way of life and, since they outnumbered Boers, would have led to the Transvaal's submersion in a British-dominated South African federation. His alternative was an Afrikaner federation in which the British provinces of the Cape and Natal, both of which contained Boer majorities, would submit to the Transvaal's paramountcy.

British governments had always had reservations about Afrikaner nationalism, and these had deepened as the gold revenues made the Transvaal rich and powerful. The expansion of Boer influence across southern Africa was considered a threat to vital British strategic and economic interests and therefore had to be contained. First there was the naval base at Simon's Town, which commanded the international shipping lanes that converged on Cape Town and provided logistical

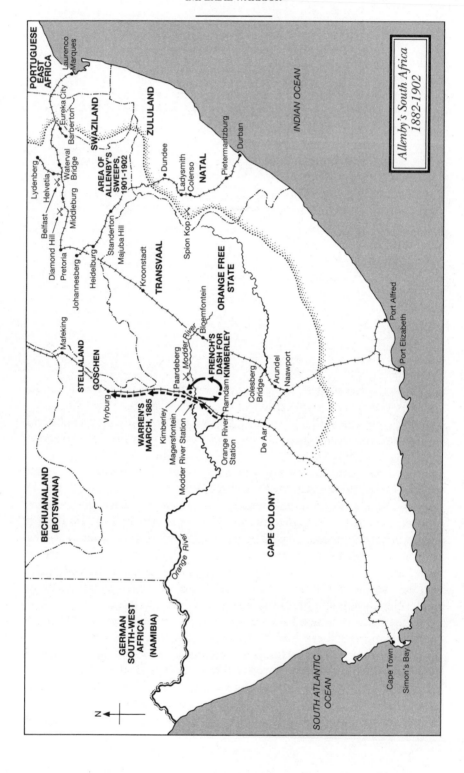

Allenby's South Africa
1882-1902

support for warships serving in African, Indian and South American waters. Secondly, the South African diamond and gold boom had attracted over £300 million in British investments and the region had become a major market for British exports. In Britain and abroad, opponents of the war seized on these economic motives and represented the Boers as a people fighting for freedom against an alliance of high finance and imperialism. They were mistaken; the war was in fact a clash between two equally acquisitive imperialisms, British and Afrikaner.

The war opened with a struggle for possession of South Africa's communications. Two Boer armies, which totalled 35,000 men, invaded Natal and Cape Colony in October and November 1899 in an attempt to capture the main railway lines and take Durban and Cape Town, so preventing the disembarkation of British reinforcements. This bold strategy was the only one available to the Boer high command, which knew that once Britain had mobilised and shipped its troops to South Africa their own forces would be heavily outnumbered. Powerful thrusts into British territory also offered a tempting political dividend in the shape of armed rebellions by the Afrikaners in Natal and the Cape, who were mistakenly imagined to be ready to desert the British.

Boer strategy failed thanks to timid leadership. By mid-November their offensive had run out of steam after their armies, having bottled up local British forces in Mafeking, Ladysmith and Kimberley, laid siege to the three towns. Static warfare soaked up manpower which the Boers needed elsewhere, and was a fatal misuse of soldiers whose strength lay in their mobility. As the Boers dug-in and began the almost leisurely long-range shelling of the beleaguered towns, the severely shaken British forces obtained a breathing-space in which to regroup and prepare for a counter-offensive. The painful results of this change in Boer strategy would be felt in the following year. In the meantime, the Boers had some cause for satisfaction; during the first three months of fighting they had taken the initiative, thrown back the British forces sent to engage them in Natal and, between 10 and 15 December, defeated armies ordered to raise the sieges at the battles of Stormberg, Magersfontein and Colenso.

The outbreak of war had caught the British Army off balance, and from the start local commanders were overwhelmed by problems. Despite the political crisis earlier in the year, no contingency plans had been prepared for operations in South Africa and a shortage of reliable maps meant that, when General Sir Redvers Buller (Commander in Chief in South Africa) began his first attempt to relieve Ladysmith in December, he had to rely on sketch-maps hurriedly drawn on the spot during his advance.[2] Not only were generals often short of even the most rudimentary local intelligence, they had virtually no experience in handling large bodies of men. There had been only four large-scale army manoeuvres held in Britain over the past thirty years, although such exercises were commoner in India.[3] Perhaps the most serious shortcoming was the Army's ignorance of Boer tactics which were summarised by one war correspondent as a combination of, 'Marksmanship, mobility, little or no baggage or commissariat train' with a good eye for and familiarity with the local terrain.[4] The British Army was forced to adapt to its adversary's methods as it campaigned, and the cost was heavy. As Buller observed of his disastrous engagement on Spion Kop in January 1900, his men 'went up recruits . . . and they came down soldiers'; a metamorphosis which over 1,000 did not survive.[5]

Allenby and the Inniskillings, short one squadron which had been delayed at Madeira, arrived at Cape Town on 11 December and were immediately entrained for Arundel, in the uplands of the north-eastern Cape, to join a unit under the command of Major-General John French (later Field-Marshal Lord French of Ypres). French was forty-seven, a dyed-in-the-wool cavalryman, but with enough imagination to experiment with new battlefield tactics. In mid-November he had taken charge of a scratch force, including Australian and New Zealand detachments, with orders to block any advance towards the vital rail junction at Naauwport and to harass a force of 3,400 Boers positioned in and around Colesberg, across the Port Elizabeth–Bloemfontein railway line.

Since then he had skilfully deployed his limited forces and undertaken a series of hit-and-run raids against the Boers, designed to throw them on to the defensive and weaken their forces with as few British losses as possible. French not only prevented an attack on Naauwport, but demonstrated to disaffected local Boers that the British Army was still a force to be reckoned with. After a month of this warfare, Allenby wrote to his wife on 15 January, 'Our present tactics are Boer tactics, and we worry, worry, worry them but do not fight'.[6]

Soon after Allenby's arrival, French felt confident enough to increase the number and weight of his forays and began to edge cautiously towards the Boer defences on the high ground around Colesberg. Here Allenby and his squadron, fighting dismounted, saw their first action, and afterwards he admitted an admiration for Boer tenacity. 'The Boers are stubborn as mules and as brave as lions in defending their positions', he told his wife, adding 'our fellows are splendid and quite amaze me with their pluck.'[7] Earlier, on 4 January, there had been a magnificent display of cavalry 'pluck' when one squadron of the Inniskillings had charged with lances a party of retreating Boers.[8] Such incidents were, however, extremely rare throughout the war, during which the Innisksillings, like other cavalry, mainly fought as mounted riflemen.

As part of his strategy of stepping up pressure on the Boers, French ordered a small flying column of horse and mounted infantry, accompanied by two cannon, to demolish by shellfire the Colesberg road bridge that lay ten miles behind Boer lines and was used by ox-wagons bringing supplies from the Orange Free State. Allenby was chosen to command this detachment, which set off from Rensberg on the evening of 13 January. The raid involved a 20-mile detour around Boer lines and early the next morning the bombardment began. After twenty shells had been fired at a range of 5,000 yards, a large force of Boers arrived 2 miles away, having been alerted, Allenby believed, by a spy. Their appearance forced him to pull back his men and they returned to Rensberg with five prisoners and no casualties.[9] Allenby was congratulated by French for his skill and prudence in a minor action that had demonstrated the vulnerability of Boer lines of communication.

This was war in the Boer style and its effectiveness impressed Allenby. In South Africa, in what was, by Army standards, an irregular war, old disciplines went by the board and new were adopted. Officers dressed like the other ranks so as not to be singled out by snipers; nearly everyone was unshaven since razors chafed sunburnt faces; and the Inniskillings slept in their boots and saddled up by three in the morning in readiness for dawn attacks.[10]

Operations around Colesberg during the winter of 1899–1900 were part of a general strategy designed to mark time. French's unorthodox tactics had distracted a small Boer army and thrown it on the defensive. To the northeast and beyond the Drakensberg Mountains, a larger British force under Buller was stumbling towards Ladysmith and holding the Boers' attention in Natal. Both campaigns achieved their objective, and gave the British high command time in which to consolidate the substantial reinforcements that were pouring into the country and to plan a massive counter-offensive. By the end of January, these preparations were nearing completion, and on the 29th French was recalled from Colesberg to Cape Town where the new Commander-in-Chief, Field-Marshal Lord Roberts, ordered him to take charge of a newly created cavalry division which would spearhead an invasion of the Orange Free State. Among the units earmarked for this force was Allenby's squadron of the Inniskillings.

Lord Roberts had landed at Cape Town the previous December and was quickly followed by his Chief of Staff, General Lord Kitchener of Khartoum. Strongly contrasting in their characters and outlook, they were Britain's most successful generals, and were considered by the government to be the only men capable of reversing the hitherto disastrous course of the war and restoring British prestige.

Roberts, then in his late sixties, was an avuncular veteran whose service stretched back to the Indian Mutiny, where he had won the Victoria Cross. He was affectionately known as 'Bobs' by the ordinary soldiers, who counted him as a friend and with good reason, since in South Africa he refused to enforce the death sentence for such military offences as desertion. Kitchener, who had commanded the Anglo-Egyptian army that had overthrown the Mahdist state in the Sudan in 1898, was a less approachable figure; contemporaries found him cold, ruthless, aloof, and a slave to ambition.

Roberts, who had pored over maps during his voyage out, had decided upon a simple, audacious but risky plan. Given that the Boers' recent successes owed much to their superior mobility, he intended to fight them on their own terms by the creation of an 8,000-strong force of cavalry and mounted infantry under French. This division would move by rail and in secrecy northwards along the Cape-to-Mafeking line, leave their trains south of the Modder River, cut across the open country far to the east of the Boer entrenchments at Magersfontein, and head towards Kimberley. On their way, the horsemen would secure crossing-places on the Riet and Modder Rivers for Roberts's main force of 37,000 men, mostly infantry.

Allenby and his squadron were attached to the first brigade of French's Mounted Division, which he joined on 29 January after a nineteen-hour train journey from Rensberg. By 10 February the entire Mounted Division had assembled and was ready for the dash to Kimberley. Kitchener and Roberts inspected the division on the 10th, and Roberts snatched the chance to address its senior officers. He promised them 'some very hard work' together with 'the greatest chance cavalry had ever had'. Something heroic was obviously called for so he summoned up memories of Henry V at Agincourt by predicting, 'You will remember what you are going to do all your lives, and when you have grown to be old men you will tell the story of the relief of Kimberley.'[11]

The following morning Allenby and the Inniskillings saddled-up and mounted by moonlight and moved off with the rest of 1 Brigade. For the next four days the snake-like columns crossed an arid landscape, their progress marked by vast clouds of dust thrown up by the hooves, and a trail of horses dead from exhaustion. Riding was best in the morning, which was mercifully cool, and sometimes cavalrymen had the good luck to find recently abandoned Boer farmsteads with full coffee pots on the hob and uneaten breakfasts on the table. Allenby survived on hard army biscuits, beef lozenges that had been sent by his wife, and tobacco-pipe and cigarettes, the soldier's universal palliatives for an empty stomach. Above all, this and subsequent marches were a test of endurance for horses, whose burden of rider, ammunition, rations and fodder sometimes weighed up to 280 pounds. The remounts, hurriedly imported from the Argentine and the United States, were unacclimatised and quickly succumbed after hard riding and long periods without water. Losses were prodigious: on 23 February Allenby told his wife that the surviving horses were 'terribly weak' while, during a 170-mile march in May, 200 of the Inniskillings' horses died.[12] Not only were the creatures overworked, but their sufferings were augmented by the clumsy horsemanship of many cavalrymen.[13]

The Boers were soon aware of the movement of the mass columns, but failed to guess their purpose. The commander at Magersfontein, Piet Cronjé, at first dismissed the advance as a decoy to lure him from his entrenched positions, and ignored it. The cavalrymen therefore faced little opposition and the dust that surrounded them confused the aim of the small parties of Boers who sniped at them. The scale and temerity of the manoeuvre had temporarily paralysed all Boer units in the vicinity so when, on the 15th, the waves of horsemen converged on Kimberley they found no difficulty in pushing their way through the besiegers' lines. This final gallop was hailed as a vindicatory triumph for old-style cavalry warfare, even though no sabre had been unsheathed or lance levelled. It was, but not in the traditional sense. The success of French's horsemen came from their weight of numbers, the boldness of their manoeuvre and the numbed reactions of their adversaries, not shock action.

Inside Kimberley the relief force was fulsomely welcomed by Rhodes, who renewed his acquaintance with Allenby at a dinner he gave for French and his officers; clearly the siege had not bitten too deeply into his larder. At five the next morning, Allenby and his squadron were again on the move, this time as part of a small force ordered by French to dislodge a Boer rearguard of 200 men which was covering the northwards retreat of the Griqualand kommando. The position on Dronfield Ridge was a strong one and, despite an effort to outflank it by Allenby and his dragoons, the attack was abandoned by nightfall. He was developing a knack for this kind of warfare; he had a fox-hunter's eye for ground, and knew how to deploy his men so that they suffered few casualties as they crawled and scrambled up hillsides.

While the Inniskillings skirmished over the kopjes outside Kimberley, a major battle was beginning further south where Cronjé, now alerted to his predicament, was attempting to escape encirclement. French's cavalry were diverted eastwards towards the Modder River to cut off his line of retreat as large bodies of infantry and artillery followed up from the west. Cronjé's army, shackled to an enormous wagon train and encumbered with the wives and children of many of his burghers, moved slowly and, by 18 February, it had been trapped along the bed of the Modder River near Paardeberg.

Roberts was unwell with 'flu and so Kitchener assumed command. Impatient for a decisive victory, he opened the battle with a sequence of poorly co-ordinated frontal attacks that cost 1,270 casualties and made no impression on the Boer defences. Shellfire, hunger and sickness did, and on 27 February, Majuba day, Cronjé surrendered his 4,000-strong army. Officers who examined Boer lines afterwards were given a glimpse into the future when they came across deep Boer trenches which had given their occupants a remarkable immunity from British shells.

Paardeberg coincided with the relief of Ladysmith and for a time the Boers were so stunned that their will to fight seemed about to dissolve.[14] From March to June, Roberts's army delivered what were imagined to be the final blows of the war. The British force followed the course of the Modder to Bloemfontein, the capital of the Orange Free State, and then shifted northwards along the railway line deep into the Transvaal, where Johannesburg fell on 29 May and Pretoria, the capital, on 5 June.

There was plenty of work for the cavalry during this advance. Allenby who, after the Kimberley ride, had told his wife that the last week was 'the longest I ever have spent', faced four more months of equally intense campaigning. The Mounted Division reverted to a more traditional role and became the advance guard for Roberts's army, scouting, probing for pockets of resistance and often holding them until artillery and infantry came up. Allenby's depleted squadron had been amalgamated with the New South Wales Lancers and was detailed for a variety of tasks. Twice Allenby undertook behind-the-lines demolition raids against railway and telegraph lines; his squadron also escorted a supply convoy, and rescued some British POWs from a camp at Waterval.[15]

The commonest and most taxing of the cavalry's duties was forward scouting. This involved fighting a number of small-scale engagements against handfuls of Boers who occupied concealed positions, usually on high ground, from where they would open fire on the approaching horsemen and then retire to deploy again on another ridge. It was an effective form of attrition since the British usually suffered a few casualties, the Boers none. The only answer to these tactics was for the cavalry and mounted infantry to work their way around the Boers' flanks, bring a cross-fire to bear and force them to pull back. Allenby, who had had his first taste of this sort of action near Colesberg and outside Kimberley, soon mastered it, thanks to his coolness, quick judgement and eye for the country.

Nevertheless, skirmishing among the kopjes of the Transvaal was always an unpredictable and dangerous business. On 10 May, during operations on the Zand River, the Inniskillings were among a small force sent to take a kopje from which to enfilade a Boer gun battery. On the way up the detachment was ambushed by Boers, concealed in a donga (ravine), and were thrown back in confusion with fifty casualties.[16] Allenby was ambushed again, late in the evening of 3 June at the Kalkheuval Pass, where a sudden attack by the Mafeking kommando, hidden in dense bush, routed several units and forced French to pull back. Allenby steadied his men and held his ground long enough for a Horse Artillery battery, a pom-pom (a heavy Maxim machine-gun firing 1-inch shells) and mounted infantry to come up.[17]

Although Allenby showed an alacrity of mind and body on the battlefield when his and his men's survival was at stake, the campaign was corroding his spirit. After Paardeberg, he found the Boers' resistance inexplicable and on 11 April he confessed to his wife, 'I am sick of this show, as are all of us, and we all feel as if we *would like* a holiday.' A week later he referred hopefully to rumours of a forthcoming peace, but imagined that he would not be home before the end of the year.[18] There were further bouts of war-weariness: on 26 April he admitted to feeling 'a bit sick of campaigning', a sentiment he repeated two months later, adding that he was mystified as to why anyone would be a soldier.[19] He was also dismayed by the news of the affair at Sannah's Post, where his friend, Brigadier-General Robert Broadwood, had led 2 Cavalry Brigade into a Boer trap on 30 March–1 April and lost several guns. There were well-founded allegations that Broadwood had been careless, which Allenby regretfully accepted. 'I can't excuse any man who is caught napping,' he told his wife, but added, 'I hate criticising and I hate war.'[20]

Allenby's disenchanted mood must have owed much to the gruelling conditions of the advance on Pretoria. As the cavalry frequently outstripped its supply train, rations were often short, although they could be augmented by slaughtered Boer cattle and sheep. The need for vigilance against sudden Boer attack meant many sleepless nights, and once Allenby complained of sleeping in the open in the rain. On top of these discomforts he had been suffering from toothache since January, and had to have treatment from a Kimberley dentist six weeks later. To make matters worse several sets of his false teeth had been broken by ration biscuits, and dentral troubles continued to vex him until the new year, when he purchased another set of teeth in Johannesburg for what he considered the grossly inflated price of fourteen guineas.[21]

With the capture of Pretoria and the annexation of the Transvaal, it appeared to Allenby that the tide of the war had turned. The Boer states were in ruins and everywhere Boer armies had been reduced to fighting limited rearguard actions in what had become an unwinnable war. And yet, in the face of seemingly hopeless odds, the Boers revived and, by the summer of 1900, a new phase of the war was beginning that would last until May 1902.

Allenby attributed the Boer resurgence to Christiaan de Wet, the commander-in-chief of the Orange Free State forces.[22] De Wet's determination, capacity for making quick responses and ability to exploit any advantage made him an outstanding partisan general. From early April 1900 he reshaped Boer strategy and attracted to himself like-minded men, all younger-generation commanders like Louis Botha, T. H. de la Rey, Ben Viljoen and, later, Jan Smuts, who were willing to continue guerrilla warfare against the British. What de Wet had in mind were small kommandos, disencumbered from their wagon trains, who would range across the countryside, drawing sustenance from and finding shelter among its largely sympathetic population, and attacking small or isolated British units. He gave striking proof of the effectiveness of his methods by the action at Sannah's Post, the first of a series of lightning raids and ambushes that embarrassed the British during the late spring and summer of 1900. The war of pinpricks waged by an elusive enemy would, de Wet and his supporters believed, make the Orange Free State and the Transvaal ungovernable, force Britain to commit vast numbers of troops and large amounts of cash, and finally undermine the national will to fight on. Exhaustion and war-weariness would drive the British government to negotiate and concede the independence of the Afrikaner states.

For all that he resented being forced to remain in South Africa for a further two years, Allenby respected the fighting spirit of the 'bitter-enders', as the Boer partisans were called. Sometimes he was infuriated by the 'abominable obstinacy of the Boers', but at least once he confessed to a sneaking admiration for their stubbornness.[23] Throughout the summer and autumn of 1900 Allenby was employed on mopping-up operations in the highlands west of Pretoria and the cutting-off of the Pretoria–Delagoa railway, the Boers' last link with the outside world. There were occasional sharp engagements, and one relaxing interlude after Allenby had led a party of Inniskillings from Barberton to occupy nearby Eureka and the Sheba gold-mine. For a short time he was military governor of a collection of zinc-roofed huts, or, as he put it, 'King of Sheba', which made Mrs Allenby 'Queen of Sheba'.[24] The climate of the hills was temperate and he found time for extended nature rambles.

Outside Eureka, the face of the war was changing. On 29 November Kitchener took over from Roberts as Commander-in-Chief, and immediately launched himself into preparations for a ruthless war against the partisans who were disrupting vast areas of the Transvaal and the Orange Free State. His answer to the free-ranging kommandos was the creation of mounted columns that would, in groups of three or four, trawl the veldt for guerrillas. By mid-1901, Kitchener had made the column commanders' work easier by ordering the construction of a network of garrisoned blockhouses linked by telephone and barbed-wire fences. From then on the mounted troops would act as beaters, flushing out the Boers and driving them into the mesh of wire. As they moved, the columns destroyed farmsteads; confiscated or burned all food and fodder found in them; killed or seized livestock; and carried off Boer wives, children and black servants and conveyed them to guarded 'concentration' camps. By these methods the bitterenders' logistical support would be eliminated, while the plight of their families might impel some to surrender.

Column warfare, which formed the pattern of Allenby's life until the end of the war, began in earnest in January 1901. He was now in command of the Inniskillings, whose colonel had returned home, and his excellent fighting record secured his appointment as a column commander. As Kitchener always made clear, he alone was the master-player and his column commanders were his creatures, to be used as he liked. He judged by results and made or broke men accordingly.[25] Allenby accepted these conditions unquestioningly and even compared himself to a single pawn on the chessboard, unable to see, let alone assess, the state of play. His quietist temperament served him well and he never, unlike some of his fellow column commanders, fell foul of the Commander-in-Chief and found himself 'Stellenbosched'; that is, sent to undertake trivial duties away from the front. (At the beginning of the war incompetent generals had been sent to the depot at Stellenbosch.)

Early in 1901 Allenby commanded a column in the eastern Transvaal, was moved in April to the Middelburg district, and spent the summer in the western Transvaal. Towards the end of the year he and his force were shifted to familiar ground of twenty years before, the Transvaal/Zululand border, and he ended the war back in the eastern Transvaal. Every operation followed a similar pattern although the 'bags' – that is, the number of Boers killed or captured – varied greatly. Each group of columns operated under a general, although his overall control and ability to secure co-operation between columns were frequently limited by distance and often rather slipshod communications. Individual column commanders were therefore left to their own devices for much of the time.

Allenby seems to have enjoyed the work, which was unusual, for many of his brother officers found it tedious in the extreme. 'One mopes and gets ill' in camp, he told his wife in January and, three months later at the beginning of another trek, he announced that he was 'off on a jaunt' through rough country which the local Boers called 'Hell'. He was still homesick and ended this letter with the news, 'I am entitled to 6 clasps for the War Medal. I don't want them. I want to come home.'[26] Nevertheless, there were compensations, for he demanded and got fried kidneys for breakfast, while sequestered Boer livestock and poultry provided fresh meat for other meals. At the outset of operations, a brother officer had arranged for a bottle of whisky to be sent daily by post from Cape Town, although delays in delivery led to alternate gluts and dearths of what must have been a necessity on campaign.[27]

Allenby was fortunate in the company he kept. He cultivated Andrew ('Banjo') Paterson, an officer in the New South Wales Lancers who was also the war correspondent for the *Sydney Morning Herald* and the Melbourne *Age*. By profession a solicitor, Paterson was better known as a poet, his most celebrated ballad being 'Waltzing Matilda', written in 1895. Allenby found the man who was considered the Kipling of the outback a delightful companion and encouraged him in his writing.

The war diary kept by Allenby's column operating in the eastern Transvaal during August 1901 gives something of the flavour of the campaign and the problems he faced daily.[28] He commanded eighty officers and just over two thousand men, over half of whom were mounted. The column was well armed for its size; there were eight artillery pieces, five machine-guns and a pom-pom. There were always difficulties keeping the force supplied, since convoys of food and ammunition were tempting targets for the Boers who were usually short of both. Communications with neighbouring columns were always haphazard. On 8 August, when Allenby stumbled on a strong Boer detachment well dug-in on high ground, he dared not attack without the backing of Lieutenant-Colonel Kekewich's column. Unfortunately no contact could be made, and by the time that co-operation had been arranged, the Boers had vanished.

To prevent such mishaps, telegraph lines were laid so that the overall commander, General Fetherstonehaugh, could synchronise the movements of all columns. On 12 August he wired Allenby with orders to hurry to the assistance of Lieutenant-Colonel Ian ('Ghazi') Hamilton. Allenby immediately obeyed, his men riding 30 miles through a moonless night. Again there was frustration; nothing resulted from this manoeuvre, and after thirty days of patrols and skirmishes Allenby's column had killed six Boers, wounded eight, taken nineteen prisoner and accepted the surrender of a further thirty-one. His own losses were four dead (including a trooper shot during an ambush of a supply convoy) and five gravely wounded. The column had also taken thirty women and ninety-eight children prisoner, after the demolition of their farms, destroyed fifteen ploughs and twenty-two wagons, and captured two hundred and sixty-nine head of cattle.

During an earlier sweep, Allenby had told his wife that the presence of Boer families and servants made his camp resemble that of 'an Old Testament Patriarch'. He saw something of the fate of these families in October 1901 when he passed a camp near Standerton, where he heard that a measles epidemic was killing children at the rate of seventy a week. No doubt repeating what he had been told by local officers, he commented, 'It's partly the fault of the mothers. They don't do what the doctors tell them. One covered her child with green paint, another covered the child with cow dung'.[29] The scandal of the high death rates in the camps had stirred up much agitation inside Britain, largely orchestrated by those who were against the war in principle. The uncontrollable epidemics which ran through the camps, notably enteric fever, which also decimated British forces, highlighted what critics of the war called Kitchener's 'methods of barbarism' and increased public pressure on the government to seek a negotiated settlement. For entirely personal reasons the war-weary Allenby was sympathetic, and in a letter to his wife of 27 October he expressed pleasure at hearing the news that his countrymen at home were 'getting tired of the show'.[30]

The demands of anti-guerrilla operations were pulling more and more black Africans into what was popularly imagined, then and later, to be 'a white man's war'. Blacks were recruited as spies, and every column Intelligence Oficer employed black scouts whose local knowledge and fieldcraft were invaluable. They were well paid, given bonuses when they captured Boers, and, despite reservations, were armed.[31] There were also plenty of blacks, motivated by an ancestral loathing for the Boers, who attacked isolated parties whenever the chance occurred. In March 1901, Allenby encountered and mildly admonished some Swazis who had recently ambushed and killed fourteen Boers; soon afterwards, his camp was visited by a body of Zulus who performed a war dance which he interpreted as an expression of 'their dislike of the Boers'.[32] In the following year 200 Zulus were attached to his column in the eastern Transvaal. All this outraged the Boers, who accused the British of fomenting a race war. Ben Viljoen, one of the guerrilla commanders, protested in August 1901 about the enlistment and arming of blacks, and the presence in scout units of NCOs from the 'degraded class' of poor whites who could never exercise authority over the natives because they were 'consorting with their women'.[33]

As the war limped on into 1902, Allenby was showing unmistakable signs of strain. During the previous year he had suffered two serious bouts of 'flu and his wife, disturbed by the gloomy tone of his letters, hurried out to join him, reaching Durban in March. He was then up-country and unable to see her until 25 May, less than a week before the final peace was signed at Vereeniging.

Like many, he found the sort of war he was being asked to wage distasteful. He felt no animus towards 'brother Boer', as he called his enemy, and in his letters he spoke warmly of individuals, including captured bitterenders, whom he met and talked to.[34] Kitchener demanded a different attitude from his subordinates; in his instructions to column commanders issued in July 1901 he ordered them to use 'every means in their power to stamp out as rapidly as possible all armed resistance'.[35] In some quarters this was taken as an invitation to extremes of ruthlessless; near Volkrust, four captured Boers were each given twenty-five strokes with a sjambok, and in northern Transvaal a court martial found two Australian officers guilty of murdering POWs.[36]

Kitchener's remorseless drive for results infected his generals, who in turn put pressure on column commanders. As this mounted, Allenby threw overboard his usual quietism and began to censure his superiors. In October 1901 he complained to his wife about serving under 'a series of difficult generals' who 'don't care a straw about horses'. On another occasion he moaned about generals with 'no more brains or backbone than a bran doll', a risky outburst given that all officers' letters were, in theory, censored.[37]

Although he felt he had much to grumble about, Allenby had done well in the Boer War. He had laid the foundations for his future career by showing himself a gallant, dedicated, hard-working and resourceful officer. His 'bag' at the end of May 1901, which would be noticed approvingly by Kitchener, was particularly impressive, including over 200 Boers killed or captured and five artillery pieces.[38] Allenby also got to know Roberts (who congratulated him on being the only officer of his acquaintance who appeared not to have aged during the war), Kitchener and French, each of whom entertained him to dinner. Like his brother column commanders, Haig, Plumer and Byng, Allenby emerged from the war as a man marked for promotion.

PART 2

HIGH COMMAND

1902–June 1917

CHAPTER 5

THE ROAD TO WAR

1902–AUGUST 1914

PROMOTION came quickly for Allenby. In 1902 he was appointed to command the 5th Lancers; from 1905 to 1909 he commanded 4 Cavalry Brigade; and early in 1910 he was made Inspector-General of Cavalry with the rank of major-general. This post assured him command of the cavalry division earmarked for the British Expeditionary Force, the army designated for service in north-west Europe in the event of England joining France and Russia in a war against Germany and Austria-Hungary.

Advancement and new responsibilities transformed Allenby. An officer hitherto noted for his good nature and affability became a caricature martinet, notorious for his prickly temper, caustic remarks and overbearing manner. Edmonds, who recorded the change, thought that Allenby assumed the role of the blusterer because he could not think of any other way in which to assert his authority. 'When later Allenby became a general, to our great amusement, he tried to play what he thought was the part and assumed a toughness of manner and abruptness of speech which were not natural to him – and became "The Bull". . . .'[1]

Stories of Allenby's 'bullishness' (though most came from his period on the Western Front) circulated widely and found their way into many diaries, letters and memoirs. Two, dating from before the war, give a vivid impression of his new abrasiveness. The first was a conversation between him and a lancer squadron commander over a report on an unsatisfactory junior officer.

Allenby: 'I call him a converter.'
Squadron commander: 'A converter, Sir, I don't understand?'
Allenby: 'A converter of good food into dung!'[2]

What must have been an extremely rigorous inspection of a cavalry barracks provoked the following exchange after the discovery of a mouldy potato in a refuse tub.

Allenby: 'What a waste of a potato!'
Sergeant-Major: 'It is a bad one, Sir.'
Allenby: 'Then it should not have been drawn!'[3]

Allenby was determined to allow nothing, however trivial, to escape his investigations, and became obsessed with minor infractions of regulations. His most celebrated, and for his subordinates most tiresome, hobby-horse was correctness of dress, in particular chin-straps. Even during the retreat from Mons in August 1914, he found time to fulminate against men who did not wear their chin-straps and officers who ignored this lapse.[4] It was after an explosion about this or some similar peccadillo during the 1909 manoeuvres that he acquired the permanent nickname 'The Bull', which replaced 'Apple Pie', a mocking reference to his exaggerated concern for neatness and order.[5]

'Pull up your socks' was the message that ran ahead of Allenby on his tours of inspection. Sudden combustion could be expected at any time for any reason, and the victims of his rage invariably felt humiliated and resentful. Gough, who had witnessed him menace an officer with a stick, detected that the mask of truculence hid a general who was out of his depth. Watching him during pre-war cavalry manoeuvres, Gough noticed that Allenby was easily perplexed and in his uncertainty followed Haig's procedures, often an unwise course. The equally unsympathetic Edmonds came to a similar conclusion: Allenby was at heart 'a good sort' who was forced to 'play-act a role for which he was not fitted'.[6]

Both judgements held some truth, especially as in private Allenby remained a loving husband and an affectionate father, and was even more interested than ever in natural history and foreign travel. Those colleagues who enjoyed his friendship or penetrated his carapace found him still an agreeable, stimulating and mentally alert companion. He was, as one put it, 'a huge Newfoundland dog', although, unlike those benevolent creatures, he snarled and bit.[7]

There were, however, other, less discernible reasons for the sudden change in Allenby's character. He was learning how to exercise authority during a period in which the Army was undergoing upheavals that had partly come about as a result of the uncomfortable lessons of the Boer War. More importantly, the Army was having to adapt to a new role, since, from January 1906, the recently created General Staff had been making plans for future British intervention in a Continental land war. If, and the latest shifts in British foreign policy pointed in this direction, the Army took its place alongside the French against the Germans then it would have to be drastically reorganised. In size the British could never match the mass conscripted European armies, but it could equal, perhaps surpass, them in efficiency.

From 1906 eficiency had to be imposed at every level, a concept that made many officers uneasy. Old habits of thought still lingered: a flabbergasted Field-Marshal Sir Evelyn Wood, on hearing proposals for reform advanced in 1907, protested, 'If you organise the British Army you'll ruin it.' What the old veteran and others of like mind feared was the destruction of the Army's peculiar ethos, which had been preserved for the past century despite structural reforms. It rested on intangibles that could never be measured in terms of efficiency and was proudly regarded as the Army's greatest strength. 'Officers may have been stupid and the men bovine', one junior officer wrote on the eve of the Boer War, 'yet each knew how to die for the other, and without mutual self-sacrifice there can be no right living in the military sense.' He added, and few would have contradicted him, that 'the height of soldiership was to be a sportsman', an ideal well suited 'to the days of sword and lance and not those of magazine rifle and machine- gun'.[8]

But the Edwardian Army, officered by gentlemen whose values were based on what they had been taught in their public schools, faced a war in which technical efficiency and professional training counted for as much as team spirit and playing the game for its own sake. At least for the time being gentlemen retained their monopoly of command, since the Parliamentary Select Committee that had discussed raising officers' pay to assist the commissioning of those without private incomes abandoned the idea in 1907 as too costly. Another committee concluded a year later 'that the majority of young officers will not work unless compelled'; that 'keenness is out of fashion' and that 'it is not the correct form'; and that 'the idea is . . . to do as little as they possibly can'.[9] This was the view from the top since the committee had taken its evidence from senior officers.

As a general officer specifically empowered to assess how regiments were measuring up to new standards of efficiency, Allenby faced an awkward and unpopular task since cavalrymen were extremely conserva-tive. He chose a minatory approach which involved riding roughshod over other men's sensibilities, and got results through intimidation rather than persuasion. As Staff College contemporaries had noticed, he was never fluent on public occasions, and so he substituted bluster for eloquence. In an institution where power flowed downwards and automatic obedience was a way of life, his conduct was not unusual. In 1895, he had been on the receiving end of, and had been deeply hurt by, a tirade from an inspecting officer who openly doubted his professionalism and commitment.[10] The Army had always contained volatile generals whose authority rested on the loudness of their voices and the shortness of their tempers: Cardigan of Light Brigade fame was the most notorious, and earlier Picton had sworn and bullied his way across the Peninsula. Allenby had chosen to follow this tradition and, interestingly, his well-known irascibility did not impede his promotion. Moreover, his behaviour, however unpleasant, could be justified on the grounds of military efficiency, since unreproved negligence in small matters encouraged it in larger.

The drive for efficiency directly affected the cavalry in a number of ways. After the Boer War, champions of traditional cavalry warfare pointed enthusiastically to the charge at Elandsgaate in October 1899 as a classic example of a successful charge on a modern battlefield, even though it had been a small-scale affair. Allenby's Kimberley ride was also cited, although with less justification, by French, who felt confident that, in a European war, 'Cavalry forces will come together, and then the rifle is of no use at all.' Haig agreed, and predicted that mass cavalry offensives would be decisive on the European battlefield.[11] Major-General Brabazon, who had served alongside Allenby, asserted in an astonishing flight of fancy that British cavalrymen should be re-equipped with battle-axes, weapons which, he believed, were ideally suited to the 'Anglo-Saxon' temperament![12]

This was merely an extreme statement of the old view that charging horsemen represented an irresistible moral and physical force that could not be deflected by rifle fire. Opposing opinion, drawing substantial evidence from what had actually happened in South Africa, held that cavalrymen would have to become mounted infantrymen. Their strength lay in a mixture of mobility and firepower. Up to a point, Allenby concurred. He certainly recognised the value of machine-guns to cavalry, and expressed his views in characteristically staccato manner to the War Office Committee on Weapons in 1902. 'I have found the Maxim very effective, up to even 3,000 yards. No Boers will face it in the open, even at extreme ranges. I should like to have one per squadron.'[13] This was exceptional, since most officers were dismissive of machine-guns, largely on grounds of their frequent jamming. He stuck by this opinion, and during a lecture on the cavalry delivered to the United Services Institute in 1910, pleaded for more machine-guns to be issued to the cavalry.[14]

Allenby's view – that in the future cavalry would need firepower – prevailed, but only gradually, and in the teeth of opposition from diehard horsemen like Haig and French, who still insisted that there was a place for sabre and lance on the modern battlefield. The result of the debate, embodied in the cavalry's new training programme, was a compromise. The horsemen underwent intensive instruction in musketry and learned how to fight as mounted infantrymen, but retained their sabres. Even Allenby, ignoring what he had seen and learned in South Africa, still hankered after traditional cavalry warfare.

The strength of his attachment to old-style mounted tactics was apparent during the annual cavalry manoeuvres, where he would insist on the rehearsal of mass, stirrup-to-stirrup charges. On one occasion, in 1909, the war-game got out of hand when the Household Cavalry charged 1 Cavalry Brigade at close range and two men were killed and several injured. Such displays alarmed onlookers, who were astonished by the facility with which senior cavalry officers resorted to the charge, often in the most adverse conditions. After the 1913 cavalry manoeuvres, General Sir Charles Douglas, the Inspector-General of the Forces, wrote despairingly that 'the present training of cavalry shows tendencies that may lead to useless sacrifice of our available cavalry force in war'.[15]

Some responsibility for this state of affairs must rest with Allenby, although both Haig and French (who from 1911–14 was Chief of the Imperial General Staff) remained unshaken in their faith in shock action. And yet to some degree Allenby redeemed himself, and got his horsemen ready to face the realities of modern warfare by pressing ahead with a training programme that emphasised deployment to cover an army's retreat, reconnaissance, alternate marching and riding to save horses from fatigue, and marksmanship. All paid dividends in 1914.

As a cavalry commander, Allenby showed no outstanding talent. He performed indifferently when in charge of a cavalry division attached to Haig's forces during a large-scale exercise in the autumn of 1912, which made Edmonds suspect his unfitness for command. Haig came off even worse; his forces were outmanoeuvred by Lieutenant-General Sir James Grierson, who made enterprising use of air reconnaissance. One thing was clear from this and similar manoeuvres: there was no sign that a supreme commander of Wellingtonian stature was emerging from the British Army.

The purpose of the huge war-games on Salisbury Plain and elsewhere, and of the pursuit of efficiency, was to prepare for the forthcoming war in

Europe. What part the British Army would play in this war was the question that dominated British military thinking between 1902 and 1914, and provided the impulse behind the thorough overhaul of the Army during this period. The steady deterioration of Anglo-German relations, and the entry into friendly discussions with France in 1904 and Russia in 1907, opened the way to exploratory military contacts between the British and French Armies in January 1906.

High-level strategic planning was conducted in secret by a small circle of senior officers, bureaucrats and cabinet ministers. Global naval and military strategy was the province of the newly formed Committee of Imperial Defence, while the Army's war plans were handled by the General Staff. It was the General Staff that initiated contacts with their French counterparts and began the covert joint discussions for future co-operation that lasted from 1906 to the outbreak of war eight years later.

At first there had been two competing strategies, both based upon the precedents of the Napoleonic Wars. One, which had strong naval backing, relied on superior British sea power and involved a series of seaborne raids on the coast of northern Europe. The other, favoured by the General Staff, called for a British Expeditionary Force to be landed for service alongside the French Army on the Franco-Belgian border. This would be the twentieth-century equivalent of Wellington's Peninsular army and, like it, would be an earnest of a permanent British Continental commitment. By the beginning of 1906, the French scheme had been endorsed by the Committee of Imperial Defence and the new Foreign Secretary, Sir Edward Grey, gave his permission for Anglo-French military conversations. Knowledge of these developments was severely restricted; the Prime Minister, Sir Henry Campbell-Bannerman, and his successor, H. H. Asquith, knew and so, in time, did Richard Burdon Haldane, the Secretary for War, Winston Churchill and David Lloyd George. Both Prime Ministers were extremely nervous about public opinion which, they believed, might accuse the government of warmongering if details of the extent of British commitment to France leaked out. Only in November 1911, and after two major international crises in which Britain had lined up with France against Germany, was the full Cabinet told of the close military co-operation between the two countries.

At the heart of strategy-shaping were two determined figures. The first, Lord Esher, held no public office but excelled in manipulating his extensive political, military and royal connections. A shadowy eminence, he provided much of the impetus for Army reform and was intimate with French and Haig, smoothing the way for their advancement. Equally influential was Major-General Sir Henry Wilson who, as Director of Military Operations from June 1910, was responsible for the evolution of strategy. An acolyte of Roberts, he was a Protestant Ulsterman who entertained Caesarean fantasies and was addicted to backstairs intrigue. A facial wound and hooded eyes gave him a languid, mocking expression and Haig, who distrusted his fluency and cleverness, imagined that Wilson was forever laughing up his sleeve at him, which was probably true. After 1914, when they became colleagues, Allenby got on cordially with Wilson since neither man threatened the other, but other generals found him conceited and dangerous.

Wilson was a passionate Francophile, with an outstanding command of the French language, who threw his considerable persuasive powers into pressing the government to go beyond military conversations and make an unequivocal pledge to fight on France's side. In August 1911 his arguments swayed the 'frocks' (as senior officers called politicians, who commonly wore frock coats) that the British Espeditionary Force was the only viable strategy for Britain; he went so far as to urge automatic intervention the moment that Germany and France went to war.

Allenby was on the periphery of the elevated and secretive circle that devised grand strategy. He did not sit on the board of senior officers that worked out the details of Britain's mobilisation plans, although it would not have been hard for him and similarly placed officers to have guessed the government's intentions towards France in the event of war. For instance, during 1912–13 the Army medical authorities were ordering stretchers specifically designed to fit in French railway carriages.[16]

While preparations for a hypothetical European war pressed ahead, the minds of many officers, including Allenby, were turning towards a real conflict nearer home. In 1912 the Liberal government had unenthusiastically passed an Irish Home Rule Bill in return for Parliamentary support given by the Irish Home Rule Party. The House of Lords, with its permanent Conservative majority, exercised its delaying powers and Irish self-government was postponed until the summer of 1914. The prospect of an Irish parliament dominated by Roman Catholics had long been an anathema to the minority Ulster Protestants, whose immediate reaction was the formation of the Ulster Volunteer Force, pledged to resist Home Rule, and a revival of the slogan 'Ulster will fight; Ulster will be right'. By March 1914, the Volunteers mustered 80,000 men, nearly a quarter of whom were armed with smuggled rifles and machine-guns. On the mainland, Conservative and Unionist politicians, notably Andrew Bonar Law and Sir Edward Carson, publicly encouraged what to all intents and purposes was an incipient rebellion.

By early 1914, and with great reluctance, the Cabinet was forced to face the fact that, at some stage in the near future, the Army would have to be employed to disarm and, if necessary, disperse the Volunteers. In March the Irish nettle had to be grasped, since Intelligence reports suggested that the Ulstermen, who were daily growing bolder, might seize and plunder undefended arsenals in the province. To meet this threat and as an earnest of the government's refusal to be browbeaten, the Cabinet ordered the General Officer Commanding in Ireland, Lieutenant-General Sir Arthur Paget, to send detachments to Ulster to protect arsenals and guard official buildings. Simultaneously, a number of men-o'-war were concentrated in Irish waters.

These precautionary measures triggered a crisis of conscience for the officers of the Irish garrison, who were almost to a man Conservative and anti-Home Rule. They were being ordered to proceed against a body of men with whom they sympathised in support of a government which most of them detested for its radicalism and hostility towards the upper classes. While Paget had been strictly enjoined to do nothing that could be interpreted as provocative, there was a widespread feeling that the Volunteers would not stand by passively and allow the government to reassert its authority in Ulster. The possible Volunteer reaction was raised on 20 March at the British Army's Dublin HQ during a tense meeting between Paget and his brigade commanders. He engaged the issue of officers' private feelings head-on and clumsily; officers whose homes were in Ulster would be excused service there, and those who had political objections to 'shooting down Ulstermen' were offered a chance to resign their commissions. If they took this course the Army would consider them 'dismissed' and they would forgo their pension rights.

Allenby had just arrived at the Curragh, a military camp outside Dublin, for the annual inspection of cavalry training and was staying with Brigadier-General Hubert Gough, commander of 3 Cavalry Brigade who came from Anglo-Irish, Protestant landowning stock. Gough was wholeheartedly behind the Ulstermen, and must have given his guest an indication of the depth of his own and his fellow officers' feelings. While Allenby went off to assess the cavalrymen's efficiency, Gough had been driven to Dublin for the conference with Paget. On his return, he and sixty of his officers from 3 Cavalry Brigade resigned their commissions in protest at Paget's offer and as a public statement of their refusal to serve in Ulster.

This news was delivered to Allenby by Lieutenant-Colonel MacEwen of the 16th Lancers at the end of the inspection of one of MacEwen's squadrons. Asked his views on the matter, Allenby prevaricated. He congratulated the squadron on its turn-out and made no comment on the Ulster situation. Soon after, on being told that an infantry battalion had been entrained for Belfast as a precaution against UVF violence, he said 'this is no place for me', excused himself luncheon in the Lancers' mess, and hurried off to Dublin where he caught the ferry for England.[17]

He was back at his London house in Wetherby Gardens by the afternoon of 22 March and was, according to his wife, 'very angry' at what he had witnessed in Ireland.[18] He proceeded to the War Office and gave a full account to French of what was happening.[19] His anger was directed towards Paget's effort to bring the officers into line for, as he wrote to Gough, 'that question should not have been put in the form in which it was forced upon you'.[20] He carefully refrained from making any suggestion as to how the question ought to have been framed, and urged Gough to reconsider his resignation since 'The country cannot afford to lose your services.'[21]

Allenby had picked up enough at the Curragh to know that officers of all three cavalry regiments in Gough's brigade were solidly behind their commander; he told a friend of the Conservative colonial administrator, Lord Milner, that he would 'stand by them'.[22] He also remarked that the other ranks were with their officers, which was far from true. One 16th Lancer trooper told his family that he was keen to go to Ulster for the excitement, and tellingly contrasted the 'aristocratic and plutocratic' Army's willingness to handle strikes with its reluctance to confront the Volunteers.[23]

So far Allenby had behaved with calculating prudence, and would do so for the rest of the crisis. Had he remained in Ireland he might have been called upon as a senior officer to lend his authority to efforts to bring the dissidents to heel. This would have been an unbearable burden, since he had some sympathy with the officers' predicament and shared their sense of outrage at the way in which they had been asked to barter their consciences for careers and pensions, a proposal that trampled on the antique but still deeply held concept of an officer's honour. Keeping to the path of correctness, he had immediately reported the whole business to his superior, and had steered well clear of the political issue which had been the root cause of the ruckus.

While he stood, a circumspect but benevolently neutral figure, on the sidelines, a wave of sympathetic resignations ran through the Army. Gough followed Allenby to London and extracted from Colonel J. E. B. Seeley, the Secretary for War, a promise that troops would not be used in Ulster, a guarantee that Seeley had no authority to give. When an astonished Cabinet made this clear, French resigned after nudging from Wilson.

In the end an embarrassed government compromised. The resignations were ignored, and on 27 March the War Office issued a general order that forbade the questioning of officers as to their reactions in hypothetical situations and insisted on normal obedience to all orders. At the same time the Cabinet jettisoned plans to impose a military solution on the Northern Irish problem and opened negotiations with the Ulstermen and Home Rulers. The former appreciated better than most what had been achieved by the Curragh Incident (some incorrectly but understandably substituted the word 'Mutiny' for 'Incident'), and congratulated Gough and his brother officers for a gesture which had effectively ruled out a policy of coercion in Ulster.

Allenby emerged well from the affair; he had behaved with judicious circumspection and stuck to the proper course of duty. Not that this mattered greatly, for others who had thrown themselves into the protest found that their careers did not suffer unduly for what was an attempt by the government's servants to dictate the government's policies. What amounted to a declaration of independence from political control by the Army anticipated the complex struggles between War Cabinets and high command in the field for the direction of strategy in the First World War. To a large extent these struggles were inevitable, but it is possible to speculate whether the confident stubbornness of the generals owed something to the knowledge that the Curragh protests had changed government policy. The incident may also have given some generals a dangerous taste for dabbling in party politics.

The affair of the Curragh and the Irish imbroglio were soon over-shadowed by events in Central Europe. The assassination of the Archduke Franz Ferdinand, heir to the throne of Austria, and Arch-duchess Sophie by Serbian terrorists at Sarajevo on 28 June precipitated an international crisis that for a time few in Britain took seriously. British detachment was impossible, however, after 28 July, when Austria declared war on Serbia. The following day, the Serbs' patron, Russia, began calling up its reservists. In Berlin decision-taking now passed to the General Staff which, like its Austro-Hungarian counterpart, had been alarmed by the scale of recent Russian rearmanent and was keen to engage Russia on terms which offered a chance of outright victory. At the same time the German High Command's meticulously calculated war plans demanded that the German Army start its mobilisation on the same day as Russia's. At midday on 31 July the German Army began mobilisation, and a day later Austria–Hungary and Germany declared war on Russia. On 2 August, the second day of her precautionary mobilisation, France, holding to the terms of her alliance with Russia, declared war on Germany and Austria–Hungary.

In the meantime, the British government wavered. On 29 July the

Cabinet, fearing the worst, agreed to enter the war alongside Russia and France if the Germans invaded neutral Belgium. It was argued, rightly as it turned out, that this affront to international law would swing British public opinion behind the war. During 3 August German units entered Belgium and gave the British government its justification for entering the conflict; war was declared on 4 August, and at ten to five in the afternoon of that day the War Office issued mobilisation orders.

Two days later, Allenby went to the War Office, where he joined his fellow generals who had been given command of the British Expeditionary Force's divisions to hear what was expected of them. They heard details of operations which had only been finalised by ministers and generals the day before, after a meeting in which Wilson had shown how the presence of the BEF in the region of Maubeuge on the French left flank would help stem the German advance through Belgium. Meanwhile, and in accordance with the French Plan 17, the bulk of the French Army would advance across Alsace and Lorraine in a push on the Rhine. If things went badly, the commanders were reassured that their position on the Franco-Belgian border would make it easier for a quick withdrawal to the Channel ports.

Allenby's work with the cavalry during the previous twelve years assured his appointment to command the Cavalry Division in France. He was fifty-three, about the average age for a divisional commander, and outwardly resembled what a subordinate called a 'pattern general'. He was 'tall, handsome and well set-up', with a firm jaw and what was, for men in his position, an almost regulation martial moustache, although not the walrus-like growths that distinguished French and Haig.[24] But was his heart really in the business of war? His consuming interests lay beyond the parade ground, but his means were limited and he needed his Army salary – he had borrowed from his mother to pay the mortgage on a London house. As a professional soldier his experience of active command had been confined to columns of less than 2,000 men in anti-guerrilla operations, but then his Commander-in-Chief, French, had never commanded more than a cavalry division. His soldierly talents were worthy rather than outstanding, and he enjoyed an unenviable reputation as a martinet.

CHAPTER 6

WITH THE CAVALRY
TO THE FRONT

AUGUST 1914–APRIL 1915

THE fortunes of Allenby and the BEF during the summer and autumn of 1914 were dictated by war plans devised over the past twenty-odd years in the war ministries of Berlin and Paris. Since 1911, the British General Staff had been aware of the broad outline of the German Schlieffen Plan, designed to outflank the French and encircle Paris by means of a massive offensive through Belgium and north-eastern France. The exact details of the plan and, most importantly, the numbers of men involved, were not known in London or Paris.

General Count von Schlieffen's plan, first formulated in 1891, appeared to be a war-winner. It solved the problem of a war on two fronts since, if the invasion of France went to schedule, there would be time enough for the victorious German armies to regroup, entrain and shift east to meet the Russians, whose mobilisation was expected to take at least six weeks, possibly longer. Confidence had increased after Russia's defeat by Japan in 1905, and the German High Command was unperturbed by the prospect of British intervention which had been anticipated as early as 1906. All that could be expected from this quarter was the occupation of Antwerp and the Channel ports, and in general the Germans set little store by the British Army.

Nevertheless, von Schlieffen's successor as Chief of the General Staff, General Helmuth von Moltke, was uneasy about the sheer risks involved in the plan and his misgivings increased once the extent of Russia's military resurgence became known. Furthermore, in the phrase later used by General Erich von Ludendorff, Germany was 'shackled to the corpse', that is, the Austro-Hungarian Army, and so men and resources would be needed to keep it in the field. In the light of these new operational problems, the Schlieffen Plan was tampered with, and as a result the size of the force designated for the big push was reduced.

The French had long known of the principle behind the Schlieffen Plan, but imagined that once they had launched the offensive embodied in their Plan 17 the Germans would be forced to shift troops from Belgium to defend the Rhineland. Plan 17 placed three French armies, nearly two-thirds of France's manpower, on the German frontier and proposed to throw them forward as a huge battering-ram against the Rhine. For its success this attack depended on what French staff officers believed were the innate aggressive qualities of the French soldier. Airy theories about superior will and the offensive spirit permeated the minds of all senior French officers, abstractions that on the battlefields of August 1914 were translated into suicidal bayonet charges.

Both grand offensives were building up momentum during the second week of August as the 100,000-strong BEF crossed the Channel and moved northwards to its assembly point at Maubeuge. British mobilisation had proceeded with few hitches and throughout the Army there was a mood of buoyant optimism. As the troops passed through the Picardy countryside they were warmly received; on 20 August Allenby told his wife how he and his staff had been showered with flowers as they rode through villages.[1]

While the soldiers marched, their Commander-in-Chief, French, consulted with his allies. When he left London, he had been told by the new Secretary for War, Lord Kitchener, that his overriding duty was to co-operate with the French, but that he could act independently when he saw fit. Between 15 and 17 August, French met first the French Commander-in-Chief, General Joseph Jacques Césaire Joffre, and then General Charles Lanrezac, the commander of the Fifth Army which was deployed on the British right flank. Stripped of his crimson breeches, blue tunic and gilded red kepi, Joffre could easily have been mistaken for a prosperous peasant who relished good food and plenty of it. There was much of the peasant in his stubbornness and determination; he was not a great strategist, but he was not easily panicked. French liked him, and was particularly struck by his calm resolution. Lanrezac, another large man, was reserved and cantankerous and, since he spoke no English and the British C-in-C's French was poor, conversation between the two commanders was stilted. French left the meeting with a suspicion that his counterpart had been less than frank.

The exchanges with Joffre and Lanrezac revealed to French that the offensive in Alsace and Lorraine was making headway and that the German thrust into Belgium was gathering pace, although there were, as yet, no precise indications as to its weight and objectives. Three days later, on 20 August, the British Army had taken up its positions on a front that ran from Condé in the east along the Condé Canal to Mons.

Up-to-date intelligence about the Germans' activities in Belgium was now vital, and the responsibility for gathering it fell to Allenby's Cavalry Division. On 20 August he had established his Divisional HQ at Givry and patrols from his five brigades fanned out northwards to discover the enemy's strength and whereabouts. Allenby had been very lucky in his choice of Divisional Intelligence Officer, Colonel George Barrow, who had asked him for the job when they had met in the War Office sixteen days earlier. Barrow quickly gave proof of his ingenuity on 20 August when he went to Mons railway station and telephoned stations throughout Belgium. A reply in French or Flemish indicated they were still in Belgian hands, silence or a German accent meant that they had been taken.[2]

Barrow was able to chart details of the direction of the German advance – which passed through Brussels on the 20th – that were confirmed by aerial reconnaissance and reports from Allenby's patrols which had discovered Germans on the Ath–Mons road. French, who visited Allenby's HQ in the early afternoon of the 21st, refused to believe what he heard and dismissed intelligence of the German advance towards his lines as 'somewhat exaggerated'. There was, his official diary recorded, 'No news of a definite nature though many rumours'.[3] As the day wore on the rumours took alarming substance: an 11th Hussars patrol reported 7,000 Germans closing in on Mons, and shortly before midnight additional intelligence reached Allenby of heavy concentrations north of the town.[4] Even more disturbing was a report that reached French during the night of 22–23 August, via the British Military Attaché at The Hague, which claimed that 100,000 Germans had passed through Liège on the 20th.[5] By this time one of Allenby's patrols had crossed swords with a party of German uhlans near Soignies.

Allenby was among the first to grasp the reality of the BEF's situation. It was lying athwart the line of advance of a formidable German army, in fact General Alexander von Kluck's First Army. Not only were the British outnumbered by at least three to one, but they were in danger of being outflanked and cut off from any line of retreat to the coast. Little help could be expected from the French; on 22 August Lanrezac's Fifth Army began to fall back to the south, closely followed by units from the German Second and Third Armies. On the same day Haig heard that Plan 17 had gone awry and that the French had suffered the first of a series of major defeats in Alsace.[6]

It was now clear that the BEF and the French Fifth Army were facing a three-pronged offensive, by three German Army corps of about one million men in total, which they were not strong enough to delay, let alone throw back. The news from the south was baleful, for after the battles there on 22–23 August the French Army was retiring. For the next fortnight catastrophe seemed very close as the BEF attempted to extricate itself and retreated south-west, first towards St Quentin and then to the region east of Paris, which was reached by 5 September. French, who was profoundly dismayed by what he considered Lanrezac's lack of help, ordered a holding action, the battle of Mons, on the 23rd, and then a full-scale retreat.

Mons was a minor triumph. The Germans were momentarily thrown off balance and, to begin with, were astonished that they were fighting a British army. Operational security and press censorship had been so tight that von Kluck only discovered he was opposed by the British forces after his uhlans had stumbled into khaki-clad horsemen on the 22nd. He soon recovered and, after having been temporarily halted at Mons, pressed forward, certain that he could catch his opponents and fulfil the Kaiser's famous order to 'Exterminate the treacherous England, walk over General French's contemptible [*verächtlich*] little army'.

It was Allenby's task to prevent this. His cavalry, which French had prudently held in reserve since the 21st, had the job of covering the infantry's retreat, keeping in contact with the Germans, and holding off their advance guard of uhlans and jäger cyclist patrols. The retreat began in the early hours of 24 August, and almost immediately Allenby discovered that he had lost control over nearly all his brigades. This was vexing but unavoidable, as the horsemen were already widely scattered, and soon found themselves split up as they were drawn into operations to protect the flanks and rear of the thirteen, often separated, infantry brigades that were retiring by parallel routes through a corridor 20 miles wide.

Confusion became endemic as detachments lost contact with each other. In desperation one officer of the 11th Hussars rang up GHQ to find the location of his brigade and when he heard that they did not know, was reduced to asking villagers whether they had seen any other cavalrymen. Eventually he discovered his brigade 'somewhat of a chaos' at St Quentin, which was filled with 'a rabble of retreating infantry'.[7] Even when cavalry detachments knew where they were going, movement was sluggish along roads clogged with refugees, infantry, guns and transport wagons.

Allenby endeavoured to keep in touch with his men, but in doing so he

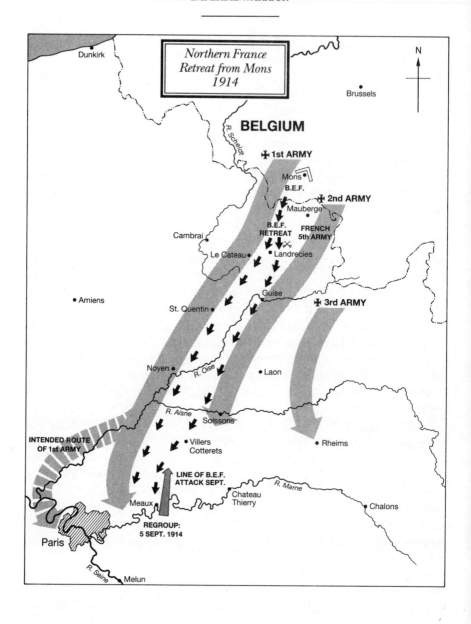

made himself elusive. On 27 August, a worried Brigadier-General Aylmer Haldane, commanding 10 Infantry Brigade, went in search of Allenby to find out if the cavalry were screening his brigade, and encountered another officer with a similar purpose. By chance they came across Cavalry HQ, where Allenby offered Haldane a welcome hard-boiled egg and some ration biscuits.[8] Supply systems had collapsed during the retreat and, as Allenby and his staff moved their Headquarters from châteaux to cottages, they had to fend for themselves and sleep whenever a chance occurred. Once Allenby was overcome by fatigue, and was found by Barrow exhausted and disheartened with his elbows on his knees and his head in his hands.[9] Somehow, and after some sleep, he rallied.

The strain of trying to co-ordinate a fragmented command was enormous. It was made worse by the wayward behaviour of one of his subordinates, Hubert Gough, who commanded 3 Cavalry Brigade which had been detailed to protect II Corps. Using the pretext that Allenby's orders were imprecise and unrealistic, Gough, off his own bat and against French's wishes, detached himself from Allenby and joined his friend Haig's I Corps.[10] Afterwards French lamely approved his temerity, and Gough continued to answer to French and not Allenby. The former Curragh ringleader was a man of easy loyalty who justified his apostasy by claiming it had been prompted by the sight of Allenby and his staff 'mesmerised' by the enemy during an engagement at Solesmes on the 25th.[11] There was also an element of panic in his decision; he told a Lancer officer, 'I am afraid we are surrounded . . . the Germans are in Amiens'.[12] Allenby shrugged off Gough's defection as 'only Gough's little way', but in private he was extremely bitter.[13] Relations between the two deteriorated and afterwards Gough never missed a chance to traduce Allenby.[14]

Throughout the retreat and under difficult circumstances, Allenby showed courage, energy and presence of mind. On the 24th, he supervised the cavalry cover during the rearguard action at Elouges during which the 9th Lancers and 4th Dragoon Guards, starved of 'real' cavalry action, somewhat unwisely charged formed German infantry. Their horses became snagged on barbed wire and they withdrew with heavy casualties; recording the action, the Lancers' War Diary proudly stated that the 'true cavalry spirit' had been displayed and that 'the moral effect was complete'.[15]

On the following day Allenby became increasingly worried about his ability to give adequate protection to Sir Horace Smith-Dorrien's (one of the five white survivors of the battle of Isandlwana, 1879) II Corps, which was falling back on Le Cateau. Allenby was a friend of Smith-

Dorrien, and at about one in the morning of 26 August he rode over to the latter's HQ at Bertry with the news that he lacked the cavalry to keep the Germans at bay and that if Smith-Dorrien did not shift his men before dawn, 'There will be another Sedan.' Like other senior officers, Allenby was haunted by the memory of what had happened in France in September 1870, when Napoleon's III's army had been herded into Sedan and forced to surrender to the Germans. Smith-Dorrien, who had already warned GHQ that his men were overcome with fatigue, consulted with his chief staff officer, Brigadier-General Forestier-Walker (a friend of Allenby's from Staff College days), and Major-General Hubert Hamilton of the 3rd Division. They confirmed what Smith-Dorrien already knew, that the men were too tired to be moved. Allenby quietly remarked, 'In that case I do not think you will get away.' 'I'll fight it out' was Smith-Dorrien's response, and Allenby agreed to assist him with what cavalry he could muster.[16]

The decision to fight a rearguard action at Le Cateau horrified GHQ and generated much subsequent acrimony. When he heard the news over the telephone during the early hours, French's Chief of Staff, Lieutenant-General Sir Archibald Murray, fainted and had to be brought to his senses with half a pint of champagne.[17] French, who was in the grip of pessimism and fearful that he was presiding over a rerun of Sir John Moore's 1808–9 retreat to Corunna, accused Smith-Dorrien of imperilling the whole army. He had long disliked Smith-Dorrien, who had been appointed to take over II Corps a week earlier only after King George V and Kitchener had overridden French's objections.[18] Relations between the two men soon became strained and Smith-Dorrien later accused French of deliberately keeping him in the dark about German movements.[19] There was more to this animosity than purely personal spite; French cherished Haig as his successor as C-in-C, and feared that, in the event of his removal, Smith-Dorrien would take over by reason of his seniority.[20] With the war less than a month old, the British High Command was already riven by jealousy and back-biting.

The battle of Le Cateau was not the disaster French had foretold. Von Kluck suffered an unexpected and savage rebuff in a day's fighting, during which he convinced himself that he was up against the entire BEF. Even French, who later gracelessly rescinded his judgement, praised Smith-Dorrien for having saved much of the army, and said as much in his Official Despatch. Le Cateau had given the retreating BEF a desperately needed breathing space and allowed it to escape; after the battle the German pressure was reduced.

Nevertheless, French remained dejected. Since 24 August he had showered the Cabinet with messages that berated the French and called for measures to be taken to secure the Channel ports for the army's evacuation. Kitchener was disturbed, and on the 26th asked, 'Please give me your candid opinion of the future resistance that may be expected from the French Army. Are they broken or what has happened to them?' French's answer did nothing to raise confidence: 'I consider I have not been treated very generously by the French commanders in allowing my retreat to be hampered by such vastly superior forces.'[21] Three days later, as those 'superior forces' approached Amiens, French was thinking in terms of an east-to-west retreat across France, and requested that the port of La Rochelle be prepared for re-embarkation.[22] On the following day, Kitchener heard from the Inspector of Communications at Rouen that the loss of Le Havre was imminent.[23]

This, together with French's plea that his army would need at least a fortnight in which to recuperate, forced Kitchener to call a midnight Cabinet meeting on 30 August, at which it was agreed that he should go to Paris immediately and see for himself what was happening. He arrived early in the afternoon of 1 September, and assured Joffre and the French Minister of War that the British Army would remain in the fight. Wearing the full uniform of a field-marshal, he took French aside and in a tense interview told him that the situation demanded that he would have to fight on. Haig, for one, felt sure that French had proved himself 'unfit' to command, and there were rumours that Kitchener had threatened the C-in-C with sacking.[24]

While Kitchener was injecting some ginger into French, the strategic situation had changed dramatically. On the 27th, Lanrezac's Fifth Army had turned on von Bülow's Second Army at Guise and severely shaken it. In response to von Bülow's request for support, von Kluck's First Army changed its line of advance and abandoned the preset course that would have taken it in a great arc across the Seine and west and then south of Paris. Now it was moving along a 20-mile front 30-odd miles north of Paris.

By 4 September, the redirection of von Kluck's army had been detected by aerial reconnaissance. The Military Governor of Paris, General Joseph-Simon Gallieni, immediately saw the chance for a mass attack on the exposed German flank, but Joffre was hesitant, arguing that it would take at least four days to concentrate the necessary forces. There was a tremendous risk involved and Joffre was uncertain whether those troops he could raise, particularly General Louis Franchet d'Esperey's First Army, would be in a condition to fight. Franchet d'Esperey was also unsure, but promised, 'My army can fight on the 6th, but its situation is not brilliant.' Neither was that of the exhausted BEF, now collected south-west of Paris, but French agreed to join in the counter-offensive across the Marne and was reconciled with Lanrezac.

The battle of the Marne (5–11 September) saved France and finally destroyed the Schlieffen Plan. What was left of Allenby's cavalry were ordered to cover the flanks of the advancing British and stay in contact with the French on the BEF's right. They were, to all intents and purposes, now fighting as mounted infantry. In an action near Faujus, the 18th Hussars dismounted and opened rapid rifle fire when they were charged by a German Guard Dragoon regiment. The Germans never made contact and were driven off with heavy losses.

There were some, Haig in particular, who hoped for something more than reconnaissance and covering actions from Allenby's horsemen. The II Corps Commander came across Allenby's HQ at Amilles on 7 September and was disappointed by what he discovered. 'I thought they were not doing much', he noted in his diary, and was dismayed to find that they had spent the night bivouacked behind the infantry. Two days later he met Brigadier-General Chetwode's 5 Cavalry Brigade moving forward at a walk, which annoyed him intensely. Believing that the enemy was in full retreat, he suggested to Chetwode 'that a little effort now might mean the conclusion of the war'. French too wanted a more rigorous cavalry pursuit.[25]

Both were mistaken. The German armies, although thrown back by the Marne offensive, were still in excellent order and their rearguard detachments of jägers with machine-guns were more than a match for galloping horsemen. Moreover the cavalry, like the infantry, continually found themselves under fire from the superior German artillery, something Allenby appreciated, even if Haig and French did not. Writing to his wife on 30 August, he observed, 'The Germans fight chiefly, so far, at long range, with artillery.'[26] This they continued to do during the Marne, and large bodies of horsemen made excellent targets.

On 10 September, von Moltke ordered his three armies in France to fall back. An early decisive victory had eluded both sides and a new phase in the war began, marked first by a German dash to secure the Channel ports and then by the creation of permanent lines, which meant digging in. Allenby was publicly congratulated by French for his direction of the cavalry during and after the retreat from Mons. This was fair; he had done much with limited resources in unfavourable conditions and he had wisely ignored demands for what would have been suicidal charges. He was proud of his men: 'Their spirit is splendid,' he told his wife, 'and they fight like tigers.' He too had behaved with great gallantry, once riding on horseback among unnerved men and rallying them under shellfire.[27]

In war, he was as bull-like as he had been during peacetime inspections and exercises. He still found time to upbraid men about chin-straps, and repeatedly revealed his peculiar aversion to a habit by which troopers would stuff a sock into their rifle-buckets, presumably to make it easier to remove the weapons. Once in battle, he showed all the symptoms of his soon-to-be-legendary aggressive spirit which made him drive men to fight beyond the limits of endurance. When, one night during the retreat, he was awoken by two colonels who confessed that they and their regiments were 'done in' and would have to be withdrawn from action, Allenby 'pulverised' them.[28] There were sharp words, too, for an army chaplain who had preached on the theme of turning the other cheek and loving one's enemies. Afterwards he was buttonholed by Allenby, who was furious at what he considered the pacifist tone of the sermon. 'I don't love my enemies,' he roared, 'I hate 'em and I'll do them all the harm I can.'[29]

After the Marne, the war entered a new stage, of which the main features were summed up by Allenby on 22 September as 'perpetual attacking and counter-attacking of local tactical positions'.[30] There was more to it than this; large-scale mobile warfare having failed disastrously, both sides struggled to seize and hold what land they could. For the British, the process involved a northwards thrust through Compiègne and Abbeville to St Omer, from where advances were made towards Ypres and Armentières, which were taken on 17–18 October. Both were occupied and subsequently defended at enormous cost in order to deny the Germans Calais and Dunkirk, ports through which reserves of men, ammunition, food and transport flowed from Britain.

Allenby's former Cavalry Division, now split in two for ease of command, the 1st Cavalry Division under Brigadier-General Beauvoir de Lisle, and the 2nd under Gough, was attached to the force allocated for the defence of Ypres. Fighting now as infantry with rifle and bayonet (Gough's heart was soon gladdened by the knowledge that his cavalrymen were adept with this bladed weapon in hand-to-hand fighting), the former horsemen were deployed on a 6-mile front along the south-eastern sector of Ypres's defences, between Dranoutre and Zaanvoorde. The medieval cloth town of Ypres lay within a landscape which has been likened to a saucer with a rim consisting of low ridges. If the Germans could gain possession of the gently undulating country around Ypres, the town would be transformed into a death-trap, overlooked and vulnerable to fire from three sides.

From 18 October until 22 November, the Germans launched a series of offensives to gain control of the high ground around Ypres. The struggle resolved itself into an extended slogging match in which the Germans enjoyed the advantage of larger numbers and a superior weight of artillery fire. As the battle proceeded, British gunners found themselves increasingly short of shells as stocks held in Britain became exhausted; some batteries were reduced to firing no more than four rounds a day. Both sides were desperately digging trenches and here the Germans were also better off, since they had begun the campaign well supplied with duckboards, hand grenades, flare pistols and trench mortars that had been originally intended for the sieges of the Belgian forts. Moreover, as Gough ruefully admitted, the Germans had made a very diligent study of trench warfare as it had been undertaken during the Russo-Japanese War of 1904–5.

The British were having to learn the skills of trench warfare the hard way. On 30 October the 9th Lancers were driven back from their trenches near Messines by enfilade fire, and the 11th Hussars had to give ground under heavy artillery fire.[31] As GHQ admitted, badly sited and shallow trenches were terribly vulnerable to shelling.[32] Command in this situation consisted of moving men around to plug gaps and, wherever ground was lost, ordering counter-attacks. It was, as Allenby told his wife on 31 October, 'Hardy and bloody fighting' in which 'our people did wonders'.[33] Losses were prodigious; during the fighting on the 30th one of the battalions under Allenby's command, the London Scottish, the first Territorial battalion at the front, lost over a third of its numbers. The 57th Indian (Wilde's) Rifles, one of the Indian regiments that had just joined the BEF, lost more than half its strength and all its officers during the heavy fighting around Messines on 31 October–1 November.[34]

Both the London Scottish and the Indians were among the units sent to reinforce Allenby's cavalry. In scale and ferocity, the fighting surpassed anything the British Army had yet experienced. By 22 November, when the Germans abandoned their offensive in the face of deteriorating weather conditions, no breakthrough had been achieved, although the British line had been pushed back closer to Ypres. In time, the Ypres Salient became a symbol of the British Army's determination to dig its heels in and fight on regardless. In strategic terms it was a vulnerable position, protruding into German lines. For this reason herculean efforts would be made to secure possession of the disputed high ground beyond the town during 1915 and 1917, latterly as a springboard for an ambitious offensive north towards the Belgian coast.

The First Battle of Ypres marked the end of mobile warfare and the beginning of a period in which the fighting line stabilised on the Western Front. By January 1915 two lines of parallel trenches extended from the Channel south-eastwards to the Swiss border. The decisive, war-winning battle had eluded the generals on both sides and now, faced with deadlock, they were forced to evolve a new strategy. Hints of the form it might eventually take were seen during the fighting around Ypres, when the conflict was reduced to a series of headlong attacks and countersallies in which men were pitted against bullets and high-explosive.

During First Ypres, Allenby had shown himself temperamentally suited to this sort of warfare; he was courageous on the occasions when he took personal charge of the fighting line, but, above all, he demonstrated an iron resolve not to let his defences be fractured, whatever the cost. Doggedness at the top would be needed if in the future the line was to be held, and, more importantly, this quality would be vital in a general when the moment came to launch and sustain an offensive. From January 1915, Allenby and the remnants of cavalry were moved behind the front lines to recuperate and to serve as a reserve. His conduct during August and September and at Ypres was not forgotten by French. On 8 May 1915, at French's bidding, Allenby succeeded Lieutenant-General Sir Herbert ('Daddy') Plumer in command of V Corps, then fighting for its life in the Ypres Salient. What was needed were the qualities Allenby had in abundance – tenacity, aggressiveness and moral stamina. Whether they were a substitute for generalship was another matter.

CHAPTER 7

AN OFFENSIVE SPIRIT

APRIL–DECEMBER 1915

ALLENBY'S independence as a front-line commander was limited. Responsibility for Allied strategy and the division of resources lay with the British and French General Staffs and War Cabinets. They worked hard throughout 1915, but the results were unpromising. No Wellington had appeared from among the British generals, and the French, too, lacked any commander of outstanding talent. Nor was there any politician with sufficient authority and vision to provide coherent and determined leadership. Asquith, during a dinner at British HQ in France, remarked, 'Strange that this war has not produced a great general.' 'Nor a great statesman,' was Wilson's tart riposte.[1] Both were correct, and it was therefore not surprising that no formula had been found to break the deadlock on the Western Front. Even if one had materialised, the British Army was as yet unready to implement it, since it was hamstrung by shortages of manpower, equipment and ammunition.

The failure of great set-piece battles during August and September 1914 to secure a decisive victory had left all high commands bewildered, although on the British side Kitchener and Haig had both foreseen a long-drawn-out conflict. By the beginning of 1915 this likelihood was universally accepted and British official thinking turned towards considerations of how the war effort could be sustained, and whether France and Russia would withstand the strain. Russia's problems appeared

Dover

Dunkirk
• Roulers
Ypres
Boulogne •   • Armentieres   **BELGIUM**

BRITISH
OFFENSIVE   Neuve Chapelle
1915: LOOS
ENGLISH CHANNEL   • Loos
B.E.F.   • Lens
Arras

SOMME
OFFENSIVE   • Gommecourt
1916   • Le Cateau
Abbeville •

• Peronne   Guise
Amiens   St. Quentin

Le Havre •

• Rouen

Soissons

N   R. Oise   **FRENCH SECTOR**   Verdun •
• Chantilly
Chateau Thierry
Meaux •   R. Marne   • Chalons
R. Seine
Paris

• Melun

Western Front
1914-1917

insurmountable and were a continual headache for her allies. In September 1914 two Russian armies had suffered calamitous defeats at Tannenberg and the Masurian Lakes, with losses that were conservatively assessed at a quarter of a million. Nevertheless, and this perplexed those pre-war experts who had predicted a brief war marked by huge, decisive battles, all the powers had shown an astonishing ability to absorb high casualties without losing the will to fight on.

Numbers now dominated everyone's strategic planning. Allied calculations, which consistently overestimated German losses, led to the conclusion that by 1917 German reserves of manpower would be exhausted.[2] By then, however, the Allies might be unable to exploit their numerical advantage. In August 1915 the British General Staff opined that Russia was well along the road to total collapse and that this would occur before the full strength of Britain's new volunteer armies could be deployed in France.[3] In this event, the Germans would be free to transfer forces from the east to the west, where they would gain a sufficient numerical advantage for a breakthrough. It was therefore imperative to keep the Russians in the war for as long as possible, tying down German and Austro-Hungarian armies in Poland and the Carpathians.

One way in which Russia could be supported was through injections of Allied aid through the Straits; that is, the Dardanelles and Bosphorus in Turkey, the sea access from the Mediterranean through the Sea of Marmara to the Black Sea. This was one of the benefits promised by supporters of the Gallipoli landings of April 1915, who argued that the forcing of the Straits would knock Turkey out of the war and so irreparably weaken her ally Germany. This was not the view held in Berlin, where the more realistic strategists saw their allies as invalids kept alive by German resources and manpower. Material assistance to Turkey and Austria–Hungary was jokingly called '*korsettenstangen*', that is corset bones, stiffening for essentially flimsy structures. As it turned out Turkey, with some German whalebone, proved quite able to take care of itself, and by September the Allies were drawing up plans for an evacuation of the Gallipoli peninsula.

This was a blow for those British strategists, notably Kitchener and Churchill, who had presented the Gallipoli expedition as a war-winner whereas offensive operations in the west were foredoomed to failure. Defending the eastern adventure in June, both argued that during the past two months Allied offensives in France had achieved tiny advances at 'inordinate cost'; the British Army alone had suffered 36,000 dead and 109,000 wounded, of whom about one third would never recover to return to the trenches.[4] At the same time French, now a field-marshal, complained that he had been starved of men. Moreover, he was under pressure from Joffre to provide active assistance in a series of French offensives.

Britain could not afford to ignore France's pleas. Throughout 1915, as Kitchener's 'New Armies' came together and trained, the French were holding most of the front-line trenches and they had, unenthusiastically, lent men and ships for the Gallipoli campaign. There was a widespread feeling inside France that the British were lukewarm allies who were dragging their feet, which was demonstrated by their refusal to impose conscription. Allenby heard something of this grumbling from Captain Capel, his intelligence officer, and he passed on the information to Wilson.[5]

The French Grand Quartier Général (GQG) insisted that the only theatre of war which mattered was the Western Front, understandably, since a large part of France, including major mining and industrial regions, was in German hands. Moreover, French strategic thinking was still dominated by pre-war orthodoxies, so that during 1915 Joffre launched a series of headlong offensives which had no result beyond casualties that France could no longer afford. *'Je les grignote'* ('I am nibbling at them') was his justification for the bloody, one-sided battles that by the end of the year had deprived his country of 1.5 million fighting men.

The British were forced to be partners in his folly, since GQG required British diversionary attacks to coincide with its larger offensives. The War Cabinet and Sir John French therefore approved British operations at Neuve Chapelle, Aubers Ridge, Festubert and, with deep misgiving, Loos. By the time of this last battle, in September, it was painfully clear to the British General Staff that while the Allies had a six to five numerical advantage over the Germans, their opponents had superior equipment, especially artillery, and more of it.

Allenby soon realised this when he assumed command of V Corps at Ypres on 8 May. On 22 April the German High Command had launched an offensive designed to drive the British from the ridges to the east of Ypres and so make the town and railhead untenable. What was officially designated the Second Battle of Ypres opened with the grisly novelty of a gas attack. The greenish-yellow cloud of chlorine that initially puzzled onlookers drove a French Senegalese battalion from its trenches and opened a gap that was hastily filled by newly arrived troops from the Canadian Division. The battle lasted until the end of May, and followed the by now familiar pattern of bombardment, infantry attack, counter-attack, with lulls during which the two sides recuperated and regrouped.

As in the previous engagement at Ypres, the defenders were at a severe disadvantage. The weight of German artillery fire was heavier, their gunnery more accurate; British stocks of artillery ammunition, already limited when the first attack was launched, dropped to dangerously low levels by the end of May. French, who had known about this dismal state of affairs since March, advised commanders to augment feeble artillery barrages with 'careful and methodical' machine-gun and rifle fire. He also demanded that whenever there had been a bombardment, an infantry assault had to follow regardless of whether the circumstances were favourable, since otherwise the precious shells would have been wasted![6] There were no prophylactics immediately available against chlorine gas, and British soldiers had to protect their mouths and noses with makeshift masks made by soaking handkerchiefs in a solution of water and bicarbonate of soda. By mid-May more effective masks became available, but they were in short supply and were issued only to machine-gunners.[7] The British were also handicapped by inadequate supplies of hand grenades (Mills bombs had become available in May) and shortages of trench mortars and machine-guns.[8]

High morale among British and Canadian units compensated for the lack of vital equipment, although Haig heard rumours that some Indian brigades were on the verge of collapse.[9] What wore most soldiers down during the Ypres contest was the continuous German shelling; one sergeant noted in his diary that the men preferred to take their chances going over the top rather than sit out a bombardment in their dug-outs.[10] There was some grumbling, and the unending pressure from above to hold the line or regain lost trenches provoked angry comment from officers, including brigade commanders, which Plumer had tried to stifle.[11] A more serious questioning of strategy had been made in April by Smith-Dorrien, who proposed the abandonment of the Ypres Salient on the grounds that the losses incurred in defending it outweighed its strategic importance. This challenge gave French the opportunity to dismiss him as commander of the Second Army and replace him with the more tractable Plumer, the V Corps Commander.

As Plumer's successor in command of V Corps, Allenby was briefed at GHQ on the general situation two days before he took over. His orders were to hold the line at all costs, and he was no doubt told that the imminent offensives at Aubers Ridge and Festubert made it all but impossible for him to expect substantial reinforcements. This must have been small comfort when he reached his HQ on 8 May. During the past sixteen days his corps had been under intermittent attack, had been forced to give ground, had lost nearly 32,000 men, and lacked the technical means to retaliate effectively. On the morning of his arrival, the Germans had reopened their attack with a push towards positions on the Frezenberg Ridge. In a few hours 80 Brigade had been all but annihilated by shellfire, and 83 and 84 Brigades severely mauled. One of the first messages Allenby read was one which reported that the 1st Suffolks were 'still grimly hanging on until apparently surrounded and overwhelmed'.[12]

The Germans kept up the pressure for the next three weeks. There was little scope for imaginative generalship and all that Allenby could do was improvise defences by shifting units to threatened or fractured sectors of line, just as he had done seven months earlier. He feared that these measures would not prove effective and became deeply apprehensive about the battle's outcome. 'I shall go down in History as The Man Who Lost Ypres!' he told his brother-in-law, 'and with Ypres on my heart like

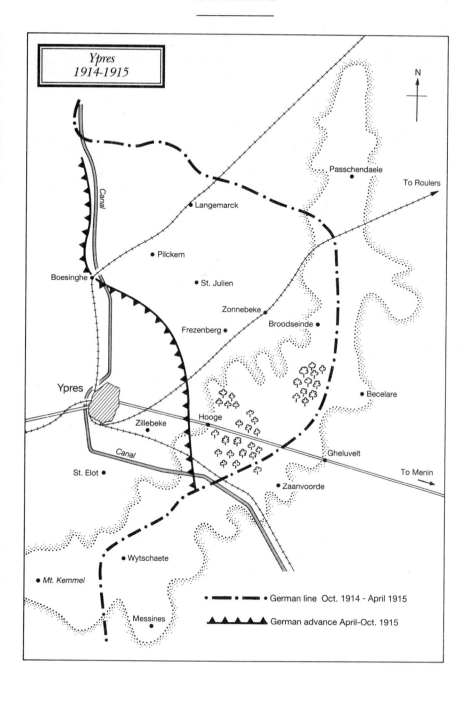

Ypres
1914-1915

N

Passchendaele
To Roulers

Langemarck

Canal

Pilckem

Boesinghe

St. Julien

Zonnebeke

Broodseinde

Frezenberg

Becelare

Ypres

Hooge

Zillebeke

Canal

Gheluvelt

To Menin

St. Elot

Zaanvoorde

Wytschaete

Mt. Kemmel

Messines

▪—▪—▪— German line Oct. 1914 - April 1915

▲▲▲▲ German advance April-Oct. 1915

Queen Mary and Calais.'[13] All that he could do was to stamp his own resolution on his subordinate commanders and transfuse them with his own aggressive spirit; not an inch of ground was to be yielded and whenever a trench was lost it had to be retaken.[14]

Allenby commanded in the only way he knew, by hectoring, and the peril of his situation made him more impatient and testy than ever. Reprimands were delivered with his customary sharpness and he squashed any officer who dared to act on his own initiative. 'It is not,' he wrote to Major-General James Briggs, commanding 3 Cavalry Brigade, on 23 May, 'for cavalry corps commanders to lay down generally how or where counter-attacks are to be launched, they usurp the authority of the commander in doing so.'[15]

This style of leadership and Allenby's abrupt manner stirred up resentment. 'Everyone hates being in Vth Corps' was the verdict of Major-General Haldane, who commanded the 3rd Division, after four weeks under Allenby.[16] Allenby was unperturbed; by a combination of sheer force of personality and intimidation he had managed to cobble together a defence of the Salient, although after just over a month of fighting the Germans had pushed forward, in some sectors, nearly 2 miles. This loss of ground meant that Ypres had become even more vulnerable.

By the beginning of June, after the German attacks had subsided, Allenby was in taurine mood and ready for a small-scale counter-offensive to retake the ruins of Hooge Château, which overlooked the Ypres–Menin road, and recover the nearby Bellewaarde Ridge. Part of Hooge Château had been seized by the Germans on 2 June as a result of what Allenby considered the maladroitness of local commanders. Their messages had given Allenby at HQ the impression that the position had been successfully held, and he was furious when he discovered later that the defenders had withdrawn and that available reinforcements had not been summoned.[17] The post-mortem at HQ was a stormy affair; afterwards Haldane believed that he now had 'a totally unsympathetic commander'. 'I do not feel,' he wrote in his diary, 'that Cavalry officers should have command of Infantry for they expect everything to gallop and in consequence are the least patient of mortals.'[18]

Haldane had confronted Allenby with the suggestion that Hooge was too battered to be worth taking and had been backed by Briggs, whose dismounted cavalrymen had until recently defended it. Furthermore, and this must have angered Allenby, Haldane believed that Allenby and his staff were handicapped by a 'lack of imagination' and were ignorant of the realities of trench warfare. Prolonged bombardment drove men to insanity – that mental condition which would come to be called 'shell-shock'. At Hooge one soldier had convinced himself he was a ticket collector, while another had fired his revolver at some engineers. Not that such knowledge would have altered Allenby's judgement and, as Haldane noticed, 'His staff seem to be too frightened of him to hold him check when he plays the bull.'[19]

There were fresh outbursts during preparations for the Bellewaarde operation. After a conference at V Corps HQ on 6 June, Haldane recorded in his diary that in Allenby's mind 'the word "retire" conjures up a vision of everyone either falling back or wishing to do so'.[20] This was so, and on 22 June Allenby sent a circular letter to his divisional and brigade commanders which ordered them to expunge the word from their vocabularies. 'In giving orders during operations in the field the word "retire" is not to be used,' he wrote. 'If it is necessary to give an order for retirement, the direction of movement will be given, or the place to which troops are to move.'[21]

The Hooge débâcle and the vinegary exchanges between him and his senior commanders convinced Allenby that he would have to take measures to assert his personal control over the battlefield. During the preparations for the Bellewaarde offensive he ordered the laying of telephone lines, in triplicate and carefully buried to preserve them from shellfire, between advance positions and divisional HQs, and some units received wireless sets.[22] His plan of attack was simple; a short bombardment would be followed by an early-morning rush against the German trenches. This was ill-co-ordinated, and some infantrymen fell to friendly fire. The 1st Wiltshires, having seized the first line of trenches, ran out of hand grenades and by 9.30 am concentrated German artillery fire ruled out any further attacks.[23]

Unperturbed by this setback, Allenby, who had been watching the engagement from 3rd Division's HQ, proposed sending in 42 Brigade, but Haldane was apprehensive. 'I told him that it would result in very heavy loss with no satisfactory result.' Allenby snapped back, 'What the Hell does that matter. There are plenty more men in England!' 'Not like these, Sir,' answered Haldane. One of Haldane's staff officers was so incensed by what he had overheard that he wanted to strike Allenby.[24] No reserves were thrown in, and Allenby found some compensation in a small gain. On the following day, 17 June, he wrote to his wife in self-congratulatory mood:

My attack was very successful yesterday; but we could not hold all the ground we won. However we have gained and held all the German front line trenches on a 1,000 yards front. We took over 170 prisoners and killed a lot of Boches. My losses were, as far can be estimated so far, that is, 130 officers and 2,700 men. I don't know what the German losses were – but big, I think.[25]

They were not, and this was a gross misrepresentation of what had been an utter disaster. British casualties were just over 4,000 (9 Brigade had lost over half its strength, and the Liverpool Scottish Territorials all but two of their officers and 378 out of 570 other ranks) and the German losses were estimated at about 300 dead and wounded and 157 taken prisoner.[26] On 19 June Allenby visited those battalions that had been hardest hit and was encouraged by the survivors' resilience. 'The men are full of cheer,' he told his wife, 'delighted to have had a success, after a long spell of defensive work in the trenches. As a matter of fact, they could not be kept in hand in attack. They broke right through and stormed trench after trench: then they came under enfilade artillery fire and machine-gun fire.'[27]

Many of the men whom Allenby encountered during this and earlier tours of the front-line trenches were soldiers of the 'New Army', the volunteers of 1914–15 who were now filtering through to France. After an inspection of 7 Brigade, he reported that the new drafts for the 3rd Worcesters were 'excellent', those for the 1st Wiltshires 'fair average', the 2nd South Lancashires 'below average', and the 2nd Royal Irish Rifles 'very bad up till about two months ago'.[28] The new officers, whose inexperience and rushed instruction courses were causing anxiety elsewhere, 'are as well trained as can be expected', but required extra coaching in such trench-warfare techniques as laying sandbags, loopholing and use of hand grenades.[29] They would have to develop these skills on the job in much the same way as their superiors were learning how to wage a new kind of warfare.

Allenby was not a fast learner. Undismayed by the imbalance of losses during the Bellewaarde operation and his dwindling stock of shells, he was planning a fresh offensive against the same target. There were purely strategic reasons for this: the Ypres sector needed strengthening, which meant regaining high ground lost in April and May that could be used as a springboard for future advances. A fresh offensive offered the chance of 'inflicting loss on the enemy', which was of paramount importance to Allenby.[30] This remark and his earlier comments about the men's spirits after the first assault on Bellewaarde were clear signs that he was a convert to the new strategic dogma preached by French and his staff. Attrition, that is, killing as many Germans as possible irrespective of one's own losses, and keeping the individual soldier's aggressive spirit at the highest pitch through a sequence of minor offensives, would sustain moral superiority and bring ultimate victory. Haig was the most passionate apostle of this orthodoxy, which underpinned his strategy from late 1915 until the end of the war. At the end of September 1914, he had convinced himself that the British soldier had achieved a moral superiority over his German counterpart and that this had to be preserved, even at the price of heavy casualties.

Maintaining the moral advantage was difficult since, from the beginning of 1915, the British trenches were being taken over by civilians transformed into soldiers. The enthusiasm of the volunteers was enormous, but they lacked discipline and the killer instinct that was thought necessary for the offensive; they therefore needed all the experience of combat they could get. By this means the Army's morale would be raised to that high level needed for a mass attack which would sever the enemy's line. Shock action was still the key to victory which, the General Staff predicted in November 1915, would always follow 'superior numbers of bayonets closing with the enemy'.[31]

French had been one of the founding fathers of the aggressive doctrine. In February he had directed all subordinate commanders to order plenty of trench raids which would 'relieve monotony and improve the morale of our troops'. The game was principally played for its own sake and, in the best public-school tradition, 'a keen spirit of rivalry and emulation' between units would emerge. Haig wholeheartedly endorsed trench-raiding as a means of fostering a fighting spirit. He succeeded French as Commander-in-Chief on 19 December, and three days later called Allenby to GHQ where he lectured him on the subject. Soldiers benefited from 'small attacks to maintain their morale and develop their offensive spirit', he concluded. Afterwards, he felt sure that Allenby, who may have had some misgivings, had been converted to what, on another occasion, Haig revealingly described as 'winter sports'.[32]

The view from the trench parapet was less hearty. Those who bore the brunt of these mainly noctunal dashes across no man's land loathed trench raids and suspected, with good reason, that they were devised by gung-ho, sporting staff officers, but to have voiced such opinions invited charges of irresolution.[33] Some raids yielded intelligence of the enemy through prisoners taken, but most were futile sallies and added to casualties.

On a bigger scale, men were kept on their toes by limited tactical forays to seize or snatch back a section of trench. This was the type of sortie that Allenby had ordered on 16 June and 25 September. The second Bellewaarde offensive had an added value since it served as a diversion for French's mass attack at Loos. It failed, like its predecessor. Ignorance of the precise location of German machine-gun nests; a bombardment that was too short and diffuse to break up the deep barbed-wire entanglements; and the impossibility of bringing up reinforcements across open ground were the reasons for the attack's abandonment. Casualties were 3,800, but Allenby drew some reassurance from the fiasco. 'The operation failed to capture any ground from the enemy,' he telegraphed GHQ, 'but POWs say [there were] heavy losses from the bombardment.'[34] Again the principle of attrition was invoked to excuse a wasteful operation.

In his general orders issued at the start of the second Bellewaarde attack, Allenby stressed that it was to be undertaken with the 'greatest vigour'. He had during the past four months sought to enkindle his men with fighting zeal and transmit to them some of his own resolution and aggressiveness. To this end he had toured divisional and brigade HQs and inspected trenches, where commanders endured those bombardments of invective for which he was becoming notorious. They won him no love and much loathing, but not from French, who prized those qualities of unrelenting determination and combativeness which Allenby's subordinates so disliked. On 23 October, French promoted him to command of the Third Army with responsibility for 71,000 men spread along a 22-mile front that ran northwards from the River Somme. It was a quiet sector – or, in Allenby's words, 'not such a storm centre' as the Ypres Salient.[35]

Allenby replaced General Sir Charles Monro, who had been temporarily shifted sideways to preside over the closing stages of the Gallipoli campaign. Monro's fate, and earlier that of Smith-Dorrien, who had been moved to the comparatively obscure command of Allied forces in East Africa, were reminders that generals who failed to manifest a thrusting, battle-hungry spirit were sacked. In the first two months of the war, over a hundred French generals had been '*dégommé*'; that is, unstuck. The expression and the process were both quickly adopted by the British Army where the hesitant or inadequate began to become 'unstuck'. On 19 August 1914 French dismissed Colonel O'Meagher of the 2nd Munsters as 'unfit to command' and, a month later, Lieutenant-Colonels J. Elkington of the Warwickshires and A. E. Mainwaring of the Royal Irish Fusiliers were cashiered after they had prepared to surrender their severely battered regiments at St Quentin.[36] (Elkington was reinstated after he joined the French Foreign Legion and was decorated for gallantry.) In 1914 and after there would be no repetition of what had occurred too often during the Boer War, when officers whose units were outnumbered or surrounded had surrendered.

The death penalty was rigorously applied to men who had shown cowardice or had deserted, again in contrast to the Boer War, when such offenders had only been imprisoned. The first deserter was shot in September 1914, and others who had fled to Paris and the pleasures offered by 'the ladies of Montmartre' had to be rounded-up by special patrols and returned to their battalions for punishment.[37]

Faintheartedness was ruthlessly dealt with at all levels. Even the trauma of shell-shock was no excuse for quitting the line; one brigadier-general who served under Allenby in the Third Army was overheard to comment, 'There is only one thing to do with a fellow who says he is or seems to be shell-shocked and that is to give him one on the point.'[38] Gough, whose dedication to the offensive spirit exceeded Allenby's, on discovering late in 1916 that it was becoming diluted among his officers in the Fifth Army, announced to his staff, 'I want to shoot an officer!' He got one 'who had momentarily failed', according to Edmonds. In all likelihood the man chosen '*pour encourager les autres*' was Sub-Lieutenant Edwin Dyett of the Royal Naval Division, then attached to Gough's command, who was under arrest for desertion. He was executed in January 1917 after Gough had overturned a recommendation for mercy from his divisional commander.[39] Allenby, while never going to the fanatical lengths of Gough, approved the shooting of at least two deserters from units under his command, although the sentences had to be endorsed by the Commander-in-Chief.[40]

Other senior officers resorted to even more desperate measures to maintain the aggressive spirit. Brigadier-General F. P. Crozier confessed to 'no regrets for having killed a subaltern of British infantry' whom he shot out of hand for running from the front during the German spring offensive of 1918. A near-psychopath who later fought against the Bolsheviks in Lithuania and in 1920 ran the Auxiliary Division of the Royal Irish Constabulary during the Irish uprising, Crozier insisted, 'My duty was to hold the line *at all costs*', and he deliberately gave commands to officers who were willing 'to act often in complete violation of all decency, chivalry, and custom in order that the line might be saved'. He imposed what he called 'public-school discipline' on his 119 Brigade, and specifically ordered trench-raiders to bring back bottles of German wine as proof that they had not funked their missions.[41] He was an ardent admirer of Allenby and Gough, whom he classified as first-rate, fighting generals, and his methods were never questioned by his superiors. Nor was he unique in his callousness. In 1916 Brigadier-General B. R. Mitford of 42 (East Lancashire) Brigade lectured his officers on what he considered the unnecessary use of their services in defence of men under court martial for desertion and cowardice, and urged them to impose the heaviest sentences if they were called on to act as judges.[42]

Protests against such attitudes, or deviance from the dogma upon which they were based, were always in vain, and ended with the dissident becoming 'unstuck' like Smith-Dorrien. Gough sacked Major-General Barrow from command of the 7th Division after he had refused to order an attack without artillery support.[43] All generals completely imbued with the offensive spirit – and they included Haig and Allenby – equated low casualties with a pusillanimous, half-hearted commander.[44] Not surprisingly, Field-Marshal Montgomery, then a junior officer, recalled that 'the so-called "good fighting generals" of this war appeared to be those who had a complete disregard for human life', a category from which he excluded only Plumer, on whose staff he had served.[45]

Further down the line of command, feeling against such generals and their staffs was even more bitter. The semi-fictional reactions of front-line soldiers in Frederic Manning's *The Middle Parts of Fortune* must have had equivalents among real Tommies. They looked on their generals as fickle gods who held total power over men for whom they cared nothing; or, in the words of one, 'Bloody swank. They don't give a fuck what 'appens to us 'uns.'[46] Allenby, even if only for his remark that 'There are plenty more men in England', must have seemed to many whom he commanded as a general cast in this hard, unpitying mould.

And yet, like his equally tough contemporaries, Allenby commanded under the constant threat of becoming unstuck for some deviation from duty or failure to keep up an offensive spirit. He showed no mercy in this quarter, nor did he expect it. In April 1917, during the battle of Arras, he asked Haig for the dismissal of Major-General James Shea after what he considered an indifferent performance.[47] Later he upbraided Colonel Charles Grant, one of his staff officers, on the subject of fairness. 'Fair, do you think I was fair to Jimmy Shea? I kicked him out and was very unfair to him, and I would kick you or anyone else out if I thought they did not do their work.'[48]

To keep men up to the mark and to preserve his own command, Allenby embraced the current dogmas of the offensive spirit and attrition. He upheld an iron discipline and relentlessly pursued those whom he thought negligent. When in charge of V Corps and, later, the Third Army, he regularly visited the front line. Haldane, who served under him throughout this period, recorded many of his idiosyncrasies, often with disgust, and word of them spread throughout the Army. Lieutenant-General Sir Thomas ('Snowball') Snow, the commander of VII Corps, recalled one incident, probably early in 1916, when Allenby came across the corpse of a soldier who had ignored regulations and died without his steel helmet and leather jerkin.

Allenby: 'Did I or did I not issue an order that no man should go up to the front line without jerkin or helmet?'

Company commander: 'Yes, Sir.'

Allenby: 'Then why has that man not got them on?'

Company commander: 'The man is dead, Sir.'

Allenby: 'Did I or did I not . . .'[49]

In another version of this exchange, Allenby imagined the man was asleep and told his colonel 'that this flagrant disobedience of orders was a disgrace to his unit'. The officer, a Territorial and a former schoolmaster, drily answered, 'Yes, Sir. Disobedience in death is to my mind even graver than disobedience in life. This man has undoubtedly lost his chance of ever going to Heaven.'[50]

Haldane was the butt for similar outbursts. He had been particularly keen to salvage equipment and rubbish from his lines in the interests of economy and cleanliness. Allenby, during an inspection early in June 1915, stumbled on one dump.

> As he delighted in making a fuss if he came upon a half-empty tin of bully beef or a horse – contrary to orders – tied to a tree and nibbling the bark, this find gave him an opportunity to let himself go. He returned to me and asked with wrath in his voice what this collection meant. I replied, 'Only some of the stuff which we have collected since we came into your area.' This enraged him as he felt, rightly too, that it reflected on his Corps.[51]

This and other similar explosions convinced Haldane that Allenby was 'not a gentleman'. 'Evil temper is very near the surface and intolerance is bursting forth at every pore.' They escaped during another inspection when an officer remarked 'Very good, Sir', to which Allenby barked, 'I want none of your bloody approbation.'[52] Such behaviour was not uncommon in senior officers, however. Lieutenant-General Sir Aylmer ('Hunter Bunter') Hunter-Weston was also notorious as 'one of the worst for spit and polish', although one junior officer who encountered him and his fads observed afterwards that there was 'a fussy old maid' just below the skin of nearly every general.[53]

Somehow Allenby's staff managed to work with him and accommodate themselves to his moods and tantrums. Those who enjoyed the everyday company of the unofficial man found him agreeable. A chef, borrowed from the French Army, prepared excellent meals for Allenby's mess, where the intellectually stimulating conversation embraced Shakespeare, Greek verse (which Allenby could quote from memory) and natural history. On occasions he was pernickety about slovenly English, and both senior and junior officers were slated for split infinitives, the use of 'padre' for chaplain, and such slipshod expressions as the 'near horizon'.

Fortunately for the smooth working of the staff, Allenby had attracted to him a circle of able and tolerant officers, in particular Lord Dalmeny, a former Liberal MP and eldest son of the Liberal Prime Minister, Lord Rosebery, who, in Allenby's words had come to France in 1914 'to see a bit of the war' and act as a staff chauffeur. He stayed, but abandoned the driving seat of Allenby's Rolls-Royce and became his Military Secretary and confidante.

Throughout his career in France, Allenby showed two faces to the world. One was that of the blustering, fault-finding general, whose dread of becoming unstuck made him toe the conventional strategic line and show what amounted to an indifference towards the lives of the soldiers he commanded. He was, his critics thought, a man far out of his depth, an old-school cavalryman fighting what was essentially an infantry and artillery war according to principles devised for the mounted warfare of a past age. The other Allenby, known to a small knot of intimates, was a genial if demanding companion, and one who showed effusive charm to the chatelaines whose country houses were his headquarters. However unattractive the public man, he had flourished; he had held, just, the Ypres Salient in May and had demonstrated a commendable offensive spirit during the summer and autumn, even though it had resulted in ten British casualties for every German. By the close of 1915, Allenby had been knighted and given command of one of Britain's four armies in France, one of which was destined to deliver the mass offensive that Haig was planning for the coming year.

CHAPTER 8

UNDER HAIG'S COMMAND

JANUARY–DECEMBER 1916

1915 had been a bleak year for the Allies, and had revealed the need for new men at the top. There had been a political shake-up in Britain where Asquith had formed a Liberal–Conservative coalition ministry in May. In December it was the turn of the generals. Out went French, discredited for his mishandling of the Loos offensive, and in came Haig after Joffre had blocked the appointment of Sir Ian Hamilton, who had lately been relieved of the Gallipoli command.[1]

Haig was on cordial terms with Asquith, but his promotion was coolly received in some quarters. 'A man of mediocre ability, slow to absorb, tenacious of what he had learnt; not a very pleasant man to deal with, though he tried to be pleasant' was the verdict of General Murray, who enjoyed the distinction of having been twice unstuck during 1915, first as French's Chief of Staff, and then as Chief of the Imperial General Staff. 'A damned stupid man' was Wilson's judgement, shaped perhaps by his own removal from active command and transfer to liaison duties at GQG.[2] Even those untainted by envy were ungenerous; Major-General Sir Philip Chetwode, one of Allenby's cavalry commanders in 1914, later remarked, 'I always regarded Haig as a very stupid man.'[3] Allenby held his tongue, although once during a trench inspection he was heard to include Haig in a general outburst of vituperation.[4]

In fact relations between Haig and Allenby seemed outwardly tranquil and warm. In January 1916 Allenby made a gift of a cob to Haig as a gesture of goodwill from one cavalryman to another.[5] And yet during weekly meetings between Haig and his army commanders, the two men appeared separated by a gulf that neither could bridge. Allenby, who was never fluent at the best of times, fumbled for words in Haig's presence, and Haig made matters worse by his frustrating tendency not to bring his sentences to a coherent end. This non-communication caused enormous difficulties during discussions of the finer points of strategy, although Allenby believed he could have got his case across more effectively in private.[6] Nevertheless, the two commanders shared a deep attachment to the cult of the offensive. Certainly Haig, who once reprimanded 'Daddy' Plumer for his kindness towards subordinates, could not complain about Allenby on that account.[7]

Haig was prepared to back Allenby even after formal complaints had been made about his short-temper and bullying. These were laid in August 1916 by Lieutenant-General Sir John Keir, who had been in command of VI Corps since March 1915 and whose refusal to wilt in the face of Allenby's tirades earned him the nickname 'Toreador'. Haig stuck by Allenby and dismissed Keir on 8 August, despite threats from the latter that he would raise the matter in London.[8]

It was perhaps reassuring for Haig that Allenby was not an intriguer, although his name was put forward, without his approval, as Haig's replacement by *The Times*'s war correspondent, Colonel Charles à Court Repington. Repington had visited Allenby's HQ in July 1916 and had been impressed by what he had seen and heard, especially from Dalmeny, who praised an 'absolutely first-class chief'. Ten days later, over lunch, Repington repeated this encomium to David Lloyd George, the new Secretary for War. Early in December, soon after Lloyd George had become Prime Minister, Repington suggested Allenby as Haig's successor 'as he combined youth, physique and character'.[9] In fact Lloyd George, distressed by the huge casualties of Haig's recent Somme campaign, was putting out feelers towards Plumer.[10] Still Repington persisted, and in May 1917 was telling guests at Mayfair dinner parties that Allenby was 'the nearest approach to the Wellington type in the Army'.[11] This was backstairs plotting by an obsessive meddler in which Allenby played no part, and of which, as far as it is known, Haig knew nothing.

The rise of Haig had coincided with that of General Sir William ('Wully') Robertson, who became Chief of the Imperial General Staff in December 1915 after persuading the Cabinet War Committee that he alone should offer it strategic advice. Robertson was a rarity in the British Army, an officer of working-class origins. He had enlisted as a cavalry trooper, much to his mother's horror, been commissioned and, through hard work and ability, raised himself to the General Staff. He was ruggedly handsome (too much so, thought Lady Carson), kept, perhaps as an affectation, a Cockney accent, and had a rough wit to go with it. After watching the government's Food Controller throw up during a rough Channel crossing, he observed that he did not seem to be very good at controlling food. He was also perceptive; early in 1915 he had told Barrow, 'Asquith must go if we are to win this war. The soldiers and the sailors can't win it. It is the people who must win it.'[12]

Robertson wielded enormous influence, most of it in Haig's interest. He worked in close partnership with Haig, whose views he agreed with, and was convinced that the war could only be won in the west by beating the German Army. Unlike Kitchener, whose power was waning, Robertson had no illusions about second fronts in the Middle East or on the periphery of Europe. When arguing against French proposals for operations in the Balkans in October 1915, he insisted that all future plans 'should be based on seeking a decision in the West, and by killing *Germans.*'[13] This was how things appeared to Haig and, for that matter, Allenby, who had had misgivings about the Gallipoli farrago.[13] During the next two years Haig would owe much to Robertson, a steadfast ally who tirelessly put the C-in-C's case to an often disbelieving War Cabinet. After the war the two men parted company when Haig, speaking at the 1919 Victory Dinner at the United Services Club, said some words in praise of their old antagonist, Wilson. Robertson was dumbfounded, and left muttering, 'I shan't go farting with 'Aig again'.

What recommended Allenby to Haig were his subordination and his aggressive spirit. One of the corner-stones of the new Commander-in-Chief's strategy was his own willpower; he believed that only by the adoption of his ideas and methods could total victory be achieved. As supreme commander of the BEF he was the driving force behind the army on the Western Front, and it was his duty to instil in all his commanders something of his own, deeply held confidence and resolution. His actual battlefield strategy owed much, if not everything, to what he had absorbed at Staff College twenty years before, and to the assumption that the stalemate on the Western Front could be ended by a decisive battle. In broad terms this would involve two phases: during the first the German front would be fractured, and during the second, mounted troops would pour through the breach, spread out and prevent the enemy from regrouping and digging new lines of defence. Allenby and his fellow army commanders heard the outline of this plan at their weekly meeting with Haig on 18 March 1916.[14]

Before this final breakthrough could occur there would be, according to Haig, an extended series of grinding battles in which the enemy would suffer heavy casualties and have his will to fight eroded. In theory attrition was the necessary preliminary to the decisive battle and, to a large extent, this was true, although there was no way of knowing when the vital point of moral exhaustion would be reached. Drawing on his own Intelligence reports which charted the growing economic hardships within Germany, caused largely by the Allied naval blockade, and on details of POW interrogations, Haig believed that this process of collapse was well advanced during 1916. And yet there were sceptics, like his own Director of Intelligence, Lieutenant-General Sir George MacDonogh, who suggested that the publication of material describing the 'desperate' conditions inside Germany would 'give rise to expectations which the facts do not justify'.[15] One of these awkward facts was the lion-hearted German resistance on every sector of the front. Never one to tolerate dissent, Haig blamed MacDonogh's doubts on his Roman Catholicism, which somehow made him susceptible to information 'from tainted [that is, Catholic] sources'.[16]

There was a fundamental flaw at the heart of Haig's strategy. It lay not in the concept upon which it was based, but in the way in which Haig translated theory into practice. His great set-piece battles of 1916–17, the Somme, Arras and Passchendaele (Third Ypres), were actions designed both to overwhelm the Germans and wear them down. All failed disastrously on the first count, and the evidence as to how far they contributed to German demoralisation is disputable. If the Allied purpose was solely to kill Germans, this task was best undertaken by artillery, which killed combatants in greater numbers than any other weapon. Yet in each battle, Haig committed vast bodies of infantry as shock troops which suffered enormous casualties and did little more than temporarily destabilise sections of the German line.

Haig's strategy demanded the total mobilisation of British manpower. At the beginning of 1916, he commanded just over a million British and Commonwealth troops. Even so, in April the Army was still 400,000 men under strength and, as forces assembled for the Somme offensive on 1 July, GHQ was forced to draft 37,500 'partially trained' soldiers into the front line.[17] The immediate shortfall and the inevitable losses that would follow future battles meant that a steady flow of fresh men had to be maintained. Conscription, introduced in January 1916, helped solve Haig's manpower difficulties, as did the hundreds of thousands of Egyptian, Chinese and black labourers who were imported between 1916 and 1918 to work on the British lines of communication in northern France.

The new mass armies which came under Haig's command for the next two years created their own special problems. Would these men make the sacrifices expected of them? Haig had some doubts; towards the end of 1917 he wrote how conscription was bringing into his army men 'from a class which like to air real or fancied grievances, and their teaching in this respect is a regrettable antidote to the spirit of devotion and duty of earlier troops'.[18] What was needed, he believed, were sermons like those he heard each Sunday from a Scottish Presbyterian chaplain, and which convinced him that 'we have no selfish motive' and were 'fighting for the good of humanity'. Such messages reinforced his own inner faith in himself as an instrument of Divine Providence, chosen to safeguard the British Empire at its moment of direst peril.[19]

The British soldier's moral stamina was tested to breaking-point during 1916. The broad strategy for the year had been hammered out during a series of Allied conferences at the end of 1915. The most formidable effort was to be made in the west, where a major offensive would coincide with a Russian push in the east (the last, as it turned out) and simultaneous pressure from a new, if far from reliable, ally, Italy, against the Austro-Hungarians.

External forces altered this grand strategy. By the turn of the year, Anglo-French Intelligence was gathering details of heavy concentrations of troops and artillery opposite the French-held Verdun salient which indicated an imminent offensive of prodigious force. This was Operation *Gericht* (a scaffold or place of execution), the brainchild of the new German Chief of Staff, General Erich von Falkenhayn. He aimed to deliver a series of blows against Verdun which the French would have to parry with all the resources and manpower they could find. 'If they do so,' he predicted, 'the forces of France will bleed to death.' According to von Falkenhayn's calculus of war, this was unavoidable, since Germany's higher birth-rate meant that there were more Germans capable of bearing arms than Frenchmen. Furthermore, von Falkenhayn argued, as France's manhood haemorrhaged, her will to fight would wither and Britain, whom he identified as the mainstay of the alliance, would be driven to capitulate.

The Verdun offensive opened on 21 February with a barrage of unprecedented weight, and two days later Joffre pleaded that France, now facing the 'decisive crisis of the war', needed the 'absolute assistance' of Haig's army.[20] In the short term all that could be managed was a stepping-up of the pace of the takeover of French sectors by British units. Among those involved in the transfer was Allenby's Third Army, which was moving into its new positions by 1 March, not always a pleasant task since French trenches were notoriously insanitary. During the move,

Haig cautioned Allenby to make no attempts to retake trenches lost by the French, but just to hold the line.[21] Allenby needed no urging on this score; shortly before Christmas he had toured the waterlogged trenches of 144 and 145 Brigades and told their occupants that they were to ignore their present conditions and hold on, orders no doubt given with characteristic vehemence.[22]

There was a period to the Third Army digging its heels in, since Haig had selected it to take part in a major offensive to be launched later in the year. True as ever to what he had been taught, Haig prescribed the objectives for the offensive and then left individual field commanders to draw up plans for his and the General Staff's scrutiny and amendment. On 23 January, Allenby was asked to prepare a scheme for an attack by fifteen divisions along a 24,000-yard front, designed to seize and occupy German front-line trenches. This assault was initially scheduled for 15 April and was largely a response to French appeals for a diversion to draw German forces away from hard-pressed Verdun. Allenby was to work in conjunction with the newly formed Fourth Army and, during the last fortnight in February, he regularly consulted its genial and perceptive commander, Lieutenant-General Sir Henry ('Cad') Rawlinson.[23]

By 6 March, Haig had decided to expand the scale and scope of the forthcoming offensive: it would now be delivered by the Fourth Army and adjacent French units against the German line north of the River Somme, and would aim for a breakthrough. The Third Army was now relegated to a subsidiary role, with instructions to mislead the Germans by a simultaneous attack on the Gommecourt salient at the northern extremity of the British front. This may have been a disappointment for Allenby, although the choice of battlefield had been dictated by Fourth Army's proximity to the sector held by the French Sixth Army, its partner in the Somme offensive.

Preparations for the Gommecourt attack were under way by the last week in April. The choice of Gommecourt for an attack was foolhardy, since it was an extremely well-fortified position on rising ground and probably one of the strongest points on the entire German line. Attacking it could not be justified in terms of attrition or a breakthrough, even though a sanguine Haig ordered Allenby to press his attack for 2 miles beyond the first line of German trenches. What made Gommecourt so formidable were its dug-outs, excavated by German engineers to a depth of 40 feet and only vulnerable to direct hits by high-explosive shells. These dug-outs gave ample protection to German soldiers from the prolonged barrages which began every offensive.

Since the Gommecourt attack was a diversion, designed to lure Germans away from those sectors to the south which were the main target of the Anglo-French attack, no serious effort was made to screen preparations from the enemy. Among these was a full-scale mock-up of the Gommecourt defence system which had been constructed behind the lines for pre-battle training. This was spotted by German reconnaissance aircraft and no doubt photographed; the defenders of Gommecourt were well aware that they would soon be attacked. Neither Allenby nor Snow, the commander of VII Corps which had been chosen to deliver the assault, were disturbed by the fact that the Germans had been alerted. Forewarned, they would shift extra troops into the threatened sector and so increase the diversionary value of the attack.

The preliminary arrangements for the Gommecourt offensive were botched. A shortage of ancillary units meant that the men earmarked to make the attack spent weeks behind the lines carrying supplies or cutting the shallow assault trenches that began to snake into no man's land. These had been intended to cut by half the 500 yards between the opposing front-line trenches, but many were soon flooded so that they caved in. By 1 July, the day of the Big Push, nearly every soldier who went over the top was already worn out by fatigue duties, sleeplessness caused by a week of bombardment, and living in waterlogged trenches.[24]

The offensive was a calamity. The four-day barrage failed to eliminate the deep barbed-wire entanglements or inflict much damage on the dug-outs. This work should have been undertaken by heavy howitzers, but these were still in short supply. The period of shell shortages had passed, but while factories had increased production technical problems remained unsolved. As a consequence, many of the shells that were fired at Gommecourt, and elsewhere for that matter, failed to explode because of dud fuses, or buried themselves harmlessly in the muddy soil. By contrast, German counter-fire was precise and devastating since their gunners had already pinpointed the forward trenches where the attacking troops mustered and those areas of no man's land across which they were to advance. Nevertheless, and with severe loss, the 46th (1st North Midland) and 56th (1st London Territorial) Divisions managed to storm the first three lines of German trenchworks. The gallant Londoners were pre-war 'Terriers', mostly City clerks and professional men, and they advanced into what one of their officers described as 'a wall of high-explosives which no living thing could pass'. Thereafter events followed the usual grim pattern with concerted German counter-attacks and artillery barrages. Allenby's response, as at Bellewaarde Ridge, was to throw in more men. At 9.30 am he ordered the 46th to make a drive against Gommecourt Wood. This was timed for 12.15, but delays in assembling the required men forced an hour's postponement. When the assault on the ridge was renewed, the fight was all but lost, and at 3.30

Army HQ received reports that 'our men were slowly retiring, in small parties, chiefly wounded'. The unequal struggle was soon abandoned, although by nightfall a handful of men still clung to some German trenches, from which they were eventually prised by grenade attacks. Already the stretcher parties were scouring no man's land; 'we had white men against us,' observed one junior officer, 'and they let us get in our wounded without hindrance as soon as the fight was over.'[25]

British casualties at Gommecourt totalled 6,800, of whom just under a third were killed; German losses were 1,242.[26] Looking back over the planning and execution of this engagement it is obvious that those involved were treated as expendable. As a diversion it had an extremely marginal effect on the operations further south, where a day's fighting accounted for 57,470 British casualties. Soon afterwards Allenby, suffering from neuritis of the arm and in great pain, was sent for treatment to Boulogne, which started rumours that he had been unstuck because of the Gommecourt fiasco.[27] They were untrue; his reputation was unblemished, for whatever else might have been said about Gommecourt it showed that the offensive spirit was alive within the Third Army.

The Germans acknowledged this spirit and recognised its strengths and weaknesses. According to the official German history of the Somme:

> The strong, usually young and well-armed British soldier followed his officers blindly, and the officers, active and personally brave, went ahead of their men in battle with great courage. But, owing to insufficient training, they were not skilful in action. They failed to grasp the necessity for rapid, independent decision. They were in many cases unequal to dealing with sudden unexpected changes in the situation.[28]

In other words, they were the victims of an inflexible system. The official British version of the Somme steered deliberately clear of any indictment of the Army's attitudes, but frankly laid the blame for some of the day's misfortunes on inaccurate gunnery, poor musketry and excessive reliance on bayonet and hand-grenade training.[29] Proficiency with these arms was of course a measure of the offensive spirit, which explains why it was encouraged.

The Somme offensive never generated the momentum needed to sever the German line, as Haig had intended. Nor was it a success in terms of attrition, since German infantry losses were less than British. Rawlinson, who detected some of the inbuilt contradictions within Haig's thinking (for which he was later 'unstuck'), imagined that the campaign was over by 1 August.[30] 'The battle has quieted down and we shall not do much more', he noted in his diary. Haig did not agree. The French position at

Verdun was still precarious, and politically it would have been unthinkable for the British Army to call it a day on the Somme while the French were still fighting for their lives. He therefore extended operations on the Somme as an exercise in attrition.

The Third Army played no significant part in the later phases of the battle of the Somme, which finally petered out in November with the onset of the winter rains. Allenby's troops, many of them units recuperating after having taken part in the Somme actions, occupied what was commonly called a 'quiet sector' of the front. This was always a comparative term, however, since no army commander, especially one of Allenby's temperament, could allow his men to hold their lines passively. The daily routine of raids, small-scale actions, patrols across no man's land (these, together with 'aggressive' raiding, were ordered to be intensified on 30 August), fatigues, training and intermittent shelling continued.[31]

Allenby kept up his own peculiar form of pressure, with regular inspections of front-line units, transport and supply lines, hospitals and ammunition dumps, to see that his officers and men were up to the mark. Wherever he detected tell-tale signs that discipline had been relaxed, such as a slow turn-out of a guard, he delivered a swingeing rebuke.[32] Among the rank and file he was nicknamed 'Tin-Hat' because of his outbursts against those who did not wear them or those who did so incorrectly, that is, without chin-straps. For officers he was, as ever, 'The Bull', a fearsome and unpredictable creature. And yet, despite his appearances in the trenches, he remained a distant figure for most men under his command. An officer of the Royal Welsh Fusiliers wrote, 'He is not popular ... and he is quite unknown to regimental officers and men.'[33]

This anonymity did not matter at GHQ where Haig believed him a trustworthy general, in tune with his own thinking and second-to-none in his adherence to the principles of the aggressive spirit and wearing down the enemy. For these reasons, Allenby's Third Army was chosen to deliver the Arras offensive in the new year. After nearly three years of senior command, Allenby was about to have the chance to prove himself as a fighting general in a major action.

CHAPTER 9

UNSTUCK AT ARRAS

JANUARY–JUNE 1917

FOR the first time in his career, Allenby had been given the direction of what he called 'a big battle'.[1] It was a task that unnerved him from the moment he and his staff began drawing up the plans for the Arras offensive, since he was uncomfortably aware that if it miscarried he would be unstuck.

Arras was first and foremost a political battle, undertaken by a lukewarm Haig under pressure from the new Prime Minister, Lloyd George, and the War Cabinet, in order to satisfy the French. The decision to fight at Arras had been taken during a series of often highly charged Anglo-French discussions during the winter and early spring of 1916–17. In December 1916 Joffre had been replaced as Commander-in-Chief of the French armies by General Robert Nivelle, an effervescent, smooth-tongued and plausible artilleryman who had made a name for himself as a field commander, and had achieved heroic status for his recapture of Fort Douaumont during the final stages of the battle of Verdun.

The self-confident Nivelle proposed a counter-stroke to Verdun to be delivered across the River Aisne. It was an ambitious plan, based on the usual heavy barrage followed by a mass infantry attack in the old French style that would, according to Nivelle's calculations, tear through the German lines. The British High Command was unconvinced, particularly Haig, who feared that co-operation with Nivelle would jeopardise the chances of his own Flanders offensive, planned for the summer. In that, he intended to deliver a blow against the German positions opposite Ypres, which would lead to a mass swing northwards to seize Ostend and Zeebrugge and thus deprive the Germans of two vital U-boat bases. Given that on 1 February 1917 Germany had reopened unrestricted submarine warfare in an all-out attempt to throttle Britain's seaborne trade, Haig's Flanders offensive made good strategic sense.

Lloyd George was wary of Haig's strategy. He had been appalled by the heavy casualties suffered during the 1916 campaigns, and found incomprehensible the General Staff's prognoses about victory through attrition. As a politician he had to answer to a public that was showing signs of becoming disheartened by battles whose only result seemed to be enormous casualties and small dents in the German line. Professional soldiers argued that the public did not understand the nature of the war. As one staff officer had written in 1914, 'As you remember in 1899–1902 we had gradually to educate the public up to what the war meant.'[2] For obvious reasons, the public was never presented with the principles of attrition, nor had the battles been explained in terms of comparative body counts. Some at GHQ could not see why. 'No spectacular progress had been made to appeal to popular imagination, unaided by detailed exposition, and the government of the day did not encourage official explanation of the results obtained,' complained Brigadier-General John Charteris, Haig's chief of Intelligence.[3]

Lloyd George did not see things through a soldier's eyes and was deeply mistrustful of Haig. The suspicion was mutual; in April, when asked by John Buchan, the novelist-turned-Director of Information, why there was friction between him and the Prime Minister, Haig naively answered, 'I am trying to work in harmony with Lloyd George but he has such strange ideas on warfare.'[4] Among his 'strange ideas' were those implanted by Nivelle, with whom Haig had been thrown into reluctant partnership. Nudged by the Cabinet, Haig had agreed to launch a series of offensives on 1 April to draw German reserves away from the Aisne.

Haig entrusted these large-scale diversions to the First, Third and Fifth Armies. The First would capture Vimy Ridge as a preliminary to an advance eastwards towards Douai; Allenby's Third would simultaneously thrust towards Cambrai and then swing south-east to outflank the new defences of the Hindenburg Line; and the Fifth would push towards Bullecourt. Operations were scheduled to begin in the first week of April. Developments during February and March, however, reduced the value of these offensives in terms of distracting the Germans. The unexpected withdrawal of German forces to their new, specially built defences of the

Hindenburg Line (constructed by Russian POWs) had reduced the length of their trenches by 25 miles and so released men from front-line duties; enough, as it turned out, to provide sufficient reserves to repel Nivelle's attack. As British forces edged forward into areas abandoned by the Germans, they discovered that the approaches to the Hindenburg Line had been carefully stripped of landmarks to confuse gun-layers, deep anti-tank ditches had been dug and, most unnerving of all, the German artillerymen had measured and squared off areas for pin-point (i.e. precisely targeted) bombardments.

Having accepted the spring offensive, Haig realised that it could be used to his advantage since the ground gained would prove valuable as a springboard for his forthcoming Flanders offensive. At the same time he saw the battles, particularly Arras, as a continuation of last year's campaigns of attrition.[5] As always, he sensed the hand of God. 'As to the battle of Arras,' he wrote, 'I know quite well that I am being used as a tool in the hands of a Divine Power.'[6] On a lower plane, he believed that the success of these attacks would stifle domestic critics.

Allenby and his staff devised the battle plan for Arras. They had command of 350,000 men and a pool of knowledge acquired during the past two and a half years about how best they might be deployed. At the same time they, and for that matter GHQ, were certain that a battle could be structured and forced to follow an exact timetable, which was what had been taught at Staff College. Alongside old orthodoxies were the products of modern technology. Allenby had at his disposal long-range heavy artillery, gas, aircraft and, a novelty less than a year old, tanks, which had first gone into action during the second phase of the battle of the Somme.

No one questioned the value of these innovations. And yet the technician officers who understood tanks closely and knew what they could or could not do were commonly relegated to minor roles when it came to preparing battle plans.[7] These remained the preserve of cavalrymen like Allenby and Gough or infantry generals like Rawlinson. They told the technicians what they needed from them, but never taxed them to discover the limitations of the new weaponry or, more importantly, the ways in which it could be most advantageously employed. So Arras, like the large battles of 1916, was basically another infantry affair in which the big guns, aeroplanes and tanks were assigned supporting parts. Nevertheless, generals were aware that the success of a battle plan owed much to the co-ordination of the new arms, but the systems of communication which could facilitate co-operation, such as wireless links between spotter aircraft and battery commanders, were still in their infancy and prone to breaking down.

Allenby was more flexible than many of his contemporaries. From the start he and his staff felt convinced that surprise would be the key to success. Beneath the ruined town of Arras was a network of cellars in which up to 20,000 men could be hidden from German reconnaissance aircraft. It was therefore possible for the concealed assault troops to stay safe from bombardment and be moved quickly into the forward trenches for the first wave of attacks. A further element of surprise would be a novel forty-eight-hour hurricane bombardment in place of the customary five-day barrages, which always alerted the Germans and gave them time in which to adjust their defences and summon reserves. This was the proposal of Allenby's chief artillery adviser, Lieutenant-General Sir Arthur Holland, an intelligent officer free from attachment to old dogmas. Allenby accepted this highly unorthodox plan, but it was rejected by his divisional, corps and brigade commanders after 'some heated controversy'.[8]

The row continued at a higher level and was finally settled by the direct intervention of Haig and GHQ, who vetoed Holland's plan. The main objections came from Haig's senior artillery adviser, Lieutenant-General Sir Noel ('Curly') Birch, who approached Allenby directly. 'I was,' Birch wrote later, 'faced with a situation I knew was wrong . . . I was devoted to Allenby and I was Chief of Staff when he commanded the Cavalry Corps, and I had to go to him and say I disagreed with everything he had said since breakfast.'[9] Allenby conceded, grudgingly, since he thought the alterations would reduce his chances of success, and on 7 February he accepted a conventional schedule for a five-day barrage.[10] Ten days later Holland was moved sideways and a new artillery adviser was foisted on the Third Army by Haig, Lieutenant-General Robert Lecky. Like Birch he was a 'safe' technician, and both men were characterised by a subordinate Gunner as 'the worst types of Horse Artillery commanders and both the laughing stock of the regiment.'[11]

The episode was dispiriting for Allenby, and the first of several in which Haig and the General Staff interfered directly in his planning and execution of the Arras offensive. He was, however, fortunate that, in contrast to his earlier, small-scale offensives, he was adequately supplied with artillery since, in the first months of 1917, earlier shortages, especially of the vital heavy howitzers, had been eliminated.[12] As prescribed by GHQ, the preliminary shelling at Arras would follow a set pattern. Over 800 18-pounders would drop a creeping barrage of shrapnel 200 yards ahead of attacking waves of infantry, a technique that had been developed at Verdun and during the later phases of the Somme and which, it was optimistically hoped, would destroy the German barbed-wire entanglements.[13] Nearly 500 4·5-inch and 6-inch howitzers

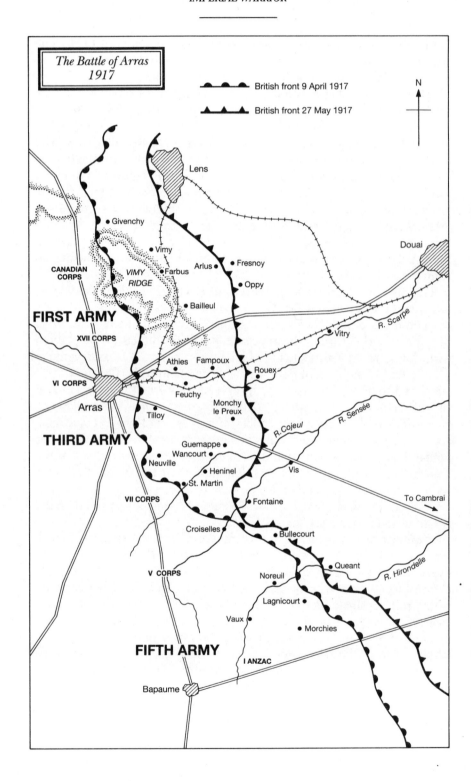

The Battle of Arras 1917

●━●━● British front 9 April 1917

▲━▲━▲ British front 27 May 1917

N

Lens

Givenchy

Vimy

Douai

CANADIAN CORPS

VIMY RIDGE

Arlus

Farbus

Fresnoy

Oppy

Bailleul

FIRST ARMY

XVII CORPS

R. Scarpe

Vitry

Athies Fampoux

VI CORPS

Rouex

Arras

Feuchy

Tilloy

Monchy le Preux

R. Sensée

THIRD ARMY

R. Cojeul

Guemappe

Wancourt

Neuville

Heninel

Vis

St. Martin

VII CORPS

To Cambrai

Fontaine

Croiselles

Bullecourt

V CORPS

Queant

R. Hirondelle

Noreuil

Lagnicourt

Vaux

Morchies

FIFTH ARMY

I ANZAC

Bapaume

would shell German support and communication trenches to disrupt counter-measures, and the big howitzers would neutralise German heavy batteries, with gas if weather conditions were favourable.

Counter-battery fire had recently become more effective, thanks to improvements in gun sighting and target identification, and to more detailed maps of enemy positions, largely based on aerial photographs. Among the new techniques to be used at Arras were aircraft recognition of targets, particularly camouflaged heavy batteries, and the direction of fire by airborne observers.[14] Unfortunately, the value of these techniques was limited. With 365 aircraft of all types, the Royal Flying Corps squadrons attached to the Third Army outnumbered their German adversaries, who had 195 machines. In aerial combat, however, the odds were weighted against the RFC, since many of their aeroplanes were obsolescent and no match for the new German Albatros and Halberstadt machines, including those of the squadrons commanded by the famous air ace, Manfred von Richthofen. In the period immediately before the offensive British attempts to secure air supremacy over the battlefield foundered; between 4 and 8 April seventy-five RFC aircraft were lost. Afterwards every reconnaissance mission had to have a large fighter escort, and losses in dogfights were heavy.[15]

Forty tanks had been allocated to Allenby, mostly ageing machines manufactured the previous year. There were high expectations for the tanks, but as yet no commander had devised a method of deploying them effectively; at Arras, for instance, they were used in penny packets and without any artillery support.[16] Nor had technical faults been eradicated; the 'Mother' types which trundled across no man's land in 1916–17 moved at 2 miles an hour, were cumbersome, and broke down readily and often.

Secrecy, which Allenby hoped would give his troops a vital advantage, proved ultimately unobtainable. On 3 March the German High Command was alerted to the Nivelle offensive after securing a copy of a memorandum with details of the French plan. Aerial surveillance of the hinterland of Arras provided indications that a Big Push was on hand and, at the end of March, POWs interviewed by Third Army Intelligence officers revealed that German front-line units were well aware that they would shortly be attacked.[17] More may have been known to the enemy: a month later a captured German wireless technician told his interrogators how German listening posts eavesdropped on French wireless signals that were obligingly sent uncoded. He added that exchanges between British battery commanders and artillery observers were also intercepted, and that British ciphers had been broken since the listeners knew all the code names for British units.[18]

*

During the week before the offensive, Haig had been busy touring the army, divisional and corps HQs of all the forces involved and checking their battle plans. Special attention was given to those of the Third Army, and on 2 April Haig visited its HQ at Bryas château near St Pol to confirm that the revised plans for the preliminary bombardment would be adhered to. His spirits were raised by what he saw and heard; 'I have never before seen commanders so confident,' he told Robertson, 'or so satisfied with preparations for cutting [the German wire with shellfire].' This was wishful thinking, since bad weather had reduced reconnaissance flights with the result that intelligence about the state of the German barbed-wire defences was patchy.[19]

British eagerness contrasted with French procrastination; on 5 April Nivelle announced the first of several postponements of his Aisne offensive, giving poor ground conditions and severe weather as his excuse. Driving rain and sleet swept the Arras sector throughout 8 April and forced Haig to put back zero hour to 5.30 am on the following day.

The morning of 9 April saw a deceptive lull in the storms and the attack proceeded to schedule. Allenby's offensive was undertaken along a 10-mile front by Haldane's VI Corps, Snow's VII, and Lieutenant-General Sir Charles Fergusson's XVII, with Lieutenant-General Sir Ivor Maxse's XVIII Corps in reserve together with a further two divisions that had been placed under Haig's direct orders. There were also three cavalry divisions put at Allenby's disposal for immediate use once a large enough gap had been made in the German front. The horsemen were, as at the Somme, essential to Haig's overall plan, which anticipated open warfare beyond the fractured German lines.

All these units were to put into effect the plan which had been carefully drawn up by Allenby and his staff over the past three months. It was a meticulously tabulated and timetabled list of objectives, each delineated by a coloured line drawn across a map. During the first phase of the advance the attacking battalions had to reach, in order, black, blue, brown and green lines, this last extending beyond the German strongpoint of Monchy-le-Preux, which had to be occupied twelve hours after the start of the offensive. Beyond this was the target for the second phase of the offensive, the Drocourt–Quéant line, called by the Germans *Wotan Stellung*, a still-incomplete extension of the Hindenburg Line that lay just over 5 miles beyond Monchy-le-Preux and 10 from the British starting-point. In terms of First World War offensives, Arras was extremely ambitious. It also, and this proved a source of unexpected difficulties, expected soldiers long used to static trench warfare to adapt to open, mobile fighting.

Allenby's chances of success depended upon units advancing at a more or less uniform, unwavering pace, and maintaining close contact between each other and their HQs. The most obvious criticism of this structured battle plan was the vast chasm between what appeared theoretically possible on a map laid across a table in Bryas château, and what could actually be achieved by men under shell and machine-gun fire as they scrambled across the wasteland that separated the opposing fronts. At the same time, the staff assumed that corps and divisional commanders would somehow keep up with events on the battlefield and control them, which in turn took for granted the maintenance of telephone links. The divergence between plan and action was always understood by those who carried out the orders, but beyond grumbling about the purblindness and ignorance of staff officers behind the lines, there was little that they could do in an army which offered no channels for criticism, however well-informed and constructive. As Haldane sadly observed ten days before the offensive, it took 'moral courage' to question obviously foredoomed operations, since the result would be a wrecked career.[20]

This was true of Allenby's command. During a crisis in the fighting near Guémappe on 13 April, when the 50th Division was pinned down by fire and unable to move forward according to plan and help the 3rd Division, its commander complained directly to Allenby that he was unsupported. The only response was a rebuke to the effect that Allenby would not tolerate squabbles between his commanders.[21] Another commander, Lieutenant-General Sir Hugh Tudor, dismayed by un-realistic orders, bypassed Allenby and Haig and denounced the latter's 'futile, half-baked attacks against fresh troops' to a highly placed friend at the War Office, and subsequently found himself in 'hot water'.[22]

Quietism was the best policy. After an on-the-spot inspection of their units' prescribed line of attack towards Rouelx, two Scottish colonels despaired. 'Let us rejoin our battalions, the more we look at it the less we shall like it,' one remarked; 'the attack looked all right on the map, but viewed from the ground it was hopeless.'[23] As well as impracticable staff plans, field commanders had to contend with more mundane human errors, unavoidable in the confusion of battle, which one battalion commander summed up as the 'Bichit, Bochit and Buggerit' factors.[24] These seem seldom to have been considered by staff officers, even those who had encountered them in the field.

Notwithstanding the many sources of mishap, the Arras offensive began well. At zero hour the first wave of assault troops mounted the trench parapets and moved forward. Despite the biting cold and a strong south-westerly wind that blew flurries of snow across a desolate landscape, remarkable progress was made, but co-ordination between units soon broke down because of poor visibility. Moreover, the rate of advance was uneven as some units came across barbed-wire entanglements and machine-guns that had escaped the creeping barrage.[25] The last should have been anticipated. In March, Third Army Intelligence officers had interrogated a captured machine-gunner who had described in some detail how the Germans had adopted a flexible distribution system for their machine-guns, keeping three in reserve for deployment after the first line of trenches had been overrun.[26]

The rate of advance was irregular and, just before noon, Haldane telephoned Allenby and asked permission for his divisions to regroup and consolidate on the second (blue) line. After congratulating VII Corps on its performance, Allenby ordered the advance to proceed immediately: 'It is important to press the enemy leaving any strongpoints to be dealt with by parties in the rear.'[27] This message, with minor variations, was repeated by Allenby throughout the next four days. He had set his heart on knocking a wide hole in the German line and, with Haig breathing down his neck, was determined to drive his men onwards at all costs.

By early afternoon the pace of the advance began to slacken. The tanks, by which Allenby had set great store, proved a disappointment. They lagged behind the infantry, developed mechanical faults, and sank in the churned-up and muddy soil. Reinforcements, needed to maintain the momentum, were delayed. 'The congestion on the road to Arras was bad enough,' wrote one eyewitness, 'but beyond that it is almost indescribable.'[28] Horse-drawn guns following the infantry were held up when their crews attempted to get them over abandoned German trenches, and transport sections found the going hard as they hurried across the cratered battlefield to carry supplies and ammunition to advancing units. By the evening, Allenby was forced to concede that his original timetable had been over-ambitious, and at 10.25 pm he ordered all units to consolidate on the brown (third) line in readiness for a renewed push at eight the following morning towards the green line and Monchy-le-Preux, an objective that should have been gained by late afternoon on the first day.[29]

Night was a torment for the exhausted men in the forward positions, since Allenby had forbidden attacking troops to wear or carry greatcoats in order to accelerate their movement. It was too cold to sleep, and at dawn a staff officer from the 34th Division encountered some 'half-frozen and very fatigued men' huddled together, one of them dead from exposure.[30]

The battle resumed on 10 April with an assault on Monchy-le-Preux. Allenby was in a state of high excitement, certain that the decisive breakthrough was within his grasp. There was every reason for optimism since his Intelligence staff, drawing on their questioning of prisoners taken the day before, claimed that the Germans had been caught off-balance, were badly shaken and only capable of small-scale, localised resistance.[31] There was also some ominous news; heavy reinforcements were on their way for a stand on the Drocourt–Quéant line. It was now a matter of urgency that the attackers should get there before these fresh German troops.

News that the Third Army's offensive might be running out of steam brought Haig to Bryas château the following morning.[32] He exhorted Allenby to keep up the pressure for at least twenty-four hours. Then, according to his diary, he advised a fresh thrust: 'If the 3rd Army is held up on the west of Monchy, I urged Allenby to push forward on the north [bank] of the Scarpe and then move south-east in the rear of Monchy so as to turn the enemy's flank.'[33] This was ideal work for the three cavalry divisions, which Allenby had been holding back since the previous afternoon after hearing that the infantry were getting into difficulties.

Haig believed he was on the verge of a breakthrough and was not going to let the chance slip away. Allenby was of similar mind, and in a mid-morning telephone call to Haldane warned him not to let his advance lose impetus and the offensive deteriorate into a 'stagnant' struggle.[34] In two days the front had shifted 4 miles, an unprecedented distance by the standards of the time, and units freed from their trenches were now fighting a battle of manoeuvre in open country. By 7.40pm Allenby felt confident enough to announce to his commanders that 'All troops [are] to understand that the Third Army is now pursuing a defeated enemy and that risks must be freely taken.'[35] Relayed to the men at the front, the message was received with incredulity.[36]

But was Allenby taking risks? Haig thought not when, in mid-evening, he visited Fergusson's HQ at Aubigny for a first-hand account of how the outflanking movement on the Scarpe was developing. He was shocked to hear that no cavalry was available to penetrate what appeared to be a widening gap in the German defences, and he angrily telephoned Allenby to discover the reason.[37] Prompted by Haig, Allenby released his cavalry reserves the next day; as they trotted off in a blizzard, some Household Cavalry, presumably officers, were heard singing the Eton Boating Song. The horsemen made little impact on the fighting and, as Allenby told his wife afterwards, were thrown back by 'wire and machine-guns'.[38]

The third day of the offensive, 11 April, opened promisingly with the capture of Monchy-le-Preux. Allenby was now convinced that the conflict had entered its decisive stage and he called for superhuman efforts from his commanders and their men. Time was running against the attackers; Intelligence had confirmed German reinforcements moving into positions on the Drocourt–Quéant line and the arrival behind it of reserve artillery batteries.[39] The weather was worsening, bringing intermittent blizzards, and after three days in action many soldiers had reached the limits of their endurance. One front-line officer warned his HQ that his men were now 'suffering from cold and were tired out'. But still Allenby demanded fresh energy for a final push.

Reviewing the situation on the morning of the 12th, Haig concluded that the opportunity for a breakthrough had passed. He was driven to Bryas, but missed Allenby, who was visiting his corps HQs. Haig therefore discussed the situation with Allenby's Chief-of-Staff, Major-General Louis Bols, who heard that an attack on the Drocourt–Quéant line was no longer contemplated since the Germans had had time to strengthen its defenders with fresh troops. 'Our advance must therefore be more methodical,' Haig argued, and the time for 'great risks' had passed. The wearing-down process would continue on the Arras sector, but 'we must try and substitute shells as far as possible for men'. The same message was delivered the following day to Allenby, who was ordered 'to arrange his advance methodically, sparing the infantry as much as possible'.[40]

This is the version of his new strategy outlined by Haig in his diary, and it seems straightforward enough. But Haig and Allenby always fumbled for words during conferences and, perhaps for this reason, Allenby was left with the impression that he was free to carry out a series of infantry attacks which, in Haldane's opinion, would merely squander lives.[41] As Haig appreciated, the balance on the Arras battlefield had swung against the attackers, who were now up against well-positioned, re-inforced and resolute defenders. When the 5th Cameronians advanced near Hénin Hill they suffered 'exceptionally heavy losses' from their own, misjudged, creeping barrage and well-sighted German machine-guns. So much for the concept of replacing men with high-explosives.[42]

These Scotsmen were among units ordered by Allenby to take 'bites' at the by now consolidated German positions between 13 and 14 April and, like everyone else involved, they were badly mauled. Allenby had utterly misunderstood what Haig wanted; instead of delivering a series of small-scale 'methodical' attacks, he had ploughed on with an intensified mass offensive. The results were calamitous.

Allenby's blunder was quickly recognised by his divisional commanders who were horrified by spiralling casualties. At considerable risk to their careers and in defiance of the traditions of their service, Major-Generals de Lisle, Philip Robertson and Percival Wilkinson (whose 50th Division had suffered the most) protested directly to Haig. They persuaded him that Allenby had misinterpreted his orders, with the result that on the 15th Haig suspended all operations on the Arras sector.[43] The trio's temerity paid off and none was admonished. For Allenby this incident was a humiliation; his capacity as a general had been called into question, he had lost the confidence of his subordinates, and Haig's faith in him had been shaken.

There was some consolation for Allenby. The results of the first five days of fighting had been impressive, at least by the admittedly undemanding standards of earlier British offensives. The Third Army had made a 4-mile incursion into German territory at a cost of just under 8,000 casualties, although this success was overshadowed by the spectacular victory of the First Army which, on 9 April, had taken nearly the whole of Vimy Ridge. Surprise had been a vital ingredient at both Arras and Vimy Ridge, as Allenby and his staff had appreciated from the start. What they and, for that matter, GHQ had failed to forecast was the resilience of the German Army and the swiftness with which its soldiers improvised defences after their forward lines had been overrun. By 13 April the nature of the battle had changed; the Third Army was facing a formidable resistance, well supported by artillery. If he was fully aware of this, Allenby did nothing to amend his orders. Moreover, matters were not helped by the ambiguity of his battle plans. On one hand he presented his commanders with a conventional, rigid timetable for carefully synchronised advances, and on the other he urged them to think for themselves and take 'risks'.

Allenby realised this, but too late, and afterwards he shifted the blame to company and platoon commanders. During a conversation with Haig on 14 April, he regretted that they had spent too long in the trenches and forgotten how to fight a war of movement across open country. They were 'like "blind puppies" . . . unable to see the features of the ground and take advantage of the cover afforded for taking out the enemy's machine-guns'. Haldane agreed, and complained about 'young and ignorant' officers who stuck to the letter of their orders and refused to act independently.[44] Both generals expected far too much from young men, many of whom had been thrown into the front line after as little as nine weeks' preliminary training under a system that prized unquestioning obedience and looked askance at individual initiative. Furthermore, Haig's strategy of attrition had caused the continual depletion of the cadre of experienced junior officers and NCOs.

The battle of Arras reopened on 23 April, Allenby's fifty-sixth birthday. Under pressure from the French, Haig had reluctantly agreed to pursue a number of limited offensives. Nivelle's overdue attack had been launched on 16 April, and had foundered almost immediately with enormous losses. The situation deteriorated to a point at which, on 30 April, large bodies of French soldiers refused to go into action. On the same day, Haig revealed to Allenby, Gough, and Lieutenant-General Sir Henry Horne of the First Army, the extent of the French collapse. Nivelle's offensive had failed and he was about to be sacked; French manpower was all but exhausted; and it was impossible for the French Army to do more than hold its section of the line until the arrival of American troops. The United States had entered the war on the Allied side at the beginning of the month, but it was estimated that at least a year would be needed in which to raise, train and equip enough American soldiers to make a decisive impact on the war. In the meantime, Haig proposed to maintain pressure on the Arras front with a series of limited sorties designed to secure 'a good defensive line' while preparations went ahead for his big push in Flanders, scheduled for midsummer.[45] Until the arrival of the United States contingent, the British Army would have to bear the brunt of the fighting in France.

This was bleak news for Allenby. His Third Army was under strength and had not yet recovered from its earlier exertions. Nevertheless, he was determined that it should fulfil its obligations and keep grinding away at the German line. 'As cool as ever', as Repington noted, Allenby watched the 6th Division's assault on Guénappe on 23 April and, as bull-like as ever, demanded redoubled efforts when it appeared to falter. Every inch of captured ground was to be held at all costs. When Haldane objected on the grounds that his men were exhausted, Allenby called for a sense of team spirit at a time when 'everyone was doing his best'. But the rallying cries of the playing field were not enough, and slowly Allenby came to realise that his men could do no more. On 28 April he 'tamely accepted' Haldane's decision to curtail an offensive for lack of men after the latter's division had been stripped of 4,000 front-line troops for fatigue duties.[46]

By 1 May, and after a week in which his Third Army had attempted the impossible, Allenby concluded that it was no longer fit for the operations that Haig demanded. He was also apprehensive about their conduct and value and, breaking his habit of the past two and a half years, challenged his superior's judgement. In a memo of 1 May to GHQ he protested against the decision taken earlier in the day to launch an attack in heavy rain. Some detachments, hampered by mud and poor visibility, had advanced without proper support and 'were left isolated and were lost, as a consequence of their gallantry'.[47] He was equally critical of the mishandling of a night attack on 3 May that had been Gough's brainchild and had gone awry when detachments had lost contact with each other in the dark. Allenby repeated his criticism of this operation during Haig's weekly conference on 7 May. The offensive had been mistimed and the

Third Army's shortfall of men had forced the commitment to battle of 'semi-trained troops unable to use their rifles properly'. He assured Haig that the Third Army remained in good heart, but large numbers of men were worn out and incapable of 'considerable operations' in the immediate future.[48]

Allenby's protest was backed by Snow and Haldane, who had already expressed misgivings about the wisdom of localised attacks on the Germans now that they were undistracted by the French and free to take effective counter-measures. The casualty figures were sombre evidence of the new German strength and made nonsense of Haig's strategy of taking 'bites' at their line. During May and June British losses totalled 126,300, German 67,000.

Haig brushed aside Allenby's doubts. He ended the 7 May conference with an emotional appeal to his army commanders, asking them to 'simulate the continuance of battle' so that the Germans would be deceived into believing that a major offensive was under way. In what was a reproof to Allenby, he exhorted each commander to submit uncon-ditionally to the 'general interest'. For the next few weeks they had no choice but to 'carry on with tired troops' and 'cut their coats accordingly'.[49] Translated to the battlefield, this homely metaphor, among other things, caused men from the 17th Division to rush German trenches without machine-gun support.[50] Nevertheless, Allenby acquiesced and the Third Army continued to stab at the German line, coming off worst in every engagement.

Allenby's behaviour during the first week of May was extraordinary for an officer who normally suppressed whatever inner uncertainties he had about the competence of his superiors. Not only did he jettison his philosophy of 'cheerful obedience', he deviated from the dogma of the offensive spirit to which, until the end of April, he had upheld with astonishing and, at times, inexplicable steadfastness. Haig, who could never differentiate between constructive criticism and censure, was ruffled by the apostasy of a hitherto passive and reliable general. On 12 May he attempted to put back the iron into Allenby's soul and, after a conversation about the objectives of his strategy, he felt he had succeeded. 'He was rather opposed to make small efforts with limited objectives to gain ground,' Haig wrote in his diary, 'but his recent successes have quite changed his mind.'[51] Allenby left no record of the exchange, and it may well have been that his customary awkwardness in Haig's presence prevented him from saying what he really thought.

Whether or not this was so, Haig was soon convinced that the time had come to unstick Allenby and replace him with a more tractable general. Allenby's dissent set a bad example which could possibly be exploited by

Haig's political enemies in London, and showed signs of becoming contagious. On 22 May, Haig was disheartened by the lukewarm response of his divisional commanders to his proposals for the forthcoming Ypres campaign, and by their distressing lack of the 'real offensive spirit'. There was also, he believed, an urgent need to remind all his senior officers of the principles which underlay his strategy, and so, on 5 June, he lectured them on attrition and explained how it was the key to victory.[52] He predicted that, 'The power and endurance of the German people is being strained to such a degree as to make it possible that the breaking point may be reached this year.'[53] On the following day Allenby was ordered to London to be briefed before taking command of the Egyptian Expeditionary Force, and command of the Third Army was given to Lieutenant-General the Hon. Sir Julian Byng, the victor of Vimy. The message was straightforward: there was no place for waverers under Haig's command.

The dismissal of Allenby had been an easy task, thanks to favourable political circumstances and the machinations of Haig's accomplice, Robertson. Both were in powerful positions, which also enabled them to secure the War Cabinet's sanction for the Ypres offensive. Lloyd George was less strongly placed as a result of his ill-considered support for the now discredited Nivelle, and he was hankering after a victory that would enhance his own and his coalition's prestige. Mistrustful of Haig, he correctly anticipated no spectacular gains from the imminent third battle of Ypres. His hopes were therefore pinned on the Middle East front; he had in mind an advance in southern Palestine that would end triumphantly in the capture of Jerusalem, an event that would cheer a war-weary Britain and encourage its allies. An 'Easterner' by inclination, he clung to the belief that the defeat of Turkey was not only possible but would fatally injure Germany. This was, in May, still a distant prospect. In the previous month, British and Dominion forces in southern Palestine had twice failed to capture the key Turkish stronghold at Gaza, setbacks that were, with some justice, attributed to the dismal local commander, General Murray. The Prime Minister realised that a breakthrough required an able, aggressive and experienced general with a reputation for getting things done. Allenby was an ideal candidate.

He had been previously recommended to Lloyd George's attention by Repington as a suitable replacement for Haig, and Robertson supported his appointment to the Middle East. At a stroke he would remove from Haig's command a potentially troublesome subordinate and, at the same time, place in the Middle East command a general who was considered a 'Westerner' at heart, and therefore extremely unlikely to make excessive demands for men and resources needed in France. So, though for very different reasons, Allenby's appointment satisfied both Lloyd George and Haig.

It did not please Allenby. He left France on 6 June in a bitter mood since he saw himself as exiled to a peripheral and moribund front as the replacement for a general who had twice been shifted downwards and sideways. On hearing the news that he had been unstuck, Allenby threw aside his usual stoicism and broke down, lamenting his misfortunes to his successor, Byng.[54] Elsewhere there was rejoicing. A jaunty Haldane was spotted whistling merrily as he walked down the steps of Allenby's HQ. The chatelaine's daughter called out, '*Vous êtes très jeu ce matin, Monsieur mon général*'. He answered, '*Par je crois le Taureau est dégommé!*'[55] That same evening, a sour Allenby arrived ostentatiously late for a farewell dinner in his honour given by Haig.

Allenby's resentment was understandable, although in fact his transfer to the Middle East would later appear a stroke of fortune. For the past year his career had stagnated and his performance as a general, the first few days of Arras apart, had been unimpressive; Edmonds later summarised it as 'one of gross stupidity from first to last'.[56] This was unduly harsh, since it ignored the conditions imposed on him by French and Haig, and the knowledge that if he deviated from their doctrines he risked dismissal. As it was, Allenby showed a gratifying willingness to accommodate his superiors, even though his generalship displayed little flair. This was not surprising, since he was a cavalryman who had been called upon to fight what the technician Edmonds perceptively described as an extended siege. The original trenches had been developed into a highly sophisticated fortification system which Allenby, in common with French and Haig, imagined could be pierced by adapting familiar methods of open infantry warfare, with artillery and such novelties as tanks and aircraft playing secondary roles. This fumbling towards an appropriate strategy was yet another sign that the hoped-for commander of Wellingtonian stature and imagination had not emerged from the Army's high command.

The thinness with which talent was spread among his contemporary commanders does not exonerate Allenby from Edmonds's charges, nor was the feeling in some quarters – that he was out of his depth and floundering hopelessly – unjustified. Opportunities for innovative planning were, of course, not open to him; he followed strategies devised by others, and whatever emerged from his HQ was liable to close scrutiny and amendment from above. What particularly marked him out was nerve which, in certain circumstances, is a supreme virtue in a general, but in his case it too often took the form of a purblind refusal to accept reality on the battlefield. When confronted with a crisis, his reaction was to insist that victory could be snatched from the jaws of defeat by an injection of the offensive spirit. From above he appeared a commander consumed by the will to win and, from below, a martinet who goaded rather than led his men, indifferent to the odds they faced.

Allenby would always attempt the impossible, and the results were predictable. From his many tours of the forward trenches and his experience of bombardment, he knew the everyday conditions that his soldiers endured, but he never let this knowledge undermine his resolve or deflect his purpose. What spurred him on and made him such a formidable taskmaster was his deeply rooted, soldierly sense of obedience and duty. He, and for that matter his fellow generals, waged war according to the codes they had learned at their public schools, at Sandhurst, and in their regiments. Allenby's loyalty, even to a man he inwardly disliked, his determination, and his belief that any worthwhile endeavour demanded sacrifice, gave him the internal strength to persevere and impose his will on those beneath him. These qualities constituted what Wavell admiringly described as his immense force of character. It did not win battles, but somehow it prevented them from being lost.

PART 3

ARMAGEDDON

JUNE 1917–NOVEMBER 1918

CHAPTER 10

MIDDLE EAST COMMAND

JUNE–SEPTEMBER 1917

ON 7 June 1917 Allenby returned to London, and a country in the grip of total war. There was rationing, accompanied by exhortations to grow and save food as the U-boat campaign against merchant shipping intensified; Zeppelin raids on the capital were being superseded by the more devastating night attacks by Gotha bombers; and there was serious industrial unrest in South Wales and the North. The last were symptoms of a widespread and growing war-weariness which alarmed the government, some of whose members were coming to the view that a victory over Germany was beyond the Allies' reach, and that some sort of negotiated peace was unavoidable.

It was against this sombre background that Allenby, accompanied by Robertson, heard Lloyd George's plans for a Palestine offensive. The Prime Minister wanted 'Jerusalem before Christmas', a victory which, he hoped, would boost national morale and, incidentally, restore public faith in the coalition government. He promised to deliver all the men and resources Allenby might consider necessary, and warned that if he held back in his demands and the enterprise failed, the blame would be his alone. These proposals were wormwood to Robertson who, 'for the sake of peace and quietness and in order to get the Prime Minister's consent to other requirements', had grudgingly agreed to approve what, in private, he called this 'Palestine rot'.[1] And yet there were excellent strategic reasons for an advance towards Jerusalem. Recent developments inside Russia made it highly likely that Turkish forces deployed in the Caucasus would shortly be shifted to Aleppo as reinforcements for a counter-offensive, code-named 'Yildirim' (lightning), that was being prepared for the recapture of Baghdad. A British thrust into Palestine would compel the Turco-German command to split their forces, or even postpone 'Yildirim'.

Broader political issues were involved. At this stage in the war, the Prime Minister and several of his senior colleagues had become convinced that the stalemate on the Western Front could never be broken, whatever Haig and the Westerners said to the contrary. Only the elimination of Germany's allies offered a chance of victory, or, taking what in the summer of 1917 was a realistic line, could secure favourable terms from the Germans in a negotiated settlement. Turkey was the most fragile of Germany's 'props' and appeared, according to Intelligence assessments, close to breaking-point. This view was confirmed by a series of clandestine peace initiatives backed by senior Turkish ministers. A hard knock, delivered in Palestine, might therefore prove fatal.

The prospect of a Turkish collapse had a further attraction, especially to the influential knot of Conservative Imperialists in the Cabinet, which included Andrew Bonar Law and Lord Milner, both ardent backers of the Palestine campaign.[2] They, like Winston Churchill and Lord Curzon, were looking ahead to post-war annexations in the Middle East that would guarantee British paramountcy in the region. A blueprint for the area's future was already in existence, drawn up by Allied diplomats who, over the past two years, had agreed the partition of the Turkish Empire. Russia had been promised Constantinople and parts of eastern Turkey, and the agreement between Sir Mark Sykes and François-Georges Picot in May 1916 settled the Lebanon, Syria and northern Iraq on France, leaving Britain southern Iraq where, by 1917, the Indian government was already constructing a new colonial administration. Palestine was to be placed under international control.

This process of parcelling out the spoils had been complicated by the upheavals in Russia – in December 1917 Lenin repudiated all claims to Turkish territory – and Arabia. In 1916 Britain had made an alliance with the ultra-orthodox and conservative Arab prince, Hussain, the Sharif of Mecca, who was soon calling himself the King of the Hijaz. Part of the price of his rebellion against Turkish rule had been the promise of a post-war Arab state, although its borders had not yet been defined. There was evidence, apparent by the summer of 1917, that Hussain would prove an embarrassing ally; he saw himself as a future supreme ruler of a 'union of Arabs', and refused to acknowledge French territorial claims in the region.[3]

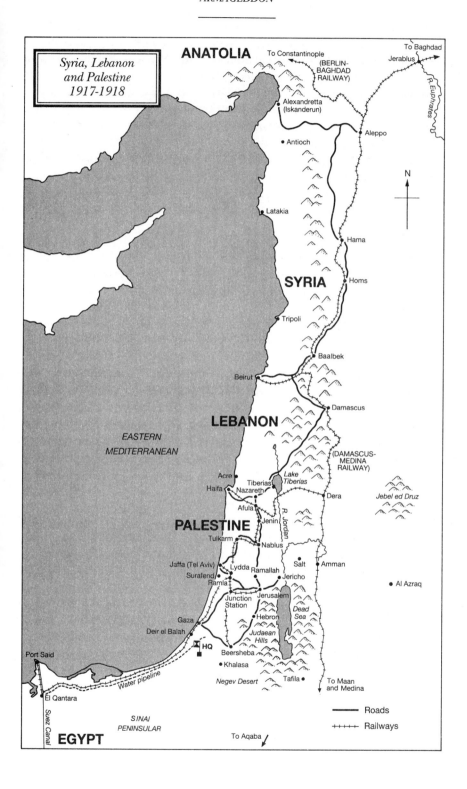

Syria, Lebanon
and Palestine
1917-1918

ANATOLIA
To Constantinople
To Baghdad
Jerablus
(BERLIN-
BAGHDAD
RAILWAY)
R. Euphrates
Alexandretta
(Iskanderun)
Aleppo
Antioch
N
Latakia
Hama
SYRIA
Homs
Tripoli
Baalbek
Beirut
Damascus
LEBANON
EASTERN
MEDITERRANEAN
(DAMASCUS-
MEDINA
RAILWAY)
Acre
Tiberias   Lake
Haifa   Nazareth   Tiberias
Afula   Dera   Jebel ed Druz
Jenin   R. Jordan
PALESTINE
Tulkarm   Nablus
Jaffa (Tel Aviv)   Lydda   Salt   Amman
Surafend   Ramallah
Ramla   Jericho   Al Azraq
Junction   Jerusalem
Station   Dead
Gaza   Hebron   Sea
Deir el Balah   Judaean
Hills
HQ
Port Said   Beersheba
Khalasa
Negev Desert   Tafila   To Maan
El Qantara   and Medina
Water pipeline
Suez Canal
SINAI
PENINSULAR   Roads
EGYPT   To Aqaba   Railways

What all this meant for Allenby was that the moment he took up his command in Cairo he was thrust into the complex and unfamiliar world of international politics. Henceforward he was an administrator and diplomat as well as a field commander, with the unenviable duty of representing a power which, on one hand, was pursuing expansionist policies and, on the other, was playing godfather to Arab nationalism. In the meantime, his first problem was to absorb everything he could about the geography of Palestine. To help him, Lloyd George presented him with a copy of Sir George Adam Smith's *The Historical Geography of the Holy Land*, remarking with a side-swipe at Robertson that it probably contained more of practical use than could be found in War Office surveys.

Allenby appreciated the gift and liked the giver. An influential body of senior officers, including Haig and Robertson, loathed the Prime Minister for his pre-war radicalism, attacks on the aristocracy and, worst of all, his open doubts about their own professional competence. Allenby thought differently. He left his interview with the Prime Minister captivated by the Welshman's energy and vision, and his judgement was confirmed by later events. Long afterwards, when the former Prime Minister had offended the Army by his criticism of Haig, Allenby was asked to add his voice to the protest. 'Attack Lloyd George?' he answered. 'But I like the little man. He won the war, though for Heaven's sake don't tell him so.'[4]

Allenby left London on 18 June and, after crossing the Channel, travelled by train to Brindisi, where he embarked on the cruiser *Bristol* for the two-day voyage to Alexandria. He arrived in Cairo on the 28th. His predecessor, Murray, had heard the news of his own dismissal on 11 June, and had been furious.[5] The Egyptian Expeditionary Force was glad to see the back of him, for he had been a remote, hesitant commander, tainted by the two recent defeats at Gaza. The news of Allenby's coming was greeted with excitement as favourable reports of his capacities had run ahead of him. Colonel Richard Meinertzhagen, recently transferred from the East African front as an Intelligence officer, looked forward to working under a decisive general known for his 'energy and push', which would be welcomed in a torpid army where staff thinking had become stuck in a narrow 'trench warfare' groove. Another senior officer also detected an atmosphere of listlessness that pervaded all ranks of a 'tired' army.[6]

Allenby lived up to expectations. Within three weeks of his arrival in Cairo and after a series of rapid tours of base camps, depots, hospitals, lines of communication and forward positions, he had completely revitalised his

Soldiers of the Queen: Allenby, standing fourth from left, with brother officers of the Inniskilling Dragoons, Natal, early 1880s.

Allenby's mother, Mrs Hynman Allenby, and his wife, Mabel Chapman aboard Mabel's father's yacht.

Mrs Allenby with their only child, Horace Michael, 1900.

On the heels of the Boer, 1901: British cavalrymen ford a river
during one of the great sweeps for Boer guerillas.

As Allenby's letters indicate, conditions were Spartan during these
operations. Here two horsemen prepare a meal; like the horses,
these troopers appear underfed and weary.

Retreating from Mons: a detachment of Lancers from
Allenby's Cavalry Division, August 1914.

Nervous moments: Lieutenant-General Sir Douglas Haig, the commander of I Corps (*left,
leaning on stick*) confers with his subordinates, Major-General Monro, commander of 2nd
Division (*second left*) and Brigadier-General Hubert Gough, commander of the 3rd Cavalry
brigade (*third left*), somewhere in France, September 1914.

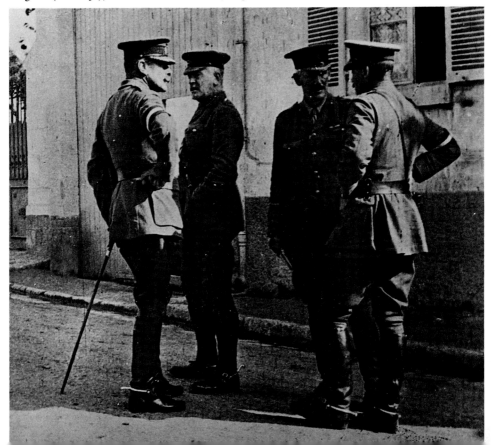

above Divided command: a distracted Allenby walks past a smiling Hubert Gough; his apparent indifference may reflect Allenby's feelings about a subordinate who had unilaterally detached himself from his command a few weeks earlier. (Near Messimes, October 1914.)

Testing the ground: Allenby, in regulation steel helmet and showing signs of strain, with King Albert of the Belgians, near Arras, spring 1917.

Offensive spirit: British infantry in good heart as they move up
to the front for the Arras offensive, April 1917.

Bogged down: One of Allenby's tanks stuck in a ditch during the Arras offensive, April 1917.

Forward with the Cavalry: Haig urged Allenby to use horsemen to exploit gaps in the German defences, but they were, in Allenby's words, repelled by 'wire and machine guns', Arras, April 1917.

Waiting for Allenby: Turkish riflemen and a machine-gun crew
ready to meet the Allied attack on Beersheba, 1917.

Cold Steel: Australian light horsemen charging
at Beersheba, 31 October 1917.

erusalem falls: The mayor of Jerusalem (*smoking, and holding stick*)
nd Turkish officers pose with two men from the 60th Londons to whom he
ad just surrendered his city. The British soldiers wear regulation shorts,
 garment of which Allenby strongly approved.

THE LAST CRUSADE.

Bernard Partridge's cartoon in *Punch* shows Richard the Lion Heart looking
down on the captured city of Jerusalem, which he failed to take in 1191.

Air power: parked machine of the Australian Flying Corps,
Palestine, 1918. Control of the skies was vital for the
success of Allenby's September offensive against Damascus.

Transport hitches: A Lewis-gun section of British infantry face a mutiny
by their mules, Palestine, summer 1918.

Colonel T. E. Lawrence serving as an aircraftsman in India in 1928.

Bloody Bull's about: Allenby steps from his staff car to receive a report from an officer during the advance on Damascus, September 1918.

The Last Push: Australian Light Horse following the road
to Aleppo, October 1918.

Ruler of Egypt: a cheerful Allenby with his wife, Cairo, 1922.

Defying the Terrorists: Allenby, in full dress uniform of a Field-Marshal, is driven through the streets of Cairo. An Egyptian policeman sits in the front seat.

ANOTHER "SERPENT OF OLD NILE."

The Strong Man and the Diplomat: Bernard Partridge's 1922 *Punch* cartoon
shows Allenby astride the serpent of sedition. He suggests to the
uncertain Foreign Secretary, 'Perhaps I'd better keep both my feet down
till you've thought of the right tune to charm him with.'

army. 'A wonderful spirit of optimism' was enkindled among the men of the 5th (Australian) Light Horse, who sensed that the dog-days of manning trenches would shortly be over as they heard reports of the 'New 'planes, more men, more guns', all promised by the new general.[7] Above all, Allenby enthused his men with something of his own energy and will, and 'a strong refreshing wind' swept through the army as he made his inspections:

> He would dash up in his car to a light horse regiment, shake hands with a few officers, inspect hurriedly, but with a sure eye to good and bad points, the horses of, perhaps, a single squadron, and then be gone in a few minutes, leaving a great trail of dust behind him. His tall and massive but restlessly active figure, his keen eyes and prominent, hooked nose, his terse and forcible speech, and his imperious bearing radiated an impression of tremendous resolution, quick decision, and steely discipline.[8]

What was emerging was a style of leadership strikingly different from that which Allenby had previously adopted, although flickers of his old, acerbic and fissile self were still present, breaking surface whenever he uncovered negligence or stupidity. What was new, and so refreshing for the men he now encountered, was his faith in them and the ultimate success of their endeavours. 'Allenby breathes success,' noted Meinertzhagen after their first meeting, 'and the greatest pessimist cannot fail to have confidence in him.'[9]

Meinertzhagen also observed that 'His manner is brusque almost to rudeness', and there were casualties in the wake of Allenby's peregrinations. 'Elderly and obese' cavalry officers disappeared and younger, lean men filled their places.[10] Many officers were discomposed by their new commander's piercing, direct stare and his laconic, penetrating cross-examinations. Allenby's old friend and former colleague, Chetwode, now in command of XX Corps, thought that his 'gruffness' unnerved many.[11] And yet Chetwode, who had had long and ample opportunity to study Allenby closely, also wondered whether his harsh manner was a mask for shyness.

Those on the receiving end of Allenby's outbursts felt differently. Once, after spotting an unconcealed ammunition dump, Allenby descended from his car and fell angrily upon the officer responsible, whom he discovered in his tent, shaving. After an apoplectic dressing-down, Allenby paused, extended his hand to his 'semi-paralysed' victim and quietly said, 'Well, good day. I am very glad to have made your acquaintance.'[12] Such sudden switches of mood were bewildering, and suggest that Allenby never understood the effect of his tantrums. For him, there was never anything incongruous about playing the censorious, fulminating commanding officer one moment and the friendly general, anxious to get to know his men, the next.

Those whom he visited were naturally more concerned with avoiding Allenby's explosions than with uncovering their psychological roots. A generous-hearted signals officer at GHQ was persuaded to transmit by wireless the coded messages 'BBA' ('Bloody Bull's about') or 'BBL' (Bloody Bull's loose) the moment Allenby set off for an inspection. The message was not always received in time and once, in New Zealand lines, Allenby was puzzled by a semaphorist waving the letters 'BBL' to an adjacent unit. Asked what this meant, a quick-thinking and probably fearful officer explained it referred to an agricultural mishap, 'Bull broken loose'. Allenby had enough humour to press the matter no further.[13]

There was a simple philosophy behind the new C-in-C's programme of rapid tours. He not only wanted to advertise himself to soldiers whom he knew were disheartened, but to show them that they were now in the hands of a fighting general who was keen to get to grips with the enemy. The point was made with a flourish on the morning that Allenby first took his seat at his desk at GHQ Cairo. He looked disdainfully at a pile of routine administrative documents piled up before him for examination, and then hurled them across the room. Supreme commanders did not shuffle papers, they led men. Many years later, when asked why Liman von Sanders, his adversary during 1918, lost battles, Allenby replied, 'He sat too much in his office. Did not go about his front to see things for himself.'[14]

Painful memories of the vast mental and physical gap that separated GHQ in France from the front line, and all the misunderstandings that it caused, made Allenby chivvy his staff from their snug Cairo quarters and set them down at Umm el Kebb, near Rafah and within range of the Turkish guns. 'You know,' he remarked, half-jokingly, 'General Headquarters' roots in Cairo and Ismailia are like alfalfa grass. They are getting deep into the ground and want pulling up. Moreover, Staff Officers are like partridges: they are better for being shot over.'[15]

The exodus of staff officers was one outcome of Allenby's hectic visits to every part of his army. He had presented himself as a dynamic figure, brimming with vigour and purposefulness, and by the sheer force of his personality he transmitted these qualities to every men he met. His success in stamping his ideas and drive on his army owed much to the transformation he had undergone since he left France. He had no longer to conform to patterns of thought dictated by Haig and his staff, and was free from that frustrating mental strait-jacket that trench warfare set on the thinking of all commanders in Europe. As a cavalryman, he now had the chance to fight the sort of battles he instinctively understood, where boldness and dexterity of manoeuvre held the keys to victory. Immense reserves of energy, which circumstances had forced Allenby to bottle up, were about to be released.

His tours of inspection revealed to Allenby a motionless army of just under 100,000 distributed in bases along the Suez Canal, lines of communication across the Sinai peninsula, and in bivouacs and forward positions along a line that stretched inland from the coast to the edge of the Negev Desert. For a general fresh from France, the most striking feature of the Palestine front was that while the British and Turks were entrenched around Gaza, their lines soon separated so that, at the point where the British positions terminated, there was a 9-mile-wide no man's land between them and the Turks. Since permanent penetration of the Negev was impractical, both armies' fronts ended 'in mid-air', allowing the possibility of outflanking attacks. This situation had been established at the end of April after two unsuccessful British assaults on Gaza, which the Turks had transformed into what Allenby later called a 'strong modern fortress' garrisoned by 5,000 men. Mesmerised by Gaza, Murray had ordered his men to dig in, and months of static, Western Front-style warfare had followed, with shelling, aerial bombardments and trench-raiding.

As he was driven through the British positions, Allenby had to consider two strategic choices. On one hand he could follow Western Front precedents and concentrate his forces for a head-on attack on Gaza, as Murray had done, on the grounds that here the Turks were strongest. On the other, he could adopt the less orthodox proposals laid out by Chetwode in his 'Notes on the Campaign in Palestine'. Chetwode had been in command of the Gaza front since May and had done much to sustain the fighting spirit of the men in the absence of Murray, who preferred to stay in Cairo. His battle plan was the outcome of careful observation, experience and a desire, natural enough in a cavalryman, to demonstrate that horsemen still had a place in a modern battle. His lucidly argued and audacious scheme involved a swift sweep around the Turkish flank by mounted troops that would compel the Turks to abandon Beersheba and Gaza. Chetwode had the means to launch such an attack; there were 20,000 well-trained, seasoned and keen Australian, New Zealand and British cavalrymen deployed on the Gaza front.

Allenby was sympathetic. He disliked the idea of horse-soldiers being restricted to dismounted duties and he shared Chetwode's faith in cavalry. But, remembering the disasters which he had witnessed in France when plans painstakingly drawn up in châteaux far away from the front were reproduced on the battlefield, he insisted on a close inspection of the ground first. Covered by screens of Australian Light Horse, he and Chetwode drove into the hills around Beersheba to see for themselves whether lines drawn across a map made sense among the wadis of southern Palestine. They appeared to, and Allenby accepted Chetwode's proposals for the offensive that would open the Jerusalem campaign.[16]

After his five-day tour of the front and with a blueprint battle plan in his pocket, Allenby turned his attention to getting the reinforcements and resources promised by Lloyd George. On 12 July he was back in Cairo, from where he wired Robertson with his evaluation of the offensive's chances and a 'shopping list'. Numbers mattered above all; Allenby wanted to attack with an overwhelming superiority, for a reverse would further damage local British prestige, which had been severely bruised by the evacuation of Gallipoli, the Kut débâcle in Iraq in April 1916, and Murray's recent rebuffs at Gaza. GHQ Cairo's intelligence assessments, made at the end of April, indicated that the Turkish rail system could not supply more than 60,000 men to the region to the south of Jerusalem where current estimates of local Turco-German strength varied between 42,800 and 49,000, with a concentration of one machine-gun to every 250 men.[17] Allenby prudently forwarded the higher figure to the War Office with a warning that it would increase once the Turco-German High Command identified the threat to Jerusalem. Furthermore, once Jerusalem was taken, he would need men to defend a line between it and Jaffa. He therefore demanded two extra divisions, fully trained and with artillery.

Turco-German air supremacy over Gaza would have to be eliminated, and so Allenby asked for five RFC squadrons, balloon observation detachments and additional wireless units. Western Front experience dictated these requests, for Allenby was anxious to have in Palestine accurate air-to-ground direction of artillery fire he had seen in France.[18] There was nothing new in the application of Western Front techniques to the Middle East, but hitherto the results had been disappointing. Six tanks had been used during the earlier assaults on Gaza, and all had attracted Turkish artillery fire which destroyed one.[19] Six were on hand for Allenby, but limitations of speed, the uneven nature of the ground, and the heat endured by their crews reduced their usefulness in a campaign that was being conceived in terms of rapid movement over large areas.

Another novelty, gas, was available to Allenby, although its debut in the Middle East had been farcical. Gas released during the second battle of Gaza had completely evaporated in the heat without the Turks ever knowing of its presence.[20] Better results were expected in the cooler season so stocks were kept in readiness and, during August, troops underwent gas training exercises.[21] In the event it was never used because of its volatility, and perhaps because of the fear of Turco-German retaliation in kind. It was heavy, pin-point bombardment which Allenby believed would break Turkish morale.

Everything depended on how many men and what equipment Robertson would release. His reply to Allenby's request, written on 27 July, was full of encouragement and warm in tone, but Robertson could not disguise his profound reservations about the ultimate value of the Palestine offensive. He informed Allenby that the recent top-level Allied conference in Paris had taken no decision on what to send to the Middle East, and reminded him that the demands of the Western Front would always remain paramount.[22] Nevertheless, he promised to do his best to procure aircraft and artillery. In the end the Cabinet prevailed; on 10 August the War Office informed Allenby of the ministers' unshaken belief in a campaign designed to 'strengthen' national morale and their determination to accommodate his needs. The same day, Robertson wrote to say that Allenby would have all that he wanted by the end of September.[23] Three days later, Robertson heard a detailed exposition of Allenby's situation and plans from his emissary Colonel Wavell, who had just arrived from Cairo. As he listened, Robertson pointedly stared at a map of France set on his office wall.[24]

Then and later, when staff in Whitehall offices could sometimes hear the rumble of the guns at Passchendaele, Robertson feared that the Palestine front would soak up invaluable reserves of men needed in France. In particular, he suspected that Allenby would soon seek to press northwards into central Palestine and Syria and become bogged down in a protracted, expensive campaign. Rather than plunge into such an adventure, Robertson wanted Allenby to follow a safer course and undertake a limited, piecemeal invasion that could last as long as three years, which was not at all what Lloyd George wanted.[25]

Thanks in part to Robertson's prevarication, and in part to unavoidable operational hitches, Allenby's reinforcements came slowly. The 10th (Irish) Division arrived from Salonika during September, with many men suffering from malaria and needing convalescence, and the 75th was ready by the end of the month, at which point Robertson bluntly warned Allenby to expect no more and make do with what he had.[26]

Aircraft were more readily obtained. The balloon observation units appeared and, most importantly, three new RFC squadrons, one Australian, were formed in Egypt. What tipped the balance and brought Allenby the air supremacy he sought was the arrival at the front, by 7 October, of five Bristol F2B Fighters. With their superior speed and aerial agility they quickly secured command of the skies over southern

Palestine, boosting the morale of ground troops. This was cheering, but Allenby was still unsatisfied and, on 27 October, he was badgering the War Office for more machines, including new DH4 bombers, to bring his strength up to seventy-two aircraft, one more than the estimated Turco-German total.[27] An enthusiast for air power who grasped its decisive value on the battlefield, he seems not to have understood that the technical quality of machines mattered more than their quantity. In the meantime, all available aircraft had been flying extensive photo-reconnaissance missions as part of the charting of the future battlefield, of which no reliable maps existed.[28]

The preparation of maps was one of the several measures ordered by Allenby as a preliminary to his offensive. Although he had never found staff work absorbing, he appreciated its value and that of the specialists who undertook it. He provided the drive, they the hard work and, ultimately, the smooth-running of his war machine. On 27 July he had wired the War Office for additional staff officers as part of a general overhaul of Murray's HQ.[29] Change began at the top with the removal of the Chief of Staff, Major-General Sir Arthur ('Belinda') Lynden-Bell, whom T. E. Lawrence characterised as a 'red general', while others recalled him as a pettifogger who insisted that all officers in Cairo wore regulation riding-breeches and gaiters throughout the hot season.[30] His place was taken by Bols, who had proved himself on Allenby's staff in France, as had Dalmeny, who remained Military Secretary. Another newcomer to Cairo was Wavell, sent there at the end of June by Robertson to keep an eye on Allenby's proceedings. Given his awkward position as the representative of a sceptical and potentially obstructive Chief of the Imperial General Staff, Wavell was disarmed by Allenby's kindness and astonished by the energy and industry of his staff.[31]

New staff officers merged with old hands. The most outstanding of these in terms of experience and talent was the Chief Political Officer, Brigadier-General Gilbert ('Bertie') Clayton, who had held a series of senior Intelligence posts since 1914. Never overawed by Allenby, he placed at his C-in-C's disposal a comprehensive knowledge of every aspect of Middle Eastern affairs. Clayton embraced the worlds of diplomacy and war: he was a link between the High Command and such agencies as the Arab Bureau (formed in 1916 to collate intelligence about the Arabs and shape policy towards them) and the High Commission in Cairo, which answered to the Foreign Office. Since the beginning of 1917 the High Commissioner had been Sir Reginald Wingate, a career warrior-proconsul who had served in Egypt and the Sudan since the mid-1880s. As High Commissioner he was, under the terms of the

British protectorate over Egypt that had been declared in November 1914, the country's virtual ruler. From Allenby's standpoint, Wingate's most important function was as a supplier of thousands of conscripted Egyptian labourers for the Army's docks, base camps and lines of communication.

The new staff presided over a reorganised army. At the end of July, Allenby restructured his command, creating three corps and appointing new commanders. The Australian and New Zealand Army Corps (Anzac) cavalry and the British yeomanry combined to form the Desert Mounted Corps under an Australian, Lieutenant-General Sir Harry Chauvel. Chetwode took command of XX Corps (10th, 53rd, 60th Divisions), and Lieutenant-General Sir Edward Bulfin, a solid dependable Irishman, was given XXI Corps (52nd, 54th and 75th Divisions). Despite having unstuck him in France, Allenby asked for and got the appointment of Major-General Shea as commander of the 60th (London) Division, a crack unit that had lately been transferred from the inert Salonika front.

The Londoners, all volunteers, were some of Allenby's finest troops. They were described, in terms typical of the age, by the war correspondent William Massey as 'a fine cheery crowd . . . the cream of British manhood'. Equal in stamina and zeal were the Anzacs, although the Australians had become a byword for insubordination and wildness, especially in Cairo. Less biddable than British soldiers, they ignored or rebelled against those aspects of military discipline which smacked of servility. And yet they were motivated by a strong, often sentimental attachment to the Empire. 'I was brought up in a wayback farm to believe in the British Empire,' recalled one for whom this faith had been the reason for his enlistment. Allenby, more than other British commanders including Haig and Murray, was probably better equipped temperamentally to handle Australians and overlook their free-and-easy, democratic approach to soldiering, for he had warm memories of serving alongside them in South Africa. Even so, as the campaign progressed, his patience sometimes wore very thin with Australian troops.

Chauvel, to whom Allenby had given command of the Australians, was a capable, well-respected and popular officer who took care of his men. Lean, rangy and self-effacing, he sustained a cordial professional relationship with Allenby, despite his habit of day-dreaming during staff conferences. Once, when he noticed that Chauvel's map was upside-down and his mind presumably elsewhere, Allenby's clenched knuckles were seen to whiten in a build-up to an eruption of rage.[32] Chauvel was never intimidated by these displays. He stood his ground when, soon after his arrival in Cairo, Allenby suggested that all Australian units be placed formally under Allenby's command rather than – and this was in operational matters a technical nicety – the Australian Imperial Force. Chauvel, backed by the War Office, got his way. Chauvel also resisted Allenby's early efforts to shake up his largely Australian staff, though with less success, for he was forced to accept a former Royal Horse Guards officer, Brigadier-General Richard ('Wombat) Howard-Vyse as his chief of staff.[33]

As Allenby had read in his Bible and in Smith's study of the Holy Land's geography, armies that were supplied with water flourished and won battles there, those without it perished and were overcome, like Napoleon's in 1799. This was an obvious truth and one that had been appreciated by Murray who, for all his shortcomings as a general, understood that logistics, and in particular water, were the key to victory in the desert. During 1916 and early 1917, when the Egyptian Expeditionary Force was edging its way across northern Sinai, its advance was followed by railway and water pipelines.

By July 1917 a sophisticated and largely efficient system had been constructed for the pumping of water from the Nile through the Sweet Water Canal to purification plants, where it was rendered safe to drink by the addition of chloride of lime. This water was then conveyed by train to the railheads at Dier el Ballah and Shellal, where containers were loaded onto camels or motor lorries for distribution to front-line troops and horses. A cavalry division was allocated 120,000 gallons a day, an infantry division 60,000, and 30,000 camels were needed to keep supplies moving.[34] When troops shifted beyond the tentacles of this water-supply network, they were driven to rely on local, usually contaminated, sources, or on wells drilled by teams of engineers.

Once the army began its advance into southern Palestine, the problem of water became acute. It was an arid district where rainfall was seasonal, and then often sparse; the only dependable supply came from existing wells that could be blocked by a retreating enemy. Allenby therefore ordered all men in training for the offensive to accustom themselves to a reduced ration of four pints daily – half that allowed troops in the Western Desert in 1940.

Water scarcity meant that opportunities for washing were only available at base camps; men of the Somerset Yeomanry went for up to twelve months without a bath.[35] Unwashed men played hosts to lice which, together with flies and sandflies, were both a constant irritation and a danger to the health of the fighting men. The burden on the preventative medical services was heavy, although they could call on the assistance of specialists who had learned their business in colonial wars fought in India and the Sudan. Strict latrine discipline, elaborate but marginally effective fly-traps and unit meat-safes reduced but never eliminated fly-borne distempers. The commonest ailments, septic sores and sandfly fever, responded to treatment so long as sufferers could be swiftly evacuated to base hospitals, where a diet of fresh food and meat speeded recovery. Malaria, endemic in low-lying, marish regions of Palestine, was reduced by draining marshes or the destruction of mosquito larvae by spraying surface water with oil. These tasks were undertaken by teams of specialists allocated to all units serving in febriferous areas.[36]

What today are called 'sexually transmitted diseases' were a further headache for Allenby's medical staff, some of whom, in moments of exasperation, equated infection with a self-inflicted wound. As more and more troops had been shipped to Egypt, the numbers of female and male prostitutes, a quarter of whom were infected with syphilis, had multiplied in Cairo (where the brothels close to Shepheard's Hotel were owned by the Coptic Patriarch) and Alexandria. The rate of venereal infection among servicemen rose alarmingly, with between 200 and 700 cases a month during the first half of 1916. Of course the rate dropped once troops were sent to the front, but the problem remained of men on leave, particularly the comparatively well-paid Australians, who often joined forces with local pimps to resist patrols of civil and military police. Measures, including army medical supervision of European whores and of some brothels, had been undertaken to reduce the spread of infection before Allenby's arrival.[37]

Allenby wholeheartedly endorsed what was being done, and launched his own forty-eight-hour campaign in which medical officers, chaplains and the YMCA joined forces in an attempt to shame and educate the army. As always, education was vital, especially about the use of prophylactics (as condoms were officially called).[38] He also asked for the transfer of West Indian troops, who seemed to succumb more easily than most to the temptations of Cairo and whose infection rate was correspondingly high.[39] Like Montgomery many years later, he took a straightforward, realistic attitude to this problem, seeking to control infection rather than impose an unworkable ban on all prostitution, a course suggested by one missionary busybody who had, with great indignation, passed to the High Commission and GHQ a sheaf of erotic postcards that were being sold to troops. They still remain, as sent, in the official file![40]

Ultimately, the invasion and conquest of Palestine depended on the huge logistical apparatus that watered men and horses, delivered ammunition and food to the front, and prevented and cured indigenous diseases. It was a fortunate accident of history that the British and Indian Armies' technical and medical services, with their long experience of colonial warfare, were more than equal to the task of sustaining Allenby's army in a land where communications were poor, water scarce, and the climate unkind. And yet the skills and ingenuity of that army's engineers, doctors and transport specialists were not enough. In the end survival rested on the Egyptian Labour Corps, fellahin who shovelled, carried stores and tended animals. Ninety thousand strong when Allenby arrived, their numbers increased to 120,000 as the scale of operations enlarged. Many were dragooned, like their country, into a war in which they had no interest.

Local co-operation of a different and better-rewarded kind was provided by the Arabs of the Hijaz. On 12 July, Allenby met and had a long discussion about these Arabs with Captain T. E. Lawrence, whose dramatic *coup de main* against the port of Aqaba six days earlier had made him the man of the moment in Cairo. He must have appeared a curious, exotic figure, for he attended the interview in Beduin costume, and Lawrence sensed that an intrigued Allenby was uncertain whether or not his guest was a charlatan. This doubt would remain for the rest of Allenby's life.

For the moment what was important was Lawrence's report of an audacious and extremely risky reconnaissance he had made deep into Turkish Syria, where he had discovered a groundswell of pro-British sentiment among local notables and tribal sheiks. Afterwards, Lawrence had distributed gold to Huweitat tribesmen who had fought an engagement with Turkish troops near Maan and had then overwhelmed the small garrison at Aqaba. Lastly, Lawrence laid before Allenby a series of proposals for co-operation between Arab forces, based at Aqaba and commanded by the Emir Faisal, Hussain's second son, and Allenby's army. These proposals added up to an intensive guerrilla campaign designed to sever the Damascus–Medina railway and distract Turkish units east of the River Jordan.

All this was good news to Allenby. The capture of Aqaba pre-empted politically motivated French plans to occupy the small port, and removed for ever the possibility of its use by the Germans as a base for mine-laying in the Red Sea. More importantly, at least so far as his campaign in Palestine was concerned, the disruption of the Damascus–Medina railway line would impede any sudden move southwards by the 'Yildirim' army. Furthermore, if the Arabs acted in accordance with Lawrence's plan, Turkish troops guarding the line would be unable to interfere with Allenby's advance on Jerusalem. With his own experience of railway raids and counter-guerrilla operations in South Africa, Allenby was immediately able to grasp the value of what Lawrence was proposing. So too, in time, was Robertson, who had once been on the receiving end of a Pathan ambush on the North-West Frontier. Moreover, Robertson jumped at the opportunity to use any non-British troops in this theatre.[41]

As Lawrence subsequently recorded in his version of events, *The Seven Pillars of Wisdom*, Allenby pledged material assistance to Arab units at Aqaba. This support appeared over the next six months in the form of British staff officers, RFC machines and personnel, French and British artillery units, armoured cars, arms, ammunition, signals detachments and field hospitals. At Lawrence's suggestion these detachments and Faisal's Arabs were placed directly under Allenby's command, an arrangement that was strenuously but unsuccessfully resisted by Hussain in Mecca.[42]

The interview between Lawrence and Allenby radically changed the nature of the Arab movement. Since June 1916, when Hussain had publicly renounced his allegiance to the Turkish Sultan, the Arab Revolt had been a damp squib. During its early stages it had nearly been extinguished by local Turkish forces and, in October of 1916, a rescue plan had been proposed that involved a possible landing by British forces. Robertson had been hopping mad, fearing another Gallipoli, but, thanks to a penetrating, on-the-spot assessment by Lawrence the scheme was shelved.[43] Since then Arab forces in the Hijaz, commanded by Hussain's eldest son, Abdullah, had conducted a half-hearted blockade of Medina while smaller units attacked the railway line causing temporary damage. Ordered by Enver Pasha, the Ottoman War Minister, to hold Medina at all costs, its commander and garrison did so with little difficulty, and in fact only surrendered in February 1919.[44]

So, in military terms, the Arab Revolt had been a disappointment, although politically it was valuable, since it had weakened the force of Turco-German Pan-Islamic propaganda. Lawrence, with his ambitious programme of railway demolitions and raids, was giving the Arabs the opportunity to play a positive part in British strategy, and this was welcomed by Allenby. What he did not realise at the time, however, was that Lawrence, backed by Clayton and a circle of Francophobes within GHQ and the High Commission, wanted to draw Arab forces towards Syria, which had been allocated to France by the Sykes-Picot agreement, where Faisal had political pretensions.

As for Lawrence the man, Allenby may have been genuinely perplexed. He had a record as an eccentric but capable and hard-working Intelligence officer, and was highly recommended by Clayton and Wingate, who had vainly nominated him for a Victoria Cross for his work behind Turkish lines. Allenby was struck by his courage and the clarity of his strategic analysis; he also discovered a young man (Lawrence was twenty-nine) of charm and learning with whom he could enjoy conversations about natural history and the Crusades, a subject which now fascinated him. Meinertzhagen, who first met Lawrence in December 1917, was unwilling to be captivated by an officer who, he believed, had 'seduced' Allenby, Dalmeny, Bols and many others by his engaging manner. He suspected that behind the façade was a glory-hunter with 'a trick of inflating the truth so that one cannot tell which is basic fact and which embellishment'.[45] It may be that this was a reaction to the colourful tales about Lawrence that were circulating in Cairo at the time.[46]

Not all that was said about Lawrence was complimentary. Colonel Charles Vickery, who had served with him during the winter of 1916–17, suspected that he was a homosexual, which explained for Vickery, the ease with which he got on with the Arabs, and Faisal in particular.[47] Even in 1917, on the threshold of his spectacular career, Lawrence attracted controversy. As it turned out, the final judgements of those, including Allenby, who were his brothers-in-arms would be moulded by events after the war, when his name and exploits captured the public imagination and he became for many the central figure of the Middle Eastern war. For the moment, Lawrence was an officer who proffered Allenby the help he needed, and seemed capable of delivering it.

As Allenby pressed forward with the preparations for his offensive, private tragedy intervened. Its advent was witnessed by Meinertzhagen:

> I was in his office at GHQ explaining our Intelligence system to him when Dalmeny handed him a telegram which brought him the news of the death of his only son. He read it, put his hands to his eyes for a moment and said 'My son' and then to me, 'Go on'. I thought it a great example of self-discipline. My heart went out to that man then.[48]

On 29 July, near Nieuport, Michael Allenby had been struck in the head by a shell splinter and had died five hours later without recovering consciousness. He was not yet twenty, but in less than eighteen months' active service he had won a Military Cross for bravery and gained the admiration of his fellow artillery officers and men for his good nature and independence of mind. Left-wing by inclination, he read the *Labour Leader*, *The Nation* and the *Manchester Guardian*, and stuck up for conscientious objectors in a mess where his views aroused tolerant amusement.[49]

His father was seared by the news; a 'pitiable figure', he asked for no sympathy from his colleagues, turning to Dalmeny for strength and support.[50] His profound grief was movingly reflected in letters – one stained by tears – to his wife and mother which not only express his suffering and deep love for his son, but echo the values he lived by. To Lady Allenby he wrote:

> You are the mother of a hero. Your son could have been no other. One letter he wrote to you is a mirror in which the whole character is shown. Devotion to his work. Humour, dry but never cynical. Joy in all aspects of life. Wide interests in literature, sport, politics. All unaffected and honest.

Four weeks later, on 29 August, he offered his wife what was in effect an obituary, which concluded:

> Whenever he came to stay with me, he was always the same; a friend on real terms; and yet, unaffectedly, he always kissed me when we met and parted – as he did when a child.
>
> Michael achieved, early, what every great man in the world's history had made it his life's ambition to attain – to die honoured, loved and successful, in full vigour of body and mind.[51]

There was some solace for Allenby in Rupert Brooke's poem 'The Dead', which he recited from memory to Wavell shortly after the telegram arrived.

> These hearts were woven of human joys and cares,
> Washed marvellously with sorrow, swift to mirth.
> The years had given them kindness. Dawn was theirs,
> And sunset, and the colours of the earth.
> These had seen movement, and heard music; known
> Slumber and waking; loved; gone proudly friended;
> Felt the quick stir of wonder; sat alone;
> Touched flowers and furs and cheeks. All this is ended.
>
> There are waters blown by changing winds to laughter
> And lit by the rich skies, all day. And after,
> Frost, with a gesture, stays the waves that dance
> And wandering loveliness. He leaves a white
> Unbroken glory, a gathered radiance,
> A width, a shining peace, under night.

These sentiments expressed an internal grief that remained hidden to all but Allenby's family and a small knot of close friends and colleagues. There were condolences from those beyond this circle, including Haig, who wrote with a heartfelt, comradely sincerity.[52] His letter was a reminder that Haig had always followed two separate codes of conduct: at a professional level he was pitiless towards anyone who stood in his way or challenged his judgement, as Allenby knew to his cost, while as a private man he was free of personal animus towards his adversaries.

Allenby could also separate completely his interior from his outer self. In the months after his son's death, he suppressed his fatherly grief and displayed his familiar public face. This stoicism must have required an almost superhuman self-discipline. His mask sometimes slipped, and his inner struggle was detected by those who watched him immerse himself in his routine work. By keeping himself busy, he mastered his emotions, but the strain must have been almost unbearable. There was some relief: during the autumn Lady Allenby joined her husband and took up residence in Egypt. Occasionally she stayed with him at GHQ near Ramlah and at least once, in defiance of War Office regulations, she visited the front. It was a hot day, and while within range of the Turkish batteries she raised her white parasol. 'I soon had that taken down,' her husband growled quietly.[53]

CHAPTER 11

THE FALL OF JERUSALEM

SEPTEMBER–DECEMBER 1917

By the beginning of September the prospects for Allenby's offensive looked good. He had at his disposal 80,000 front-line troops, against the 46,000 Turks of Freiherr General Friedrich Kress von Kressenstein's Eighth Army which occupied the Gaza–Beersheba line. Moreover, thanks to his endeavours over the past two months, he commanded an army imbued with a high degree of dedication and sense of purpose that looked confidently towards him for leadership. Lastly, he had inherited a logistics system capable of bearing the strain of the offensive, and possessed a carefully prepared plan of operations.

His adversaries were in a state of disarray. The Turco-German High Command was temporarily paralysed, unable to decide whether to concentrate the 'Yildirim' army group for an all-out offensive against Baghdad, or to siphon off substantial forces to meet the threat in southern Palestine. By mid-September and under pressure from General Erich von Falkenhayn, who had operational command of the 'Yildirim' army group, and his German staff it was agreed to detach reinforcements, to be known as the Seventh Army, for the Palestine theatre. The decision was too late for, when the battle began, the bulk of the additional units were either waiting for entrainment at Aleppo or else in transit. Moving troops and their equipment in the Ottoman Empire was always a cumbersome and trying business. Stoppages and delays were plentiful because of slovenly staffwork, an overloaded railway system that tottered on the brink of collapse, and shortages of motor transport and pack animals.

Turkish administrative sclerosis exasperated German and Austro-Hungarian officers with higher standards of efficiency, and created a permanent tension between them and their Turkish counterparts. 'In Turkey,' General Liman von Sanders, Commander of Yildirim units in Palestine and Syria, observed, 'one can make the most beautiful plans and prepare their execution by drawings and perfect orders, and something entirely different will be done or perhaps nothing at all.'[1] Among the recurrent and insoluble problems were corruption, which led to military trains and rolling-stock being diverted for civilian use; shortages of coal and spare parts for engines; and soaring desertion rates.[2] Mismanagement was universal and inevitable in an empire where the processes of regeneration and modernisation, begun in 1908 by the Young Turks of the Committee of Union and Progress (CUP), were too late and too few to prepare its people and government for the test of modern war. The Empire and its institutions, like those of Russia, could not sustain the pressure placed on them by the war effort and, by late 1917, the cracks were showing. Moreover, as the Empire's weaknesses were exposed, Turkish ministers and generals became increasingly suspicious of their highly critical and impatient German advisers, who behaved as if Turkey was already a German dependency.

The Palestinian front had its share of the muddle and incompetence found everywhere: von Kressenstein's operations were bedevilled by an inadequate stock of artillery and transport horses, which was to be expected given that the veterinary corps for the entire Turkish Army of just under 2 million men was only 250 strong.[3] All that he and his fellow commanders could do was to rely upon the remarkable stamina, dogged fighting skills and quietism of the ordinary Turkish soldier.

And yet for all its shortcomings the Turkish Army was still a force to be reckoned with, and its fighting capacities were always treated seriously by Allenby, his staff, and the War Office. Throughout the summer and early autumn, the latter was constantly agitated by a flood of alarmist reports which indicated that the 'Yildirim' army group was ready for a mass offensive. These reports were forwarded to Allenby, together with instructions that he was to abandon his timetable and launch his offensive the moment the 'Yildirim' army group made a precipitate move against Baghdad or turned its attentions towards Palestine.[4] The appearance of von Falkenhayn in Jerusalem at the end of August added to these fears that a Turco-German offensive was in the offing.

Assuming, rightly as it turned out, that the 'Yildirim' army group remained preoccupied with its logistical problems until mid-September or later, Allenby was free to choose a date at the end of October for his offensive. This choice was to a large extent forced on him by local weather conditions. These remained temperate until the second or third week of November, after which winter rains could be expected in the Judaean Hills. Bearing this in mind, Allenby decided to open his bombardment of Gaza on 27 October and deliver the surprise attack on Beersheba four days later. If this succeeded, he had a fortnight in which to deploy his cavalry north and west of Gaza, where they would fall upon the remnants of the Eighth Army as it retreated northwards.

Everything hung on taking von Kressenstein unawares. A campaign of disinformation was contrived to convince him that Allenby would follow Murray's example and throw the weight of his force against Gaza. The trick did not prove too difficult since, soon after his arrival, Allenby's Wireless Intelligence Unit had delivered to him an intercepted and deciphered Turkish signal which read:

> The enemy's commander, General Allenby, was on the Western Front this year. It's understood he is wont to attack after a violent, but short bombardment.[5]

Von Kressenstein would therefore interpret the barrage against Gaza as a clear sign that it was the objective of the attack. To make absolutely sure he had no second thoughts, Meinertzhagen devised a stratagem by which a staff officer blundered into a Turkish patrol and threw away his notebook as he made his escape. The captured data indicated an imminent attack on Gaza, and was confirmed by a sequence of bogus wireless messages in an easily breakable code that would be picked up by Turco-German listening-posts.[6]

Once the offensive was under way, additional confusion about its purpose would be created by a small party of Arab and Sudanese camelry under the command of Colonel Stewart Newcombe, a daring and resourceful officer who had led raiding parties against the Hijaz railway. Newcombe's force would slip surreptitiously around the Turkish flank and take up a position on the Hebron road, from where it could hinder the movement of reinforcements to Beersheba. At the same time the formidable firepower of Newcombe's party, which was well armed with Lewis light machine-guns, would mislead the Turks into thinking that they had stumbled on a substantial unit making a sortie against Jerusalem.

The most ambitious of Allenby's clandestine operations was undertaken by Lawrence, who was ordered to lead a small Arab guerrilla unit into southern Syria where they would demolish the Yarmuk railway bridge and so cut the track between Dera and Haifa. At a stroke, Turco-German communications in Palestine would be thrown into chaos and the movement southwards of reinforcements from the 'Yildirim' army group would be halted. Lawrence was briefed on the importance of his mission by Clayton on 12 October, and set off from Aqaba for his operational base at al Azraq twelve days later. In setting Lawrence this task, Allenby took his first step into a political labyrinth. For some time, French liaison staff attached to the Hijazi army and Allenby's HQ had been disturbed by the scope of – and the secrecy surrounding – Lawrence's undercover work in Syria, a province earmarked for post-war French control. They suspected, with good reason, that Lawrence was using his position to foment anti-French Arab nationalism and promote Faisal as Syria's future ruler.[7] Accordingly, an official request was made to Allenby for a French officer to accompany Lawrence. Allenby, persuaded by Clayton, refused, the first sign that he was coming under the influence of those within his staff and the High Commission who were prepared to do all within their power to undermine any post-war settlement that would allow French paramountcy in Syria.[8]

In purely operational terms, Arab assistance was of greater value to Allenby than French goodwill. But Arab loyalty was fragile and they needed careful handling. Allenby was reminded of this on 5 October when he received a telegram which reiterated the Cabinet's desire to secure Jerusalem and added that its capture might force the Turks to sue for peace.[9] The diplomatic signs were promising: since August there had been covert diplomatic exchanges with the Turkish Grand Vizier, Mehmed Talaat Bey, about the possibilities of a negotiated settlement, and the Cabinet mistakenly imagined that the loss of Jerusalem would finally force the CUP to throw in the towel.[10] Allenby was uneasy about a development that could imperil his forthcoming campaign. On 9 October, he warned Robertson that rumours of any arrangement which left the Arabs unsatisfied would turn them into enemies, for 'the question of continued help from [the] Arabs depends on their continued belief that we shall keep our promises'.[11] Hitherto, all his strategic calculations had taken for granted Arab co-operation, particularly that of the forces based on Aqaba; its withdrawal would jeopardise the advance on Jerusalem. Fortunately for Allenby the Anglo-Turkish *rapprochement* came to nothing, but the incident was an uncomfortable reminder that the Arabs would only continue fighting as long as they believed that the British would deliver them political rewards after Turkey's defeat.

On the morning of 27 October the first shells fell on the Turkish trenches around Gaza. The bombardment, from artillery and a flotilla of British and French men-o'-war, was intense and confirmed the enemy's predictions that Gaza was Allenby's objective. In the meantime, and in

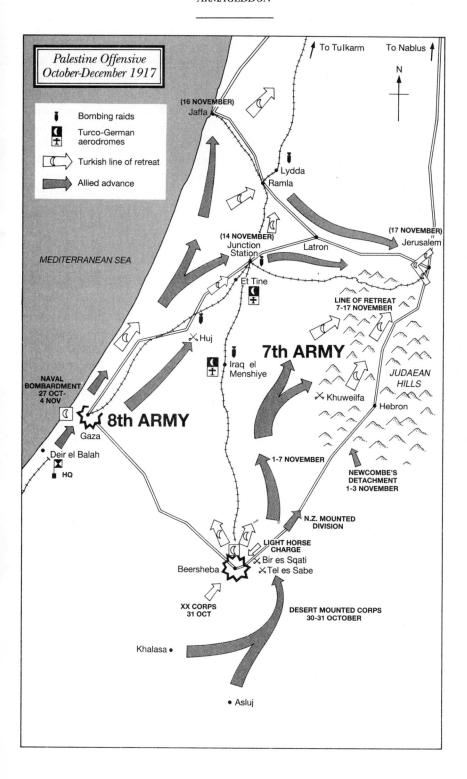

**Palestine Offensive
October–December 1917**

Bombing raids

Turco-German
aerodromes

Turkish line of retreat

Allied advance

To Tulkarm

To Nablus

N

(16 NOVEMBER)
Jaffa

Lydda

Ramla

MEDITERRANEAN SEA

(14 NOVEMBER)
Junction
Station

Latron

(17 NOVEMBER)
Jerusalem

Et Tine

LINE OF RETREAT
7–17 NOVEMBER

Huj

7th ARMY

Iraq el
Menshiye

JUDAEAN
HILLS

Khuweilfa

Hebron

NAVAL
BOMBARDMENT
27 OCT–
4 NOV

8th ARMY

Gaza

Deir el Balah

HQ

1–7 NOVEMBER

NEWCOMBE'S
DETACHMENT
1–3 NOVEMBER

N.Z. MOUNTED
DIVISION

LIGHT HORSE
CHARGE

Bir es Sqati

Tel es Sabe

Beersheba

XX CORPS
31 OCT

DESERT MOUNTED CORPS
30–31 OCTOBER

Khalasa

Asluj

secrecy, a striking force of 40,000 troops converged on Beersheba. During the night of 30–31 October Chetwode's XX Corps approached the town's southern defences while Chauvel's Desert Mounted Force left their concentration points, Asluj and Khasala, and swung in a huge arc to the east. At nine in the morning and according to plan, the horsemen were deployed in a semi-circle on sloping ground to the north-west of Beersheba, which appeared like an island of greenery among the stark Judaean Hills. Some Australians were reminded of the outback settlements of their homeland.

While Brigadier-General Edward Chaytor's Anzac Mounted Division moved northwards to seal off the Hebron road, the Australian cavalry turned their attention to the defensive outposts at Bir es Sqati and Tell es Sabe. Both were attacked, with horse artillery and machine-gun support, shortly after nine, at the same time as Chetwode's infantry assaulted the heights 3 or 4 miles to the west of the town. These were occupied by midday and immediately heavy guns were hauled up for the close-range bombardment of Beersheba. The Australians faced tougher resistance which was only overcome, after hard fighting, at three in the afternoon, leaving between one and a half and two hours of daylight in which to pierce the north-western perimeter defence works and enter the town.

The lion-hearted defenders of Bir es Sqati and Tell es Sabe had bought time and played havoc with Allenby's schedule. Chauvel, who had watched the fighting from his battlefield HQ on a hill 4 miles away, was desperately anxious about the condition of his men's horses, some of which had not been watered for twenty-four hours. Unable to decide between their needs and the demands of a battle plan which required Beersheba be taken by nightfall, Chauvel sent a worried message to Allenby, who was at XX Corps HQ at el Buggar, asking for permission to withdraw the Desert Mounted Corps' horses for watering.

The reply was characteristically direct and peremptory: 'The Chief orders you to capture Beersheba today, in order to secure water and prisoners.'[12] Allenby could not afford an overnight delay which, while it might give relief to Chauvel's horses, would deprive his forces of the element of surprise and give the Turks time in which to block the Beersheba wells. Among his staff officers there was astonishment at what was considered Chauvel's faltering behaviour. Meinertzhagen thought he had acted with 'stupidity and slowness', while Brigadier-General Arthur Temperley recalled later that 'Chauvel did nothing; Chaytor did nothing, while the New Zealand Mounted Rifles Brigade simply deployed into a thin skirmishing line without any depth in an open plain and waited for something to happen.'[13]

Something did happen as a result of Allenby's order – a spectacular, full-scale cavalry charge, almost the last of its kind. At his C-in-C's prompting, Chauvel instructed Brigadier-General William Grant, commanding the 4th Australian Light Horse, to rush the Turkish trenches and take Beersheba. Whether this enterprise would be another Charge of the Light Brigade depended solely upon the accuracy of the latest aerial photographs of these trenches which appeared to be unprotected by wire and without any forward anti-cavalry ditches. At four, Grant drew up his squadrons in loose order, 300 yards apart, and ordered a general advance downhill towards the Turkish positions, with each man grasping his sharpened bayonet as a sword. At first the troopers cantered but, galled by rifle and machine-gun fire, they soon spurred their chargers into a gallop. Mercifully, neither wire nor traps barred their way and the Turks, stunned perhaps by the temerity of the attack, shot wildly. Their trenches were soon overwhelmed, and while some riders dismounted to engage the defenders with rifle and bayonet others rode on into Beersheba. By six, the town with its precious wells was in the Australians' hands, although for some time they came under fire from the gunners of XX Corps, who were unaware of what had happened.[14]

Allenby had what he wanted, water for the horsemen and a springboard for a pursuit of the Turkish Eighth Army, which was now enduring the fourth day of bombardment. Sappers laboured through the night to get all the Beersheba wells working while the horses, many of them frantic after forty hours without a drink, were watered. The supply was not up to expectations, thanks to a recent drought, and the following day the Australian Mounted Division was pulled out and moved south, where more reliable supplies were available. Meanwhile to the north, Chaytor's New Zealanders probed along the Hebron road and Newcombe's isolated camelry, mistaken for a more formidable force, was tying down six Turkish battalions sent from Hebron. After a heroic two-day battle, Newcombe surrendered.

For the next six days (1–7 November) Allenby's plan more or less ran according to schedule. Mounted units fanned out northwards from Beersheba, while the pressure on Gaza increased with aerially directed pin-point shelling. The ferocity of this barrage coupled with advances made by infantry from XXI Corps made Gaza untenable, and von Kressenstein decided gradually to evacuate the garrison. By the 7th the now undermanned outer defences collapsed and the ruined town was occupied. As the Turks retreated northwards, the stage was now set for the final, decisive phase of the battle with the pursuit and cutting off of the Eighth Army as it struggled across the coastal plain.

Having been driven from their positions and forced into the open, the Turks showed remarkable resilience. Mounted and infantry units probing northwards from Beersheba were held up by a series of determined rearguard actions, and it took three days for the 53rd Division to occupy the powerfully held position at Tell el Khuweifa, 10 miles north of Beersheba. For Allenby's forces, water now became a serious problem as the cavalry pressed forward into an upland area where there was no exact way of knowing where it could be found or in what quantities. The only answer was to pull back units to areas where sources could be relied on, which reduced mobility and freedom of manoeuvre.

Even though horsemen were constantly distracted by the need to find water, the momentum of the advance was somehow kept up and there were several opportunities for cavalry charges in the classic style. On 8 November, a detachment from both the Warwickshire and the Worcestershire Yeomanry, which had run out of water overnight, charged German and Austro-Hungarian positions on a ridge near Huj. It was, according to the Worcestershires' Medical Officer, 'a wonderful and terrible sight' as the horsemen rode into shell and machine-gun fire. Afterwards he crossed the field, which was 'strewn with horses and fallen yeomen, many of whom were lying close to, and some beyond, the batteries, surrounded by Austrian and German gunners, many of whom were dead or wounded'. He noticed that 'every single casualty we inflicted was caused by our sword thrusts'.[15] The gallant yeoman cavalrymen suffered 66 casualties, and lost 100 of their 170 horses.

German and Austro-Hungarian units always fought back vigorously; many hungry and exhausted Turks, dismayed by the scale and weight of the offensive, were easily overawed. Trooper Idriess of the 5th Australian Light Horse recalled with exhilaration the moment his detachment overtook a fleeing Turkish gun battery:

> The squadron dug in the spurs, stood in the stirrups, waved bayonets and roared! It was enough! The artillerymen lost their heads, a mounted officer struck out in mad desperation, then the officers leaned over their horses' necks and galloped along the road, the artillerymen ran for their lives. The squadron roared for their lives.

Having scared their enemies, the Australians dismounted and peppered them with rifle fire. 'The panting artillerymen must have coughed up their hearts, for by Jove they ran until they fell. How great it was – spurts of dust kicking around their desperately moving legs.'[16]

Far more demoralising and deadly were Allenby's aircraft which relentlessly bombed and strafed the retreating columns (a technique first tried out against tribal rebels in the Sudan a year before). It was possible, Massey grimly noted, to trace their path by the stench of unburied and burnt bodies. At the same time as harassing the Turks, Allenby's fighters and bombers temporarily neutralised Turco-German air power in two mass raids, involving eighteen and twenty-two aircraft. On 8 November the German aerodrome at Iraq el Menshiye and a nearby railway station were hit, and three days later the target was the airfield, storage depots and railhead at es Tine. In all, at least eleven German machines were destroyed, and in the last air raid the bombardment was so heavy as to panic hundreds of Turkish troops, who fled pell-mell, some as far as Jerusalem.[17] Allenby was clearly impressed by the terror and destruction caused by his air force; on 25 November he asked the War Office for a further twenty-five machines, up-to-date Nieuport Scouts, to be sent from France.[18]

On the ground the battle had dissolved into a sequence of relatively small-scale actions in which Turkish detachments attempted to hold off their pursuers. Notwithstanding this resistance, forced detours in search of water, and the hot, choking khamsin which blew intermittently, Allenby's forward units were always hard on their opponents' heels. Having been caught off balance, the Turco-German High Command tried first to organise a counter-attack and then consolidate along the railway line between Lydd and Jerusalem. A wireless signal to von Kressenstein giving details of these operations was intercepted on 9 November, and preventive measures were immediately put in hand.[19] They proved unnecessary, however, since the attack by the Seventh Army against Allenby's eastern flank was fended off without much difficulty by the Australian Light Horse and, by 11 November, the counter-offensive had run out of steam.

Any hint of a Turkish resurgence had to be taken seriously since their rail network in northern Palestine was still intact. Lawrence's mission to sever the Dera–Haifa line had failed after the defection of one of his party, Abd al Qadir, a Turco-German agent, who had alerted the military authorities at Dera. The possibility still existed that reinforcements might pour south from Aleppo, although it was admittedly a remote one, given that a decrypt of a Turkish wireless message sent on 9 November indicated a chronic shortage of engines and rolling-stock north of Dera.[20]

A lack of transport added to the already enormous problems facing the Turco-German High Command. Von Kressenstein's Eighth Army, scattered north-west of Jaffa and in need of a breathing space, was no longer a threat. During the first week of the British advance a wedge had been driven between it and the Seventh Army, which had been shepherded back towards Jerusalem. As his adversaries had retreated, Allenby's advance guard pushed forward to occupy key communications centres. Junction Station was taken on 13–14 November, and two days later the New Zealand Brigade rode unopposed into Jaffa, cutting road and rail links between Jerusalem and the coast.

Allenby had every reason to congratulate himself and his army. In less than three weeks, the Turks had been prised from the Gaza–Beersheba line and then had been systematically pummelled in an advance of over 60 miles. The measure of Allenby's achievement was apparent in a telegram to him, dated 11 November, from a Cabinet which, unused to advances on such a scale, cautioned him not to take risks with extended lines of communication and reminded him of the misfortunes that had followed a similar push in Iraq during the autumn of 1915, when General Townshend's army had outstripped its supply lines and been forced to retreat to Kut-al-Amara where it later surrendered.[21] Nevertheless, the order to take Jerusalem remained unchanged, and ten days later Allenby received detailed instructions of the arrangements to be made once the city was in his hands.

Allenby was well aware that the battle for Jerusalem would be something of a gamble, with considerable odds stacked against him. With the possession of Jaffa and the road from there to Jerusalem, he had the means of shifting men and supplies to the front. But it was a brittle and unreliable link: material and men disembarked at Jaffa had to be carried ashore in surf-boats manhandled by specialists imported from West Africa and from Rarotonga in the South Pacific, and the road, like others in the region, was unfitted for heavy and continuous military traffic. Moreover, the second half of November saw the onset of the cold, rainy season and the start of a winter that proved one of the harshest in living memory. Many of the troops advancing into the Judaean Hills were still in their light summer uniforms, without greatcoats and wearing shorts, the latter an innovation which Allenby regarded as 'indecent and abominable' and banned for cavalrymen.[22] Geography, as well as climate, was against his army for, as he knew from his study of biblical and Crusading campaigns, the passes on the road from the coast to Jerusalem offered an enterprising and well-prepared commander the opportunity to fight a series of delaying actions that would wear down his adversary.

The Turks were never able to take advantage of this terrain. The Seventh Army was kept under constant pressure from Allenby's forward units and forced to fall back until it took up defensive positions west of the Jerusalem–Nablus road, its only remaining link with the rest of the Ottoman Empire. In Nablus, according to an Intelligence analysis of 27 November, the Turco-German High Command was desperately endeavouring to create a new army which, the evidence suggested, would remain on the defensive.[23] Given the resources at their disposal, it appeared most unlikely that the two local commanders, von Falkenhayn and Jemal Pasha, would mount a major operation to relieve Jerusalem.

Although this was not known for certain at Allenby's HQ, the German High Command in Berlin had already accepted the abandonment of Jerusalem as inevitable. On 28 November, the *Frankfurter Allgemeine Zeitung* prepared its readers for the worst, with a report that because of poor communications Jerusalem could not be rescued, but that its loss was of no strategic significance.

Nevertheless, Allenby could not afford to give the Turks any time for recovery and consolidation. His plan for taking the city was simple: having established control over Jaffa and the coastal plain, the bulk of his forces would turn inland, fanning out on either side of the Jaffa to Jerusalem road. Warned by the British government of the possible international repercussions of fighting in the city or its suburbs and of potential damage to Christian, Jewish and Muslim holy places, he aimed to isolate Jerusalem from Nablus and force a withdrawal of its garrison. The weight of his offensive would therefore be directed towards the Nablus road.

By 21 November British forward units were in contact with the Turks, who were strung out along a 30-mile front which extended northwards from Bethlehem and ended in the hills to the north of Jerusalem. There followed an untidy battle which lasted for a fortnight and consisted of a series of hard-fought struggles for the possession of hilltops and ridges. Total Turco-German strength around Jerusalem was 16,000, and despite a steady flow of desertions, the Turkish front-line soldier showed his characteristic hardiness and determination. Whenever ground was lost, the Turks counter-attacked; some observers suspected that German instructors had adopted Western Front methods and selected and trained special 'storm-troop' units for these sallies.[24]

There was equal stubbornness on the British side in what became a test of sticking-power and stamina. Barrow's Mounted Yeomanry Division, which held the extremity of Allenby's right flank, bore the brunt of some of the toughest fighting. Isolated for eight days, the yeomanrymen suffered 400 casualties, a third of their strength, mostly from sickness and fatigue. In some instances horses went without water for up to seventy-two hours, and without fodder for sixty-eight.[25] When, on 27–28 November, the horsemen were relieved by 7 Brigade, they resembled Falstaff's tatterdemalions, for Barrow remembered them as 'a ragged crowd, lean, unshaven and unwashed, with clothes torn and stained and boots cut to pieces'.[26] In this condition they were reviewed by Allenby, who warmly thanked them for their exertions, which had bought him time and denied the Turks vital ground.

What saved Allenby's offensive was his superior weight of numbers, and equipment which enabled him at moments of crisis to put fresh or rested troops into positions held by units, like the Yeomanry Division, that were close to breaking-point. The 52nd and 75th Divisions, which held the centre of his line until 26–27 November, were replaced after six days of hard fighting by the Londoners of the 60th Division. The strain on transport was less easy to relieve, however, despite improvisation by some units like the Australian Light Horse, who purchased donkeys locally, and a hurried programme of road-building. A combination of the problems of communication and the doggedness of Turkish resistance west of the Nablus road compelled Allenby to reconsider his strategy on 24 November. No longer sure that he could dislodge the Turks north of Jerusalem and occupy the Nablus road, he decided to shift his line of attack to the south.

From 4 to 7 December the British forces regrouped, with the 60th Division concentrating to the west of the city while the 53rd approached from the south-west along the Hebron road. The attack opened at daybreak on 8 December in heavy rain, and soon proved too strong for the depleted and weary Turks, who by evening were preparing to evacuate Jerusalem. Inside the city there was pandemonium as Turkish soldiers and officials hurriedly commandeered transport and began a helterskelter rush along the only escape routes still open, the Nablus and Jericho roads. Unaware of this, the 60th Division pressed forward to the outskirts, the 53rd continued its advance from Bethlehem, and a detachment of the Worcestershire Yeomanry descended on the Jericho road.

It was left to Jerusalem's mayor to surrender his now abandoned city. With a small party under a white flag and carrying the city's keys, he set off towards British lines, where he stumbled into Privates Church and Andrew of the 60th Londons, who accepted his surrender. They conducted him to a sergeant, and eventually he was taken to General Shea who undertook the official formalities.

This accidental encounter was the prelude to a more elaborate ceremony which had been carefully planned by a government keen to exploit to the full the propaganda value of the capture of a city venerated by Christians, Jews and Muslims. On 21 November Allenby had received detailed instructions from the Cabinet about the arrangements to be made once Jerusalem had fallen.[27] Lloyd George intended to announce the city's capture personally in the Commons, a *coup de théâtre* that required no premature press statements or communiqués from Allenby's HQ. Allenby's entry was to be carefully stage-managed. He was, at Robertson's suggestion, to walk into the city, in striking contrast to the Kaiser who, when he had visited Jerusalem in 1898, had ridden wearing a plumed helmet and white cloak, like a latter-day Crusading Teutonic Knight.[28] In similar bombastic vein, he had placed in the Kaiserin Augusta Victoria hospice images of himself and his consort dressed as a medieval Hohenstaufen Emperor and his Empress. The artwork was kitsch, but the political message was clear: Wilhelm II was the true heir of both the old Holy Roman Emperors and Europe's Crusading tradition, and the new German Empire was about to assume paramountcy in the Middle East. To dilute these Christian pretensions and placate Muslim feelings, the Kaiser laid a massy bronze wreath on Saladin's tomb in Damascus, a token that was later removed by Lawrence, who shared the Kaiser's sense of historical destiny, and given by him to the Imperial War Museum.

There would be no such crassness in British handling of local, or for that matter international, religious susceptibilities, nor any hint of sectarianism. Allenby was ordered to proclaim that the shrines and hallowed places of all faiths would be treated with equal reverence, and the rights of the religious communities which looked after them upheld. In particular, he was to demonstrate Britain's goodwill towards Islam and respect for its faith by the announcement that he would follow the generous and honourable gesture of the Caliph Omar, who had put the Holy Sepulchre under his personal protection, and place the Mosque of Omar under Muslim control, with a guard of Indian Muslim troops. Allenby understood exactly the delicate nature of his task, and on 26 November asked the War Office for confirmation of his assumption that no Allied flags were to be flown over the city.[29] He entered Jerusalem in humility and on foot, as a liberator, not a conqueror.

Accompanied by members of his staff, including Lawrence, together with French, Italian and American officers, Allenby walked in to Jerusalem at midday on 11 December. Further emphasis that this was an Allied victory was given by the presence on the city's streets of English, Scottish, Welsh, Irish, Australian, New Zealand, French and Italian detachments. It was a crisp, windless and sunlit day, which suited the film camera crew sent by the War Office to make a record of the event, which was shown in British cinemas a few months later. The crowds who watched the entry and listened to Allenby's conciliatory proclamation – delivered in English, French, Arabic, Hebrew, Russian and Greek – appeared happy with their new rulers. After the ceremony, Allenby informed the War Office that he and his statements had been well received, although he confided to his wife that he had felt uncertain whether the popular enthusiasm was 'real or feigned'.[30] Perhaps the onlookers may have had doubts about the permanence of the Allied occupation, since they could hear distant shellfire as Turkish units fought a rearguard action on the Jericho road. The better-informed who followed events in Europe may have had misgivings about whether the Allies would ever win the war.

Lloyd George was unwell, and thus unable to make his dramatic Parliamentary announcement of Jerusalem's capture. Instead it was delivered on 10 December, squeezed somewhat incongruously between Parliamentary questions about National War Bonds and the Wigan Friendly Society, by Andrew Bonar Law, the Leader of the House.[31] His bald statement was greeted with cheering and, no doubt, relief, for he had ended by drawing Members' attention to the fact that final taking of the city had 'been in some degree delayed in consequence of the great care taken to avoid damage to sacred places in and around the city'.

As a propaganda exercise, the occupation of Jerusalem was a considerable success. From the start, the government had been determined to exploit its religious significance for Christians and Jews throughout the world without offending Muslim sensibilities. Naturally enough Christian and Jewish communities celebrated the event with the greatest enthusiasm and services of thanksgiving. A *Te Deum* was sung in the Roman Catholic Westminster Cathedral within hours of Bonar Law's statement; the bells of Southwark Cathedral rang out over the East End of London where the Jewish community was rejoicing; and on the following day Stanford's *Te Deum* was sung in St Paul's. The Anglican weekly magazine *The Guardian* applauded the 'dignified simplicity' of Allenby's entry into the city, which had 'struck the right note'.[32] The Moderator of the Church of Scotland, preaching at a united service in Edinburgh on the text 'The Lord hath redeemed Jerusalem', struck a different note by his expression of the hope that Edinburgh might itself become 'a Jerusalem where drunkenness would not ravage God's children'.

Britain's Jews were exhilarated by the news. The Chief Rabbi expressed his delight, and the *Jewish World* of 12 December proclaimed that by its conquest of Jerusalem Britain had now become the greatest Christian, Muslim and Jewish power. A Jewish volunteer battalion of the Royal Fusiliers, in training in England, wired congratulations to Allenby and received the cheery reply, 'Your congratulations are warmly welcomed. Wish you had been with us'. Inside Jerusalem, Massey reported his meeting with a Jewish woman, who told him, 'We have prayed for this day and today I shall sing "God save our gracious King, long live our noble King". We have been starving, but now we are liberated and free.' There was, Massey discovered, a similar sense of emancipation among the Arabs, one of whom, a former officer in the Turkish Army, said he would shout 'Hip hip hurrah' for England as Allenby's procession passed through the streets.[33]

All this was a godsend for a far from popular government beset by crises. For the past weeks the newspapers had been brimful of baleful news: in Italy British reinforcements were attempting to shore up an ally severely shaken by its devastating defeat at Caporetto in October, and on the Western Front the battle of Cambrai, from which much had been expected, had ended in the usual stalemate. Most perturbing of all were reports of the anarchy in Russia, the Bolshevik coup in Petrograd and Lenin's peace overtures to Germany and Turkey, which appeared to signal the final collapse of a major ally. Against such a background it was no wonder that the government and press made all they could of Allenby's victory.

Allenby, hitherto a little-known general, was a beneficiary of this publicity, and enjoyed a spell of public adulation which was, in the circumstances, to be expected, since victorious Allied commanders were few and far between during 1917. The *Spectator* considered that 'The whole campaign is enormously creditable to the brain which planned it',[34] and credit was also extended to Robertson for backing Allenby with men and material. The latter's alacrity in following up his breakthrough at Beersheba and Gaza was singled out for praise in the *Saturday Review*, which compared his swift response to the lassitude displayed by commanders at Cambrai, who had allowed victory to slip from their grasp.[35]

There was wide coverage of the Palestine campaign in the illustrated press. The *Illustrated London News* of 15 December included fifteen pages of official photographs of the advance on Jerusalem as well as drawings by James McBey, the official war artist attached to the Egyptian Expeditionary Force. Photographs of Allenby in his staff car, cavalry and stock pictures of Jerusalem and the Holy Places appeared in the *Sphere* of 22 December. The official photographs of Allenby's entry into Jerusalem were released in January and, again in the *Illustrated London News*, were contrasted with drawings of the Kaiser's passage through the city 'arrayed like a Crusader as seen in pantomime'.[36]

The taking of Jerusalem was naturally given prominence in the Allied press, but treatment of the story varied according to national preoccupations. *Petit Parisien* was aggressively imperialist in tone and predicted that 'The way to Syria is now open and France can play the due part of her traditions.' An American, and anti-imperialist, view was presented by the *New York Sun*, which saw Jerusalem's capture in terms of its release from an oppressive colonial power and as an indication of imminent Ottoman collapse. Neutral newspapers gave the event limited coverage and saw it as harmful to Turkey rather than Germany. *Osservatore Romano*, a Vatican mouthpiece, reflected the pleasure of all Roman Catholics at the freeing of Jerusalem, although Pope Benedict XV remained prudently silent so as to not to compromise his self-appointed role as a peacemaker. Where they gave it attention, the Central Powers' press dismissed the loss of Jerusalem as being of minor strategic importance.

For the British government Allenby's Palestine campaign and its triumphant culmination had some psychological value, even though the celebrations and press puffs could not dispel the mood of war-weariness that was creeping over the country during the winter of 1917–18. Nor could they balance the gloomy reports from other fronts. Furthermore, Cabinet predictions that the loss of Jerusalem would accelerate the collapse of the Ottoman Empire proved to be wishful thinking.

Nevertheless, Allenby's victory made an impression on the public imagination that would outlast the war. With the invasion of Palestine, the war in the Middle East acquired a historical significance in both Britain and the United States, where journalists and commentators were quick to draw parallels with the Crusades and, most importantly, to point out that the battlefield encompassed a land which was familiar to everyone who read the Old and New Testaments. British and Dominion soldiers crossed a landscape which had been traversed by the armies of the Pharaohs, Alexander the Great, the Romans, and Richard the Lionheart. Names such as Gaza, Beersheba, Bethlehem, Jericho and Jerusalem recalled stories from Sunday School and, to generations for whom a knowledge of the Bible was an essential feature of schooling, the war in Palestine was assured a special place in public consciousness. In an editorial, the *Saturday Review* observed that the conflict in Palestine 'touches the imagination and stirs in the most sluggish mind distant religious and historical emotions'.[37] Further reminders were offered by the pictures of 'biblical' landscapes, often with Arab figures, printed in newspapers and illustrated journals which pointed out that they portrayed a world unchanged since the time of Christ.

The fighting men shared this fascination, none more so than Allenby, who had always been a Bible reader. On tours of inspection or at the front, he seldom missed a chance to draw his companions' attention to some landmark and explain its historical significance. Surveying the XX Corps positions north of Jerusalem, he suddenly exclaimed to Chetwode, 'Look at that big rock in front of us! That must have been just about the place where Jonathan and his armour-bearer climbed up and attacked the Philistine garrison.' Chetwode, who had other more pressing matters on his mind, attempted to stem the flow of Allenby's account of the subsequent battle by taking him to another position, which prompted a further enthusiastic exposition, this time on an engagement fought nearby by Joshua.[38] Amateur archaeology flourished in some units; William Maitland Woods, the Senior Chaplain to the Anzac Division, ran biblical archaeology classes and superintended digs behind the lines near Gaza.[39] Allenby too indulged in this pursuit and, having identified what he took to be a Crusader arch on a building near his HQ at Bir Salem, got into a huff when it was demolished by an Engineer subaltern. He was rescued from his Commander-in-Chief's obloquy by the intervention of Clayton, who revealed that what Allenby considered a medieval artefact was in fact just fifty years old.[40]

Allenby was on firmer ground as a naturalist, and he enjoyed acquainting himself with new and unfamiliar birds, plants and insects which he would describe in letters home. He also acquired an extra-ordinary pet, a Galeodes fighting spider whose jaws could sever a scorpion's tail, which he named 'Hindenburg' after the equally formidable Prussian field-marshal who, with Ludendorff, controlled the German war effort. 'Hindenburg' was matched in a contest with Meinertzhagen's Galeodes spider and was overcome; as the beast died, Meinertzhagen saw a flicker of fury cross its owner's face which was suppressed with difficulty.[41]

Not long afterwards, in January 1918, Meinertzhagen was transferred to London. Looking back over six months under Allenby's command, he concluded that 'If any one man has by his personality and influence won a campaign it is Allenby.' A similar verdict was delivered by Chauvel the day before Jerusalem fell.

The Commander-in-Chief . . . has been everywhere. He is the most energetic commander I have yet come across. I like him immensely and he appeals to my Anzacs tremendously. He is just the kind of man we wanted here. He knows what he wants and sometimes explains it in no measured terms but he generally gets it done. The great thing is he gets about amongst the troops, looks in at hospitals etc., has a cheery word for the wounded and does not have a fit if he's not saluted, all of which appeals to the Australians and I think to the other troops also. . . .[42]

CHAPTER 12

MARKING TIME

JANUARY–AUGUST 1918

F ROM the moment his army pushed its way past Gaza and Beersheba, Allenby became the head of Occupied Enemy Territory Administration (OETA). Henceforward he was both supreme commander and a proconsul responsible for the governance of a poor, backward region whose often fractious inhabitants were divided by race, religion and politics. He had to lay the foundations of an impartial and equitable government that would secure the tranquillity of an area that was soon filled with base camps, hospitals and depots, and across which ran the army's lines of communication.

The technicalities of administration bored Allenby, and until November 1918 all his energies were concentrated on waging war. He therefore left the business of governing Palestine to Clayton as Chief Political Officer, and Lieutenant-General Sir Arthur Money was made Chief Administrator. Day-to-day administration was, at Allenby's insistence, to be conducted along the lines set down in the *Manual of Military Law*, but wherever possible 'the Turkish system of government will be continued and the existing machinery utilised'.

While Allenby could delegate the humdrum duties of administration to subordinates and, when required, could call upon their advice, there were occasions when he had to intervene directly. He had therefore to cultivate the talents of a diplomat as it became clear that the contradictory policies devised in London threatened to set Arabs and Jews at each others' throats. There were also problems created by the French Consul-General, François-Georges Picot, who was always ready to make a fuss whenever he believed his country's rights were being ignored or overridden. In many respects Allenby was temperamentally unsuited for this type of work. He lacked the emollient qualities of the diplomat and it was not in his nature to temporise. These deficiencies were more than compensated for by his pragmatism, determination, common sense and adherence to the rules of fair play. There were even times when his martial bluntness and vehemence were political assets. The Zionist leader, Chaim Weizmann, discovered that Allenby never minded when spoken to in language as forthright as his own. On the other hand, a mentally bruised Picot complained to his superiors about being treated with *'une brusquerie toute anglaise'*.[1]

Putting a Frenchman in his place was a diversion for Allenby. War, not politics, occupied most of his time during the first half of 1918. Having consolidated his front between the Mediterranean and Dead Seas, and having temporarily neutralised Turkish forces east of the Jordan, Allenby was keen to restart his offensive with a push northwards. Lloyd George had set his heart on a decisive Middle Eastern campaign that would culminate in the occupation of Beirut, Damascus and Aleppo, which he felt certain would force Turkey's capitulation. Advised of this, Allenby and his staff drew up an appropriate battle plan, which was submitted to the War Office on 20 December 1917. He promised that, by July at the latest, he could advance as far as a line between Haifa and Nazareth. He added a proviso: no offensive could be contemplated without reinforcements if the local Turkish strength rose above 60,000. Furthermore, if the Prime Minister wanted him to reach Aleppo he would need between sixteen and eighteen extra divisions, along with a substantial corps of engineers and railway troops to build a broad-gauge track to connect Haifa with his front line.[2]

No one knew for certain how many troops the Turks might deploy to meet the attack. On 2 January, Robertson forwarded estimates made by Military Intelligence in London which indicated that by mid-February the Turks would have as many as 80,000 men, including 11,000 Germans, in northern Palestine and Syria. Logistics experts predicted that the local transport system could sustain a further 20,000 troops without undue strain.[3] The same conclusion had been reached by Allenby's staff which, in an assessment made on 2 January, put Turkish strength at 100,000.[4] These figures turned out to be wildly exaggerated and based upon the assumption that, having signed an armistice with Russia on 18 December 1917, the Turks would automatically reinforce their depleted armies in Syria and Palestine.

Nothing was further from the truth. Ever since September, when Intelligence had first heard details of fraternisation between Russian and Turkish troops in the Caucasus, the War Office had expected at least 400,000 men to be shifted from the Russian to other fronts.[5] It was taken for granted that, once augmented, Turkish armies in Iraq and Palestine would mount offensives to recover lost Ottoman provinces. In fact, the Minister for War, Enver Pasha, and the dominant group within the CUP had completely revised Turkey's grand strategy. By February 1918 it had been decided to concentrate the bulk of Ottoman men and material in eastern Turkey for an offensive towards the Baku oilfields and the western shore of the Caspian Sea. The invasion of Russian Central Asia was undertaken by 'The Army of Islam' under Enver's brother, Nuri Bey, who, proclaiming a new jihad, hoped to win over the local Muslim population. In the long term, Enver hoped to penetrate Turkestan and from there foment Muslim uprisings in northern India.[6]

Such an ambitious strategy made colossal demands on an already overburdened war machine. The new Russian front had absolute priority and General Liman von Sanders, the former head of the German Military Mission to Turkey who in March had taken over the Palestine front, realised that he could expect few, if any, reinforcements. He gloomily concluded that Enver had all but abandoned Palestine and Syria, a judgement that was confirmed in the summer when troops stationed there were withdrawn for Russia.[7] And yet, much to von Sander's annoyance, Enver refused to strengthen the armies in Palestine and Syria with troops from the garrisons strung out along the Damascus–Medina railway. Of course, having lost Mecca, Baghdad and Jerusalem the CUP was anxious to retain one Muslim holy city as a matter of prestige.

What was a fundamental change in Ottoman policy was undetected by Allied Intelligence, which continued to believe that the Turks would concentrate on the reconquest of what had been lost over the past three years. This possibility gave Allenby some passing concern. In a plea for extra troops, sent to Robertson on 7 December, he warned that any withdrawal from Palestine 'would alienate the Arabs and result in disaster'.[8] Not that any such course of action would have been considered. Rather, on 21 January, the Supreme War Council endorsed Lloyd George's scheme for a large-scale offensive aimed at Aleppo, and a week later the War Cabinet despatched General Jan Smuts to the Middle East to discuss with Allenby his manpower needs.

The decision to back Allenby's offensive had been strenuously opposed by the new French Prime Minister, Georges Clemenceau, who wanted an end to all Middle Eastern operations, and by the Westerners on the

General Staff headed by Robertson. In his letter of 2 February, informing Allenby of Smuts's mission, Robertson could not hide his bitterness. Nothing whatsoever would be gained by an advance on Aleppo, and Allenby was to keep uppermost in his mind the needs of the most vital front of all, in France, when he outlined his requirements to Smuts. 'Very heavy fighting' was expected there shortly, so provisions of men and resources to the Middle East might easily be curtailed at short notice.[9]

Smuts's extended discussions with Allenby and his staff ended on 15 February. Despite sightseeing excursions to Jerusalem and Luxor, Allenby found the business extremely tedious.[10] Smuts, a benign figure, had some knowledge of soldiering, but none of the Middle East. He was an English-educated Afrikaner lawyer who, having established his nationalist credentials by fighting the British in the Boer War, became a leading South African statesman and an Anglophile. He had commanded Allied troops in East Africa, and since 1917 had been attached to the War Cabinet with a particular interest in manpower. He explained to Allenby the Cabinet's wish to take Aleppo and adumbrated a cautious plan for its capture. First, Allenby's forces would cross the Jordan and permanently fracture the Damascus-Medina railway near Amman. With the coming of spring, there would be a general advance to a line between Haifa and Lake Tiberias. The last phase of the offensive involved a push northwards along the coast to Beirut, from where attacks would be launched against Damascus and Aleppo, supported by local pro-British elements of whom the Druze were believed to be the most reliable. To facilitate communications, railway detachments would construct a broad-gauge line from Haifa to Beirut.

At the heart of the exchanges had been the question of how many troops the government was prepared to release for this enterprise. Allenby wanted at least sixteen divisions, the War Office believed nine would do, and Smuts finally agreed to deliver fifteen, including one of Indian cavalry who were presently redundant in France.[11] This was a disappointment for Allenby since, very much against his wishes, he had had to accept three Indian infantry divisions, one of which had arrived from the Iraq front at the end of January. In principle he objected to the use of coloured troops anywhere in the Middle East; in July 1917 he had asked for the replacement of West Indian by European troops 'owing to the prestige attached to the white man' by Egyptians and Arabs.[12] Again, when writing to Robertson about reinforcements, he demanded 'for political as well as military reasons' that the majority should be British.[13]

Events beyond Palestine made a nonsense of these quibbles. There were objections from Iraq about relinquishing troops at a time when the Bolsheviks were opening a campaign of anti-British subversion in Persia.

As a result the Cabinet reduced Allenby's reinforcements to one division, which was scheduled to reach Egypt in May.[14] Specialist railway troops proved unobtainable, which ruled out any plans to lay a track north of Haifa.

These frustrations did not stop Allenby from going ahead with the first phase of the strategic plan he had agreed with Smuts. On 19 February the 60th Division advanced on Jericho, which fell two days later. The second, far more formidable sally, Dalmeny's brainchild, was directed towards Salt and Amman and began on 21 March under the direction of Shea.[15] It was soon in very serious difficulties, caused by a combination of heavy rain, primitive roads and a rugged terrain that offered an abundance of good defensive positions to the Turks, who fought with their usual tenacity. After a tricky crossing of the swollen Jordan, the mounted advance guard entered Salt unopposed on 25 March. Australian and New Zealand cavalry reached Amman on the afternoon of the 27th and encountered determined opposition. The fight for the town lasted until 31 March, when the British position here and at Salt had become precarious because of Turkish and German reinforcements, some of which had been brought up by rail from Maan. The objective was not worth the casualties, and rather than get bogged down in a Western Front-style battle of attrition, Shea, with Allenby's approval, pulled out his by now exhausted men.

In the middle of this inconclusive battle, Allenby's HQ received sombre news from London, although it had long been expected. Since November 1917 the German High Command had shifted over forty divisions from the moribund Russian front to the west in preparation for the *Kaiserschlacht* ('Kaiser's battle'), a massive, war-winning offensive scheduled to be launched on 21 March. On that day the Germans, striking on the Western Front at the junction between British and French lines, advanced an astonishing 40 miles. The crisis worsened as British reserves of manpower dwindled; in the first five weeks of fighting Allied casualties totalled 250,000. Immediately the scale of the German attack was understood, orders were sent to Allenby to rush men to France. Between 23 and 26 March the 52nd Division, the 7th Division's artillery and nine yeomanry regiments were recalled, and, five days after a fresh German push on 9 April, the 74th Division was withdrawn. These losses were, in time, made good by Indian troops, and forced Allenby to overhaul the entire structure of his army with a series of amalgamations at brigade and divisional level.

The process of reorganisation did not deter Allenby from mounting a second foray east of the Jordan, an undertaking he justified on the grounds that it would deceive von Sanders into thinking that the main

British offensive would come in that area. The attack had been originally intended for 15 May, but once it was discovered at HQ that vital co-operation offered by the outwardly pro-British Bani Sakhr tribe would not be forthcoming after the first week of May, the date was put forward to 29 April.[16] The battle had been planned in two phases. The first involved a frontal attack by the 60th Division against Turkish positions at Shunet Nimrim athwart the Jericho–Salt road. Once the Turks were fully engaged, Australians of the Desert Mounted Corps would sweep north and east and seize Salt. Turkish reinforcements from Amman would be intercepted as they crossed Bani Sakhr territory, leaving the Shunet Nimrim force isolated and unable to retreat.

This audacious plan failed, thanks entirely to the Bani Sakhr tribesmen, who remained paralysed in their camp.[17] The Turks were therefore free to move additional men towards Shunet Nimrim and, by 3 May, the Australian Horse were in peril of being trapped between a column from Amman and the Turkish 3rd Cavalry, who were rapidly converging on Salt. Allenby, who had been following the course of the battle by wireless at Chauvel's HQ, seemed oblivious to the danger until the last moment. At three in the afternoon of 3 May, with the remark 'I can't lose my mounted troops', he ordered the Australians to pull back from Salt. Within an hour and in great haste the horsemen moved out, many cursing the Arab 'deserters' whose cravenness had lost the battle. Allenby brushed aside any suggestion that he had suffered a reverse. 'Failure be damned! It has been a great success!' he told a sceptical Chauvel.[18]

Allenby's two incursions across the Jordan had revealed the limitations of Arab co-operation. On both occasions the Turks had been free to transport troops by rail without any serious hindrance; in the middle of the contest for Amman on 27 March a train had delivered Turkish reinforcements from the south.[19] Neither Arab saboteurs nor, for that matter, British demolition parties had been able to sever the railway line permanently. Arab attempts to penetrate and hold the country between the Dead Sea and Maan had met with mixed success. Under the skilful direction of Lawrence, Arabs, mostly regulars, had taken Tafila on 25 January and beaten off a Turkish counter-attack. The strongpoint was, however, soon lost once Hussain's lumpish younger son, Zaid, took command.

Both Allenby and Robertson, swayed by the arguments of Lawrence and the Arab Bureau, had been led to expect much from the Arabs, and had accordingly included them in plans for offensive operations during 1917 and 1918. And yet there was always a gulf between what the Arabs promised and what they actually delivered, as Robertson was one of the first to admit. On 8 December 1917 he confessed to Allenby that he had been 'somewhat disappointed' by Arab exertions during the advance on Jerusalem.[20] After the performance of the Bani Sakhr during the second raid on Salt the feeling in many quarters was that the Arabs were a broken reed, and were never to be trusted again.[21]

Allenby was never blind to Arab deficiencies, but he stayed firm in his commitment to Faisal, sending him all he needed in the way of men, equipment and ammunition. His relations with Lawrence, who was now established as Faisal's chief political and military adviser and the intermediary between him and GHQ, continued to be smooth. Junior staff officers heard Allenby speak highly of Lawrence and what he had achieved with what was generally regarded as unpromising material.[22]

In the spring of 1918 Lawrence appeared an indispensable figure, the mainstay of what the Arab Bureau presented as 'the Arab Movement'. This was a deliberately misleading phrase, since it implied to the outside world that most, if not all, the Arabs within the Ottoman Empire supported Sharif Hussain's bid for independence. The same impression, made stronger by Lawrence's description of a coherent Arab sense of national consciousness, is conveyed in his *The Seven Pillars of Wisdom*, which he began writing in 1919 and which was finally published, privately, in 1926. It became public property soon after its author's death in 1935, since when it has coloured the world's view not only of the Arab Revolt but of the whole Middle Eastern campaign. It is a compelling account of the Arab part in the war, full of exciting incident, rich in rhetoric, and strong in political polemic. *The Seven Pillars of Wisdom* elevated the Arab Movement to something it had never been, a noble, selfless struggle for national emancipation in which Lawrence emerged as a dominant force. At the same time as exalting the Arabs' sense of purpose, and sometimes exaggerating their military usefulness, Lawrence appeared to play down the achievements of Allenby and his army, something for which many would never forgive him.

Other, less celebrated, eyewitnesses to the war offered very different testimony about the Arabs and their activities. In the first place they recognised that many Arabs, especially in Sinai and Palestine, wanted no part in a movement of national resurgence sponsored by alien, infidel powers. Clayton, reporting to the War Office on opinion in Palestine in January 1918, put forward the official view, which was that the population distanced itself from the war, but looked forward to a post-war Muslim government.[23] Pro-Turkish elements also existed even after the fall of Jerusalem. At the end of 1917 a party of Turkish POWs were welcomed by the inhabitants of one village, who took them to be the advance guard of the returning Turkish Army. When the British escort appeared, the Arabs' mood changed and their 'faces fell with a bump and they slunk disconsolate into hovels'.[24] More common than open sympathy for the Turks was a malevolent neutrality. Wherever the opportunity occurred, Arabs plundered camps and stores and sometimes attacked isolated servicemen.[25] Even Faisal's army at Aqaba was not immune; during August 1918 local tribesmen rustled some of its stock of camels.[26]

Allied troops found such behaviour intolerable; they also found it very hard to obey Allenby's general orders to treat all Arabs with civility.[27] Australian and New Zealand units, who suffered badly from depredations, developed an intense and violent loathing for every kind of Arab, fighting men as well as civilians. 'Unreliable, feeble-hearted, overpaid', was the verdict of the Australian official historian, Henry Gullett, on the Arab Army, while his New Zealand counterpart wrote 'The Arab Mohammedan is without humour, sympathy, or cleanliness; and his smile is the smile of deceit.'[28]

There was, as more realistic British officers knew, no reason why Arab populations anywhere in the Middle East should have been well disposed towards Allied troops. The Arab Revolt, which Allied propaganda claimed was a movement of national rebirth, had in fact been conceived by its British backers as a device with which to splinter Islam and diminish the impact of the jihad declared against Britain, France and Russia by the Turkish Sultan, Medmed V, in November 1914. Hussain, the movement's figurehead, equated Arab nationalism with the extension of his family's political power into Syria and Iraq, and was widely distrusted by Arab intellectuals who were well aware of his anti-liberal views. His local power base was rickety, for his Arabian pretensions were challenged by the pro-Turkish Ibn Rashid and the cautiously pro-British Ibn Saud; by August 1918, the latter was making incursions into the Hijaz.

Hussain's rebellion presented all Arabs within the Ottoman Empire with a far from welcome crisis of conscience. They could remain loyal to the Sultan and maintain Islamic unity in the face of Christian aggression, which most did; follow a course of prudent neutrality; or else join a nationalist movement tainted by Anglo-French patronage. Those who did back Hussain were warned by the Emir Shekib Arslan, a Syrian nationalist and one of that country's deputies in the Ottoman Parliament, that they would fragment the Arab peoples and ultimately deliver them to the 'fate of Tunis, Algeria, Morocco etc.'.[29] This argument carried weight at all levels. Arab POWs who volunteered to join Faisal's regular army in training at Aqaba were taunted by their comrades with jeers of 'You are going to fight for the British and French'. There were also apolitical opportunists who were willing to sell their services to the highest bidder, Britain, which paid in gold. Moreover, the Beduin tribal sheiks and their followers needed little coaxing to raid the Damascus–Medina railway which, since its opening in 1908, had deprived them of payments formerly extracted from pilgrims who crossed their territory. Some tribes, like the Anazah, played a double game and took subsidies from British and Turks.[30]

As the Arab Revolt proceeded, its political contradictions and apparently cynical manipulation in the interests of Anglo-French imperialism were exposed and exploited by Turco-German propagandists. Their version of Allied motives gained added credibility on 2 November 1917 when the British government issued the Balfour Declaration, which pledged support for the creation of a Jewish 'homeland' in Palestine. Six weeks later, the Turkish authorities in Damascus published copies of the secret Allied wartime treaties that had just been made public by Lenin.

Arab opinion had long been aware that Britain and France intended to annex and partition sections of the Ottoman Empire, so the Russian revelations did not come as a great shock. The Balfour Declaration did, however; Allenby, realising its potential for mischief, immediately had it banned in Palestine.[31] His attempt at censorship failed, for copies were produced by the Turks and were soon circulating in Palestine and beyond, where they aroused Arab fears of mass Jewish immigration and colonisation, both with British encouragement. On 15 January 1918 a worried Clayton reported to the War Office that Faisal and his inner circle were 'somewhat apprehensive of signs indicating the rise of Jewish influence and possible predominance in Palestine'.[32] An indication of how far Faisal's faith in his allies had been undermined was his encouragement of covert approaches to him by Ottoman officials that had been first made at the end of December.

Allenby's first political priority had always been the preservation of the Arab alliance, which held the military key to the security of his eastern flank. Unwilling to be distracted by and possibly drawn into the Arab-Jewish imbroglio, he left the job of calming and reassuring the Arabs to the experts, Clayton and Lawrence. Their work was made more difficult when Faisal's confidence in the Allies was further shaken during the spring and summer by reports of German advances in France. Since these indicated the possibility of an eventual German victory, Faisal continued to entertain the secret proposals for a Turco-Arab *rapprochement* that were put to him intermittently until early August. He was a disingenuous negotiator, and it soon became apparent to Lawrence and other officers who monitored the clandestine intercourse between him and the Turks that he was playing for time.

The political ferment across the Middle East during the winter and spring of 1917–18 was such that it became impossible for Allenby's political staff to keep up a bureaucratic detachment. Clayton was sympathetic towards Arab aspirations; understood the Arab leadership's uncertainty about the future of the region and about the implications of the Balfour Declaration; and sincerely hoped that a just settlement would be reached after the war. Lawrence passionately wanted an Arab state in Syria with Faisal at its head, and disregarded all official pledges made to France. Placing private sentiment before official duty, he once encouraged Faisal to make terms with the Turks the moment he took possession of Damascus, even if this involved leaving his allies in the lurch.[33]

Lawrence's was characteristically an extreme position, but there were others among Allenby's staff who shared his feelings for the aristocratic sheiks and emirs and who respected the simple, warrior-manliness of the Beduin tribesman. Romantic Arabism, where it flourished, often went hand-in-hand with mistrust of the Jews, although many servicemen were impressed by the cleanliness, order and industry of Jewish settlements in Palestine, which contrasted with the squalor of Arab villages.[34] Such admiration did not wholly offset the home-grown anti-Semitism which permeated the Army's officer class which had its roots in pre-war opposition to Jewish immigration from Russia and Eastern Europe, and in middle- and upper-class hostility towards Jews who had advanced themselves in society.

This residual resentment had lately been given a new and deeply unpleasant edge by the tendency of the right-wing British press to identify the Jews with Bolshevism. This was manifested in the Egyptian Expeditionary Force during March of 1918 when there had been alarm about the presence in the three Jewish volunteer battalions, the 38th, 39th and 40th Royal Fusiliers, of men with Russian, American, German and Austrian backgrounds who appeared to constitute 'an element of danger'. After seeking War Office guidance, Allenby had the matter investigated; a number of Russian Jews were discharged and a similar enquiry was made into personnel of the Zionist Mule Corps.[35] This alarmism was partly explained by the circulation among some officers of Allenby's army of typescript copies of *The Protocols of the Elders of Zion*, brought back from Russia by former British liaison officers with the Imperial Army.[36] *The Protocols*, which were to gain a baleful notoriety throughout Europe during 1919, were a piece of mendacity fabricated by Russian anti-Semites to prove the existence of a Jewish conspiracy aimed at global domination, and so were valuable ammunition for anyone who wanted to represent Bolshevism as Jewish-inspired. Eventually, in 1921, the *Times* correspondent in Constantinople, Philip Graves, who had been one of Allenby's Intelligence officers, exposed the base origins and falsehood of this document.

While Allenby's Political Officers attempted to placate the Arabs and maintain a provisional government in occupied Palestine, the government in London was trying to disentangle the mesh of pledges made to its European allies and produce a new policy for the region that took account of recent developments. Allenby could not escape involvement. On 26 November 1917 he had been cabled by Robertson with secret orders not to 'entertain any ideas about a joint administration' with the French, whose government was taking the line that Palestine was an integral part of Syria. The view in Whitehall was that Palestine must eventually pass under British control, but Allenby was to reveal nothing of this to the French Consul-General, Picot.[37] The Frenchman was very persistent, and went so far as to importune Allenby about setting up a French administration in Jerusalem during the lavish luncheon party at XX Corps HQ given just after the official entry into that city. Allenby was dumbfounded, and his reaction was recorded by a delighted Lawrence. 'His face grew red: he swallowed, his chin coming forward (in the way we loved), whilst he said grimly, "In the military zone the only authority is that of the Commander-in-Chief. Myself." '[38]

Allenby again became directly involved in local politics during the spring of 1918, when Palestine was visited by the three-man Zionist Commission headed by Weizmann. The decision to send this mission was one of the first of the new Middle East Committee, which had been set up by the Cabinet on 15 January 1918 to formulate new policies for the region. The Zionists' purpose was to examine the possibilities for post-war Jewish settlement in Palestine, and some of Allenby's staff feared that their arrival would encourage Arab agitation. Notwithstanding these misgivings, Allenby wired approval for the visit on 30 January.[39]

Allenby met Weizmann for the first time at his HQ at Bir Salem on the morning of 3 April. Over breakfast, the C-in-C appeared preoccupied with military business although, unknown to Weizmann, he had just exploded after discovering that a well-meaning but ill-informed officer had suggested giving the guest bacon and eggs.[40] Later the two men discussed Palestinian politics, and Allenby expressed his amazement that the Jews could see a future for themselves in such an inhospitable and backward region. As for arrangements for future immigration, Allenby reminded Weizmann that 'We have to be extremely careful not to hurt the sensibilities of the population.' When, the following day, his 'polite even kind' host offered Weizmann a lift to Jerusalem, it was refused. In the circumstances his appearance in the Commander-in-Chief's car would be both impolitic and embarrassing. Grateful that Weizmann had understood his problems, Allenby stepped out of the car, extending his hand. 'You are quite right,' he said, 'I think we are going to be good friends.'[41]

Allenby was right; a free and friendly relationship developed between him and Weizmann, although at first he could not appreciate the fervour and scope of the Zionist's vision. He did give his backing for a conciliatory meeting between Weizmann and Faisal early in June which, although inconclusive, indicated the possibility of some later accommodation. Allenby had hoped for, but not secured, Lawrence's presence during the interview.[42] He also lent his assistance to a scheme for the foundation, in May, of a Hebrew University in Jerusalem, despite his doubts about the timing and feasibility of the project. 'You have chosen the worst possible time,' he told Weizmann. 'The war in the West is passing through a most critical phase; the Germans are almost at the gates of Paris.' There was even, he suggested, a chance that the Turks might attack and regain lost ground, including Jerusalem.[43]

The war came first for Allenby; rightly so, for only when it ended could detailed attention be given to unravelling the political problems it was creating. Throughout May, June and July Allenby devoted all his energies to his army and the evolution of an offensive strategy with which to end the stalemate in Palestine. Operations were limited and, by and large, confined in this period of intensive heat to aggressive patrols into no man's land, designed to keep his own forces and the enemy on their toes.[44] Even in a period of comparative inactivity, Allenby insisted on high standards; staff officers were discouraged from taking leave in Britain and eccentricities of summer uniform were reprimanded.[45]

It was, however, the numbers of men under his command rather than what they wore which was Allenby's main concern at this time. As the Germans continued to make headway in France he was forced to relinquish units for service there. By the time of the departure of the 74th Division in mid-April, he had lost a total of 60,000 men, all well-seasoned and experienced troops. The War Office's demands continued. On 12 June the Cabinet asked for one Australian mounted division to be shipped to France the following month, along with the 54th Division. Allenby protested that he could not countenance any further withdrawals, arguing that in the previous November and December he had pushed forward too far and that if he was called upon to advance further he needed all the men he now had. Furthermore, the 68,000 Indians he had received as replacements were far from efficient. The Cabinet considered his plea and, on 21 June, agreed to let him keep the Australians.[46]

Allenby was unsatisfied, however, and continued to fight to hold on to the 54th Division. He was assisted by the sympathetic attitude of Sir Henry Wilson, who had replaced Robertson as Chief of the Imperial General Staff on 18 February 1918, and by Dalmeny, who was now serving in the War Office. On 26 June, Dalmeny and Sir Mark Sykes, the most influential figure on the Middle East Committee, finally persuaded Wilson to sway the Cabinet in favour of keeping the 54th in the Middle East.[47]

Allenby's tenacity in retaining as many white troops as he could was in part explained by his belief that they enjoyed a peculiar prestige among Arabs and Egyptians. During June, as more and more Indians took the place of British and Australians, rumours were being spread in Egypt to the effect that the Allies were already beaten in Europe, that the white soldiers were being withdrawn to save them from a forthcoming Turco–German offensive, and that the Indians had been sent as sacrifices.[48] These canards discomposed Indian soldiers, who were also receiving Pan-Islamic propaganda leaflets printed in their own languages, and were subject to verbal subversion by pro-Turkish Egyptian troops and labourers. Twenty-nine per cent of Allenby's Indian troops were Muslim and, on 1 July, he reported to the War Office that since only a handful of cases of unrest had been uncovered among them there was no call for immediate alarm. He could not, however, speak for the future, as signs of discontent were hard to detect given that so many officers were 'out of touch' and could not speak their men's tongues. Allenby therefore wanted no Indian artillerymen, who 'would be dangerous should a wave of sedition intervene'.[49] Other reinforcements created political problems. Neither Allenby nor the War and Foreign Offices wanted the French units dispatched to the Middle East theatre in March. These included the mounted Légion d'Orient, recruited from Armenians naturally anxious to avenge the genocide of their countrymen that had been undertaken by the Ottoman government since 1915.[50]

To avoid the complications which, he believed, would follow the importation of too many Muslim or French troops, Allenby applied on 2 June for three or four Japanese divisions.[51] The request was refused by the War Office, but was not so far-fetched as it might have seemed, since there were already a dozen destroyers of the Imperial Japanese Navy serving in the Mediterranean. In the end, Allenby had to make do with what was available. The French and Armenians arrived as did two battalions of West Indians (who would prove their mettle during operations close to Amman during September), and two battalions of Nigerians were due to join what had become a polyglot army in October.

Among the new units was the Jodhpur Lancers, raised and commanded by the seventy-year old Maharajah, Sir Pertab Singh, who announced that his greatest ambition was 'One good charge and die for the King'. When one of his sons, aged seventeen, was denied such an honour because he had been ordered to man a telephone, Sir Pertab complained. He had not brought his sons to the front 'to do telephone duty, but to die for their King Emperor and that nothing would make him happier than to know they were dead on the battlefield'. After all, he added, 'All British sahibs getting their sons killed, why not I getting some killed?'[52] His strange wish was to be granted before the campaign was over.

Regiments like Sir Pertab's lancers were amalgamated into divisions alongside experienced British and Anzac units during the late spring and summer. Following Indian Army custom, established after the 1857 Mutiny, no all-Indian division was permitted, and so every division included a mixture of British and Indian brigades. One division, Chaytor's, contained Australian, New Zealand, West Indian, Indian and Jewish brigades. There was an unseemly protest from three Jewish battalions who objected to being included in a brigade with West Indians, but in the end the arrangement worked smoothly.[53] As the new divisions reorganised and the recently disembarked became acclimatised, all units underwent a rigorous programme of training.

To compensate for the loss of the yeomanry regiments, some Australian squadrons were armed with sabres. The cavalry charges of the previous November were considered proof that shock action could still succeed, even against adversaries who were backed by machine-guns and artillery. There seemed, therefore, some truth in the pre-war wisdom about the psychological terror imparted by charging horsemen armed with bladed weapons. Old theories were accordingly resurrected: the general orders for Barrow's 4th Cavalry Division exhorted every trooper to keep in mind the ancient traditions of the cavalryman. He was to be ready 'to gallop the Turkish infantry with a light heart', for he possessed a 'moral superiority' against a foe who 'dislikes our cold steel and the sight of it makes his fire erratic'.[54]

At the end of July there were no indications as to when and where the Turk would flinch before cold steel. Early in June, Allenby had told the War Office that with his present strength he could not deliver a blow hard enough to bring about Turkey's capitulation. With an extra three or four divisions he could immediately push his front as far as a line between Acre and Lake Tiberias by the onset of the October rains.[55] Wilson's response was lukewarm. The still-fragile Italian front had priority for manpower, Aleppo's strategic and political value had dropped now that it was clear that Turkish efforts were concentrated in Central Asia and Persia, and no extra troops could be transferred to the Middle East before December.[56]

Allenby therefore had to rethink all his plans, a process which involved forgetting all about the ponderous and piecemeal advance northwards that had been agreed with Smuts. Circumstances still favoured an attack. He commanded 12,000 mounted men, 57,000 infantry and 540 guns, and possessed aerial superiority. Against him von Sanders mustered 3,000 poorly mounted cavalry, 26,000 infantry and 340 guns. On 1 August, Allenby returned from a morning's ride and announced to his surprised senior commanders that he had evolved a plan for an extremely bold and ambitious offensive designed to bring about the total extinction of Turkish power in the Middle East.

CHAPTER 13

OUT FOR BLOOD

SEPTEMBER–NOVEMBER 1918

STEALTH, boldness and flexibility were the essential ingredients of the battle plan that Allenby outlined to Chetwode, Chauvel and Bulfin on 1 August. The three divisional commanders heard details of a sledge-hammer blow to be delivered against Turkish positions close to the coast that would fracture the line and stun its defenders. Through the gap would pour the cavalry, who would then sweep northwards and eastwards, seize lines of communication and harass the retreating enemy. Everything depended on speed, momentum and quick, independent thinking by individual commanders.

To fight and win such a battle required a style of generalship uncommon at the time, and far removed from that which had so long obtained in France. Allenby would not act as a remote, directing intelligence following events on a map and delivering orders by telephone. Instead he saw himself as a dynamic source of fighting spirit and energy, qualities he transmitted to subordinates by frequent contact and exhortation. At staff conferences during the next seven weeks, he repeatedly and with characteristic vehemence told his generals what he expected from them. 'The Turks must be completely destroyed'; there was to be an 'elastic system of advance' without restraining timetables; commanders must think for themselves and when checked at one point, they should withdraw and attack elsewhere.[1] In his own words, Allenby was 'out for blood', and he would be satisfied with nothing less than the annihilation of the three Turkish armies in Palestine and Syria.[2] Such was the force of his personality that the battle plan captured the imagination of his generals; on 19 September the day of the attack, he told his wife that Chetwode was 'as keen as a boy'.[3]

In broad principle, Allenby followed the formula adopted by Chetwode for the Gaza–Beersheba breakthrough. Like its predecessor, Allenby's plan relied on deception to secure surprise. From mid-August elaborate and often ingenious measures were contrived to convince von Sanders that the main thrust of Allenby's attack would be against positions to the east of the Jordan. At the suggestion of aerial reconnaissance experts from the Royal Air Force (created from the old RFC and the Royal Naval Air Service on 1 April 1918), dummy camps were laid out and furnished with 15,000 mock horses. To give complete verisimilitude and fox spies, sledges were regularly drawn across the ground to throw up clouds of dust and give the impression that the 'horses' were being watered. A bogus GHQ was established in a Jerusalem hotel, which had been commandeered and stuffed with appropriate paraphernalia. Evidence of a build-up of forces was provided when West Indian battalions were marched to the Jordan front by day, and then driven back to their camps in lorries at night to set out again the following morning. Arab agents, directed by Lawrence, spread disinformation west of Amman by placing secret orders for vast quantities of fodder to be kept in readiness for the arrival of Allenby's cavalry.[4]

It was of the utmost importance to make von Sanders believe that the bulk of the cavalry was concentrated on the Jordan sector, since the Turco-German High Command believed, rightly as it turned out, that Allenby intended to include a mass mounted attack in his offensive. It was therefore necessary to keep real as well as replica cavalry in the Jordan Valley. It was the hot season, a time when, according to the official military handbook of the region, 'no civilised human being' could survive the climate. So men and horses endured temperatures which rose to 120 degrees Fahrenheit and exposure to malaria, which hit Indians hardest. During September 1,200 men became infected, and when the offensive started thousands more were incubating the disease.[5]

It was a high price to pay, but the bluff worked. Documents later captured at 'Yildirim' Army Group HQ at Nazareth indicated that von Sanders and his staff had remained convinced that Allenby would attack across the Jordan. Among the papers was an aerial reconnaissance report dated 15 September, which read: 'Some regrouping of cavalry units apparently in progress behind the enemy's left flank [where in fact there were over 10,000 horsemen]; otherwise nothing unusual to report.'[6]

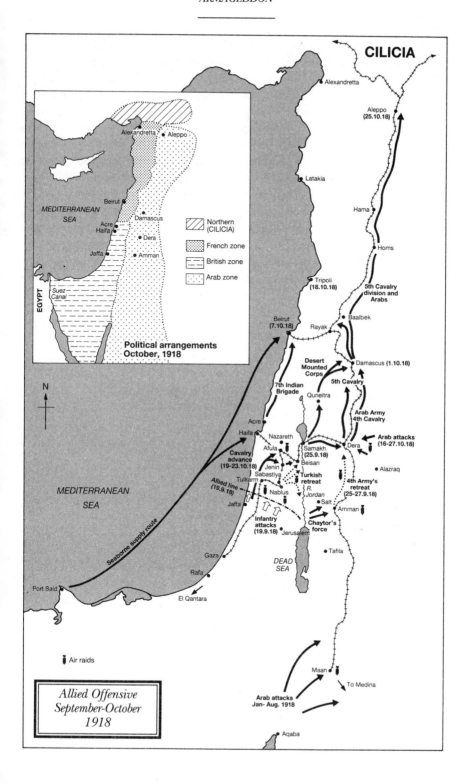

CILICIA

Northern (CILICIA)

French zone

British zone

Arab zone

**Political arrangements
October, 1918**

MEDITERRANEAN
SEA

Alexandretta · Aleppo

Beirut

Acre
Haifa · Damascus

Jaffa · Dera

· Amman

EGYPT

*Suez
Canal*

N

Alexandretta

Aleppo
(25.10.18)

Latakia

Hama

Homs

Tripoli
(18.10.18)

5th Cavalry
division and
Arabs

Beirut
(7.10.18)

Rayak · Baalbek

Desert
Mounted
Corps

Damascus (1.10.18)

7th Indian
Brigade

5th Cavalry

Quneitra

Arab Army
4th Cavalry

Acre

Haifa

Nazareth

Arab attacks
(16-27.10.18)

Afula

Samakh
(25.9.18)

Dera

Cavalry
advance
(19-23.10.18)

Beisan

Jenin

Alazraq

Sabastiya

Turkish
retreat

4th Army's
retreat
(25-27.9.18)

*Allied line
(19.9.18)*

Tulkarm

Nablus

*R.
Jordan*

Salt

Amman

Jaffa

Infantry
attacks
(19.9.18)

Chaytor's
force

Jerusalem

MEDITERRANEAN
SEA

Tafila

Seaborne supply route

Gaza

DEAD
SEA

Rafa

Port Said

El Qantara

Maan

To Medina

Air raids

**Arab attacks
Jan- Aug. 1918**

*Allied Offensive
September-October
1918*

Aqaba

Field security was extraordinarily strict, at Allenby's insistence. Battalion commanders were not informed of the offensive until 9 September, and he made a point of telling each unit commander only what he needed to know to carry out his orders.[7] There was one last-moment hitch when, on the day before the attack, an Indian sergeant deserted to the Turks and revealed that an attack across the plain was imminent. This was vague intelligence and the Turco-German High Command, remembering the planted intelligence notes found before Beersheba, may have regarded it as a red herring. In any case, it was too late for von Sanders to make effective changes in his dispositions.[8]

At the time that Turkish and German Intelligence officers were evaluating the Indian's interrogation, they were receiving further, convincing evidence that a big push was about to be made across the Jordan. On 16 September, Dera, the focus of rail communications in northern Palestine and southern Syria, was attacked by substantial raiding parties backed by armoured cars. During the previous week a body of Beduin, stiffened by Arab regulars, Egyptian camelry and Algerian mountain gunners, had secretly moved to al Azraq. Under the command of Nuri es Said, a capable ex-Turkish Army officer with a taste for whisky, assisted by Lawrence, this force was under orders to create diversions around Dera and, if possible, sever the rail lines that radiated from it. The track suffered some damage which was repaired by German troops, and on the 19th the Arab forward base was detected by German aviators whose attacks brought operations to a standstill. The tables were turned by Lawrence, who summoned machines from British and Australian squadrons which quickly gained control of the air over Dera and subjected the town to heavy bombing.

In the meantime, Allenby was making his final dispositions. His cavalry were assembled in orange groves north of Jaffa, having been moved, unobserved, by night from their camps near the Jordan. The infantry, likewise, had been shifted to their attack positions by nocturnal marches, each man carrying a bottle of water, a day's rations and 170 rounds of ammunition. Gas respirators were issued as it was feared, mistakenly, that the Turco-German forces were equipped with gas.[9] Close behind the assault troops were chlorination units under orders to move forward and secure a supply of potable water the moment the attack began.[10]

The grand offensive began at dawn on 18 September with a fifteen-minute bombardment of Turkish positions, which almost immediately eliminated the enemy's artillery. At 4.45 am the infantry advanced, slicing through the thinly held Turkish line within two hours. By 7.30 am the 5th Cavalry Division, followed shortly by the 4th, was passing through a gap which by the evening would be 10 miles wide. As night fell, the horsemen had ridden for over 20 miles along the coast and were ready to turn inland towards Nazareth and Nablus.

Resistance was sporadic and often half-hearted. The Turks had been caught off balance and many units were fighting blindfold since the 'Yildirim' communications system had completely collapsed. Guided by aerial photographs, RAF bomber pilots had pin-pointed and destroyed the telephone exchanges and telegraph offices at Afula, Nablus and Tulkarm. By seven a bewildered von Sanders had lost contact with his front-line commanders.[11] His own air force was impotent; round-the-clock raids on his main air base at Jenin grounded all machines there. From the first moment Allenby had achieved what arguably proved to be the key to victory, air supremacy. For the next seven days, the RAF dominated the skies and relentlessly bombed roads, railways, aerodromes and troop concentrations. Among the bombers was a novelty that astonished the Arabs who watched it in action over Dera, a twin-engined Handley-Page 0/400 which carried a payload of over a ton of bombs.

On the ground, Allenby's cavalry made astonishing headway. By the evening of 20 September detachments of the 5th Cavalry Division were at the outskirts of Nazareth, which was occupied the next morning after stubborn resistance by von Sanders's staff. Their commander's first instinct had been to cut and run the moment he heard sounds of firing and, still in his pyjamas, he was driven off in a staff car. Remembering that he was a German officer, he later dressed and returned to collect some papers from his HQ. Further south, the Seventh and Eighth Armies were in headlong retreat with Allenby's infantry close on their heels. At the same time the 4th Cavalry Division occupied Afula and Beisan and by the evening its advance guard, the 19th [Indian] Lancers, was within 10 miles of Lake Tiberias.

Everything had gone Allenby's way. On the first day of the battle he had predicted to his wife that his horsemen would be 'irresistible'.[12] Two days later he was confident that the Turkish Army had been destroyed as an effective fighting force. He was correct: in forty-eight hours the Turkish Seventh and Eighth Armies had fallen apart, and fragmented units were hurrying north and east in a desperate attempt to avoid encirclement. Allenby, driven in a Rolls-Royce flying the Union Flag, had followed the fighting line, praising and encouraging his men. On the 22nd, he encountered Chauvel and asked how many prisoners the 5th Cavalry Division had taken. On being told 15,000, he laughed and exclaimed, 'No bloody good to me! I want 30,000 from you before you've done'.[13]

As he motored across the foothills of Samaria he saw for the first time the extent of the damage to men, material and animals inflicted by his bombers. 'I was at Tulkarm today,' he told his wife on the 20th, 'and went along the Nablus road. It was strewn with broken lorries, wagons, dead Turks, horses and oxen, mostly smashed and killed by our bombing aeroplanes.'[14] Once the enemy line had been broken, Allenby's strategy had allowed the Turks no time in which to extricate themselves, recuperate and regroup. Thousands were herded along the road from Tulkarm to Sabastiya, from where the remnants of the Turkish XXII Corps scattered northwards towards Jenin. The detritus of the Seventh Army and the Asia Corps passed through Nablus and tried to escape along the road to Beisan or down the Wadi Fara to the River Jordan.

Funnelled along these three roads, the retreating columns and their transport were strafed and suffered what would later be called saturation bombing. There was no respite; along the Beisan road machines attacked at two-minute intervals throughout one day. The results were horrendous as panic-stricken men and animals strained to escape their tormentors. According to the RAF's official history:

> At one part of the road lorries, abandoned in motion, had crashed forward into guns which had been carried with their teams into other transport wagons, and the accumulation had gone tearing on, shedding lorries and guns over the precipice on the way, until at last it had been brought to a standstill by its own weight. Along the length of the defile lay the torn bodies of men and animals. There were found in all about 100 guns, 55 motor lorries, 4 motor-cars, 837 four-wheeled wagons, 75 two-wheeled wagons, and 20 water-carts and field kitchens.[15]

One cavalry patrol encountered some human survivors of this ordeal hiding in a state of 'utter demoralisation and terror'.[16] Some who flew these missions were repelled by what they were doing and 'got so sick of the awful havoc they had created that they asked to be relieved of the duty, and it was left to the gunners to smash up the rear of the column'.[17]

The bombing sorties undertaken during the first stage of the campaign sealed the fate of von Sanders's Seventh and Eighth Armies. From the beginning neither had been in a fit state to meet, let alone fend off, Allenby's blows. There were two anti-aircraft guns for the entire 'Yildirim' army group in Palestine; for months no fresh troops had replaced front-line units; pack animals died for lack of fodder; and hungry, often ill-clad men deserted. Over 1,000 broke ranks in the four weeks before the offensive, many enticed from their duty by leaflets which promised comfort, food and clothing in a British POW camp. Sometimes these inducements were put in packets of cigarettes dropped on Turkish trenches. Once, just before the Beersheba offensive, Meinertzhagen had proposed lacing the tobacco with opium, a suggestion which Allenby rejected because it was 'sailing too near the wind of dishonesty'. Meinertzhagen went ahead and, more than ten years later, confessed his disobedience to Allenby, who remarked, 'You should have known that if you had told me at the time I should have backed you up.'[18]

In the end it was the ferocity of Allenby's offensive, the cavalry sweeps that cut off lines of retreat and the pursuit by RAF aircraft, which shattered the nerve of soldiers already at the end of their tether. It was the same story beyond the Jordan where, on 20 September, Chaytor's attack against the Fourth Army drove all before it. During the initial fighting, the hitherto underrated West Indians showed exemplary valour and won widespread admiration. Amman surrendered on the 25th and Maan two days later. In both instances the Turkish garrisons demanded and got Chaytor's protection against bands of Beduin marauders determined to murder and kill fugitives and prisoners. At Amman, Turkish officers and men were permitted to keep their rifles, and one group of POWs had to be defended by Australian machine-gun fire against Bani Sakhr tribesmen who had rediscovered their courage once they realised the Turks had been beaten.

The engagements fought between 19 and 25 September came to be collectively known as the battle of Megiddo, after the fortress by the Musmus Pass through which the 4th Cavalry Division had debouched on to the plain of Esdraelon as it advanced on Afula. It was the site of many Old Testament contests and is associated with that great battle of nations, Armageddon, described in the Book of Revelations (16:16). Megiddo was a decisive victory; by the evening of the 25th three crippled Turkish armies were staggering along roads that converged on Damascus, and were close to extinction. This was the result Allenby had anticipated when he had first introduced his plan. His strategic instinct, his daring use of cavalry and, above all, his resolution, had brought victory. He had wanted a fluid battle of manoeuvre and had been ruthless with those who had failed to sustain the momentum of advance. Two cavalrymen, Howard-Vyse and Brigadier-General Philip Kelly, were both unstuck after their brigades got into a mess, although the fault lay with circumstances rather than their commanders' lack of nerve.[19]

By 25 September Allenby, the bit now between his teeth, had set his sights on Damascus. The fall of Samakh that day opened the road to Dera along which Allenby ordered Barrow's 4th Cavalry Division, while Chauvel's 5th was instructed to approach the city by the route which swung north of Lake Tiberias and through Quneitra. Contact had already been made with Faisal's contingent, which was continuing operations in the vicinity of Dera; together with the cavalry divisions, it was to continue rounding-up Turkish fugitives.

The decision to go for Damascus opened up a political can of worms for Allenby. A city of 300,000 mainly Arab Muslim inhabitants, it lay in a region, roughly equivalent to modern Syria and northern Iraq, where according to the terms of the Sykes–Picot Agreement, French influence was to be paramount. The French government was already anxious about what sort of administration Allenby would establish in the area, and had made some representations to the Foreign Office on the matter. The response had been firm, and on 25 August Wilson had assured Allenby that whatever was decided would be 'subject to your authority' and that, so long as the war continued, military considerations would always take first place.[20] When news of Allenby's breakthrough reached London, MacDonogh, who was both Director of Military Intelligence and a member of the Middle East Committee, advised him to stick to the letter of Sykes–Picot. If an Arab government emerged in Syria, and this seemed very likely, it was to be given French advisers.[21]

Since there was as yet no way of knowing the outcome of the campaign or the reaction of the Syrians, Allenby ordered Chauvel to follow the precedents taken when Jerusalem had been occupied; that is, rely on the local *vali* (Turkish governor) and existing administrative structures. 'What about these Arabs?' queried Chauvel. 'There is a rumour that they are to have the administration of Syria.' 'Yes, I believe so,' was Allenby's answer, 'but that must wait until I come and, if Faisal gives you any trouble, deal with him through Lawrence, who will be your liaison officer.'[22] Five days before, Allenby had forbidden any Arab dash to Damascus on the grounds that such an enterprise would force them to abandon their operationally more important work near Dera.[23] As the overall situation had changed, he sent an order on the 25th which relaxed the ban, but insisted that the isolation of Dera continue to have priority.[24]

Allenby's arrangements for the administration of Damascus took for granted the fact that Lawrence would comply with official policy and counsel Faisal accordingly. This was not so, however; the Sykes–Picot Agreement and the prospect of Syria under an Arab government answerable to France were wormwood to Lawrence. He had seen Allenby's campaign as an excellent device with which to further Faisal's cause, and had urged him to snatch Damascus when the chance occurred and claim both the city and the right to rule Syria by conquest. Allenby was completely in the dark about Lawrence's views and the passion with which he held them, but they had been detected by Osmond Walrond, a Foreign Office official in Cairo attached to the Arab Bureau. On 1 October, he warned Lord Milner that Lawrence intended to install Faisal in Damascus as Governor.[25]

When Allenby's message permitting him to press on to Damascus reached Faisal, his army was in no position to act on it. Scattered detachments were still engaged around Dera. Once it became clear that Ottoman authority was withering and the Turkish Army had crumbled, more and more Beduin attached themselves to Faisal's army, driven solely by rapacity. Their looting and cruelty towards prisoners revolted British and Anzac soldiers and deepened the widespread contempt felt for all Arabs. When the 21st (Indian) Lancers approached Dera on the morning of 28 September, areas of the town were on fire and a massacre of Turkish wounded and prisoners was underway. 'Arabs murdered in cold blood every Turk they came across,' was the comment in the 4th Cavalry Division's War Diary.[26] Barrow reached Dera soon afterwards, summoned Nuri es Said and Lawrence, and rebuked them. An acrimonious exchange followed, during which Lawrence refused to intervene and left Barrow to impose order and expel the marauders.[27]

During the previous day's fighting, a Turco-German rearguard that included a Turkish lancer regiment had murdered women and children at Tafas, 10 miles north of Dera. This incident provoked a general slaughter in which not only soldiers from the column were killed. Lawrence later excused what was random retribution as justifiable vengeance, but some eyewitness accounts suggest that he did what he could to stop the killing.[28] He was quick to tell Allenby what had occurred at Tafas when they met a week later, perhaps to forestall protests against Arab brutality from other officers.[29] Ironically, the commander of the Turkish lancers was taken prisoner by British cavalrymen and later entertained in the 4th Cavalry Division's mess.[30]

There were parties of demoralised Turks strung out along the roads to Damascus, and none offered any serious resistance to their pursuers. There was, however, no way of knowing whether once in the city they would join forces with troops already there and make a stand. Allenby wanted to avoid either a siege or street fighting and so, in orders issued on 29 September, he revived the strategy he had used against Jerusalem and instructed the Australian Mounted Division to swing north-east of the city and block the road leading to Homs. The practical details of setting up this cordon were left to individual commanders, who were reminded in a message from Allenby's HQ that 'If possible no troops were to enter [the] town.'[31] This was received at 8.45 am on the morning of 1 October, over two hours after the 3rd Australian Light Horse had passed through Damascus. Other detachments quickly followed: Major-General Macandrew orderd his 14 Brigade through the middle of the city rather than send it on a lengthy detour around the southern outskirts. He was at the Meidan station at 9.30 am where he met Major White, the Brigade

Major of the 4th Cavalry Division, whom he told to keep quiet about what had been an infraction of Allenby's orders.[32]

Allenby was untroubled by his cavalrymen entering Damascus, moves undertaken on purely operational grounds. And yet a series of comparatively minor incidents during the early hours of 1 October were subsequently the subject of a rather sour controversy which arose from Lawrence's claims that Faisal's troops had been first in to the city, and were therefore its liberators. This was untrue: Major Olden, commanding the advance guard of the Australian Light Horse, encountered no Arab forces as he rode through the city, although he saw plenty of Turks attempting to leave. He did find a collection of leading citizens who had declared themselves the government and one of them, Muhammad Said, a former Turco-German agent, formally surrendered Damascus to him. During the short exchange Said said nothing to the effect that he was acting on behalf of Faisal.[33]

Meanwhile Lawrence had precipitately left Barrow's HQ and, after a series of misadventures, entered the city at about 7 am in a Rolls-Royce driven by Major Hubert Young, a fellow liaison officer with Faisal's army, with an escort of Indian cavalrymen.[34] He quickly stage-managed a coup in which Muhammad Said and his brother Abd al Qadir (the man who had betrayed Lawrence's mission in November 1917) were deposed and the pro-Faisal Shukri el Ayubi installed as Governor. At 8.30 he introduced Shukri as the new Governor to Chauvel, who had just arrived and was looking for the Turkish *vali* who, according to Allenby's order, was to head Damascus's interim government. According to Lawrence, Shukri had been elected by a majority of Damascenes, and so Chauvel, ignorant of the events of the past few hours, accepted him.

By mid-afternoon and through the agency of Major Young, Chauvel discovered the truth, namely that Shukri was Faisal's nominee and his supporters were a minority within the city. He acted quickly and decisively; Ali Riza Rikabi, a former Turkish Army officer and an Arab nationalist, was appointed Governor, and a parade of British and Australian units was arranged for 2 October to remind everyone that the city had been liberated by them and not Faisal's army.[35] At the same time Chauvel's troops restored order, a task which Faisal's regulars were disinclined to do, and drove out the hordes of Arab and Druze looters who were terrorising Damascus.[36]

Allenby was at his forward HQ at Tiberias while this charade was being played out. During 1 October he heard that Australian units had entered the city and that a local government had been set up overnight.[37] Chauvel's actions had asserted British paramountcy in Damascus which Allenby confirmed by his visit to the city on the 3rd. Leaving Tiberias at five in the morning, he was driven to Damascus where he arrived at one in the afternoon. On the last stage of the journey he was accompanied by Chauvel, who explained his conduct of the city's government. Allenby approved, but was less than happy to hear that, by arrangement with Lawrence, Faisal was due to make a triumphal entry at three. 'Triumphal entry be damned,' Allenby exclaimed, 'I cannot wait till three as I have to go back to Tiberias tonight. You must send a car for him at once. He can go out again for his triumphal entry.'[38] The Arab leader was summoned and duly appeared, none too happy about being upstaged.

Faisal, accompanied by Lawrence, was received by Allenby and Chauvel and their staffs in the Victoria Hotel. With Lawrence interpreting, Allenby outlined the future arrangements for Palestine and Syria. What followed was described by him as a 'long and satisfactory' talk with Faisal. Its conclusion was summed up in a letter to his wife written the same day: 'He [Faisal] will take over the administration of Damascus, in the same way as Money in Palestine; or, rather, will put in a Military administrator.'[39] His cable to the War Office was more specific, and indicated that he accepted an Arab military government east of the Jordan between Damascus and Maan, assisted by a British and a French liaison officer and under Allenby's control.[40]

These brief statements gave no indication of the temper of the meeting, which was recalled by Chauvel some years later.[41] Through Lawrence, Allenby explained that France would have supervision of the administration of Syria, which would remain for the time being in Faisal's hands. Palestine would stay under British governance and the Lebanon was allocated to France. Faisal protested.

> He said he knew nothing of France in the matter; that he was prepared to have British assistance; that he understood from the Adviser that Allenby had sent him [Lawrence] that the Arabs were to have the whole of Syria, including the Lebanon but excluding Palestine, that a Country without a Port was no good to him; and that he declined to have a French liaison officer or to recognise French guidance in any way.

A bewildered Allenby then asked Lawrence, 'But did you not tell him that the French were to have the Protectorate over Syria?' 'No Sir, I knew nothing about it.' Allenby pressed him further, 'But you knew definitely that he, Faisal, was to have nothing to do with the Lebanon?' 'No Sir, I did not,' answered Lawrence. Three days later Allenby, still puzzled, cabled the War Office with the news that 'Arab leaders have never been officially notified of the terms of the Anglo-French agreement.'[42] This was, of course, not so, although Faisal and Lawrence may have been genuinely astonished to discover that the terms of Sykes–Picot were going to be carried out exactly, at least in the immediate future. Allenby ignored the bluff and bluntly told Faisal that he was officially a lieutenant-general in the British Army and therefore bound to obey his superior's orders. The Arab acquiesced, partly reassured by Allenby's promise that the business would be sorted out when the war had ended.

Then, according to Chauvel, Lawrence announced his own refusal to serve alongside a French officer and asked permission to take overdue leave in England. 'Yes, I think you had,' was Allenby's curt answer. Lawrence's version of the parting suggested that it was a good-tempered affair and that Allenby had pleaded with him to stay. This seems strange, since the C-in-C must have known from Chauvel that Lawrence's behaviour over the past few days had been tantamount to insubordination, and that his claim, made when they had first met in the Victoria Hotel, that he and not Chauvel had quelled the disorders in Damascus was false.[43] In the light of this knowledge, and of news reaching GHQ of a pro-Faisal coup in Beirut, Allenby may have been inwardly glad to be rid of an officer whose defiant attachment to the Arab cause clouded his judgement and drove him to disobedience. Lawrence was replaced as Faisal's mentor by Lieutenant-Colonel Kinahan Cornwallis, a judicious choice, according to Osmond Walrond. 'Faisal,' he told Milner, 'is a weak character but as long as he has an Englishman at his elbow he won't go far wrong,' and Cornwallis was 'an Englishman before everything'.[44]

On the same day that he settled the governance of Damascus, Allenby was confronted by a new political crisis. Reports had reached his HQ of a coup in Beirut, engineered by local nationalists acting in Faisal's interests and with his encouragement. A collision between the Arabs and French forces now seemed a possibility – and a dangerous one, not least because Beirut, with its rail link to Baalbak, had been earmarked by Allenby as the supply base for all forces in northern Syria. A message was immediately sent to Vice-Admiral Thomas Jackson, the senior naval officer in the Eastern Mediterranean, asking him to discover exactly what was happening in Beirut.[45] At dawn on 6 October the armed motor yacht *Managem* approached Beirut harbour and discovered the French destroyer *Arbalète* at anchor and French transports unloading stores.

Beirut lay within the region set aside for French government and Allenby acted with precise propriety. His own troops, Bulfin's 7th Indian Division, were approaching the port from the south and arrangements were made for them to enter the town at the same time as French seaborne forces.[46] The vanguard arrived during the evening of the 8th with orders to remove all Hijazi flags and recognise the local rights of the newly appointed French Governor, Colonel de Piépape, who was, however, reminded that he remained solely under Allenby's command.[47]

This incident and all that it implied discomposed Faisal. He protested to Allenby, who agreed to discuss matters with him on 17 October. The talks were accompanied by what Allenby, a good judge in such matters, called an 'excellent dinner'. It was also his first chance to study Faisal closely; afterwards he sent his largely favourable impressions to Lady Allenby. The prince was 'a keen, slim, highly strung man. He has beautiful hands like a woman's; and his fingers are always moving nervously when he talks. But he is strong in will and straight in principle.'[48] The talk had been political and Allenby had found Faisal 'very distrustful of French intentions, fearing that French military governors will take advantage of their official positions to carry on propaganda'. Allenby reminded him that all present measures were provisional, and added the reassurance that 'the French were our Allies, an honourable nation, fighting for the same cause and with the same ideals'.[49]

In private Allenby was already entertaining doubts about French motives and the practicability of French control in the region. There were disturbing signs that French officers were forgetting that they were still under Allenby's orders and that he was the source of all authority throughout the occupied territories. He had had to make this clear to de Piépape, who seemed to think that the Lebanon was already a French colony; later, he refused to bargain with Picot who, in his eyes, was just a subordinate liaison officer.[50]

Allenby's contact with Faisal and Ali Riza Rikabi (the latter he found to be a capable and hard-working official) had convinced him of the depth of local Francophobia. 'This fear and dislike of the French is universal among the Muslims in Syria,' he told Wilson on the 19th. For this reason he would not allow a special Syrian base to be established for the French units under his command, and he asked Wilson to ensure that there would be no interference from the French government.[51] Four days later he issued new instructions for the administration of occupied territory: the British zone in Palestine remained and the French were given control over a coastal strip from Beirut to Alexandretta, while a third region, stretching from Aqaba to Aleppo, was placed under an Arab governor, al Rikabi. In deference to Faisal's wishes, the *qazas* (Ottoman administrative districts) of Baalbak, Rushiya and Hasbiya, formerly in the French zone, were permitted to keep their Arab administration pending an assessment of local feeling.[52] Supreme power remained in Allenby's hands. It was a fair allocation of political authority, and showed that he was willing to accommodate local Arab opinion. At the same time, the new arrangement avoided what he feared the most, a clash between Arab and French forces.

While Allenby was endeavouring to play the political ringmaster, operations in Syria continued, although on a smaller scale. Since the fall of Damascus the remains of the Fourth, Seventh and Eighth Turkish Armies continued their retreat northwards, and Allenby ordered his cavalry to maintain the pursuit. Macandrew's 5th Cavalry Division entered Rayak on 6 October, Homs on the 16th and Hama on the 21st, but the 4th Cavalry Division and Chauvel's Desert Mounted Corps had to be withdrawn from action during the second week of October, as both were suffering epidemics of malaria contracted in the Jordan Valley. Weakened men also fell victim to a wave of the Spanish influenza pandemic which would reach Europe by the end of the year. Four times as many Australians died from these diseases as had been killed by Turkish action during the campaign despite the vigorous efforts of the medical staff.[53]

In spite of the loss of two of his cavalry divisions, Allenby decided to press on to Aleppo with Macandrew's 5th assisted by Arabs. The Arab contingent, under Nuri es Said, proved invaluable during the street fighting that preceded the capture of Aleppo on 25 October. After taking the city, cavalry units followed on the heels of the Turkish rearguard, which was commanded by Mustapha Kemal Pasha (Kemal Atatürk), an energetic officer who had, during the past fortnight, attempted to reorganise his men and rekindle their fighting spirit. A measure of his efforts was a fiercely fought rearguard action at Haritan, 5 miles north of Aleppo, on the 26th.

What turned out to be the final action of Allenby's offensive involved a cavalry charge by the Mysore and Jodhpur Lancers. The horsemen encountered what they took to be a small Turkish detachment isolated on a ridge and rode it down. 'The charge got home,' wrote Major Lambert, a staff officer attached to the unit, 'the horsemen galloping through lines of infantry, mostly German, lying down. Fifty of the enemy were killed and over twenty taken prisoner.' The next moment the scattered lancers discovered that they had blundered into nearly 3,000 Turkish and German troops and, unsupported, they fell back in haste. Some of their prisoners picked up rifles and fired at them as they rode past. Astonishingly, the Indians suffered only eighty casualties.[54]

Four days later the 5th Cavalry Division, now on the Alexandretta road, heard by wireless that the Turkish government had signed an armistice which would take effect at noon on 31 October. Three weeks before, as the news of the calamities in Syria were reaching Constantinople, the war party within the CUP found itself isolated politically and began to disintegrate. A new government was formed under Izzet Pasha, and was almost immediately confronted by the news of the continued German retreat in Belgium, the collapse of the Austrians in Italy, and the whirlwind Allied Balkan campaign which had forced the Bulgarians to sue for peace. The Turks had no choice but to follow Bulgaria, and agreed to what was in effect the complete capitulation of their armies on all fronts and, most galling of all, occupation of the Straits by Allied men-o'-war.

Allenby had been the architect of a remarkable victory. Measured in purely statistical terms, his army had, in the space of five weeks, advanced just over 300 miles, taken 75,000 Turkish prisoners and 360 guns, and itself suffered fewer than 6,000 battle casualties. In the course of operations three Turkish armies had been destroyed and three provinces, Palestine, the Lebanon and Syria, liberated. The credit for this was Allenby's; the battle plan had been his conception and its faultless execution owed much to his iron-hard faith in its success and to the impetus he provided, whether in staff conferences or driving along dusty roads, to encourage his forward commanders. There was still much bullishness in his manner, but by now his men knew him as 'the Chief', a name which betokened respect and perhaps even affection. To the peoples he emancipated he had been, since his arrival in the Middle East, *'el Nebi'*, a prophet who, according to legend, would free them.

At the time and for some years afterwards, Allenby's success was entirely attributed to his deployment of cavalry, which had, in Europe at least, played a cinderella role in the war, much to the chagrin of cavalrymen. Up to a point this assessment was correct: the horsemen had raced through the gap in Turkish lines on 19 September, penetrated deep into enemy territory, barricaded lines of retreat and made it impossible for the Turkish High Command to rest and regroup its armies. Exceptional stamina had been required from men and horses. Out of 25,618 horses in Allenby's command, 3,245 were casualties of which 904 returned to service thanks to the army veterinary services. Some units lost no horses at all, their men mindful of Allenby's advice that a good cavalryman cared diligently for his animal until the moment came for battle, and then he rode it hard. There had been plenty of occasions for hard riding, and advocates of cavalry charges were more than satisfied with those which ended successfully, forgetting that on these occasions the galloping horsemen had been supported by horse artillery, machine-guns, and sometimes armoured cars.

Less notice was taken of the part played by the RAF, which between 19 and 25 September had wreaked havoc on exposed Turkish columns jammed along narrow passes. Not as glamorous as the cavalry charge but infinitely more deadly, the continual bombing and machine-gunning of retreating men assured Allenby's victory. From the beginning to the end, Allenby had had total air supremacy, a fact which, revealingly, was given only one paragraph in the official military history.[55]

The RAF's terror attacks settled the fate of an army tottering on the brink of collapse. A year before, Mustapha Kemal had reported from the Palestine front that 'Our army is very weak. Most of our formations are now reduced to one-fifth of their prescribed strength. The Seventh Army, which constitutes our only organised strength, has been shaken without exchanging a single shot with the enemy.' The process of deterioration of both manpower and morale continued alongside a disintegration of the medical services. Malaria and pellagra (a skin infection) were common and were made worse by malnutrition and exhaustion. During the September and October advance, the hospitals of the Desert Mounted Corps had to cope with 2,000 sick Turkish POWs and a further 8,000 had to be admitted to makeshift hospitals in Damascus.[56]

Allenby's army undoubtedly enjoyed a higher morale than its adversary, as well as an immense material superiority. In these circumstances a general might have been tempted to rely solely upon these advantages and crush his opponent. Allenby was wiser: he beat the Turks by speed and dexterity of manoeuvre, and so spared the lives of his men. He had learned much since leaving France.

PART 4

IMPERIAL
PROCONSUL

NOVEMBER 1918–JUNE 1925

CHAPTER 14

WHITE MUTINIES
AND BROWN MISCHIEF

NOVEMBER 1918–JUNE 1919

VICTORY added to Allenby's burdens. From 1 November he was both Commander-in-Chief of an Allied army which totalled, including conscripted Egyptian civilians, a quarter of a million and the ruler of about a million Palestinians, Syrians, Lebanese and Armenians. His satrapy extended from Cilicia in the north to Sinai in the south, and from the Mediterranean coast to the Syrian and Arabian deserts. He was, in his own words, responsible for 'the maintenance of order and the establishment of an impartial, non-political administration' that would endure until Allied statesmen, who gathered at Paris in January 1919, resolved the region's political future.[1] In the meantime he had to play the part of a benevolent autarch presiding over an improvised government, uncertain about when and how his responsibilities would cease. 'I haven't the foggiest idea what is going to be the future in the near East,' he confessed in March. All he could do was to 'walk warily' and trust, as ever, in his common sense.[2]

He faced a massive and complex task. His 1918 victories and the dissolution of Ottoman power marked the beginning of an extended period of chronic instability throughout the Middle East. A political vacuum had been created in a part of the world where, before 1914, political activity had been curtailed and where 'Western' concepts of nationalism, individual freedom and representative government were

179

understood only by a tiny educated minority. There had been plenty of political ferment, much of it generated by the 'Young Turk' revolution of 1908, which increased dramatically as the war progressed. New ideas had spread slowly and unevenly across the old Ottoman Empire. In Damascus and cosmopolitan Beirut an élite thought in terms that would have been recognisable to European liberals, and racial groups such as the Kurds and Armenians were groping their way towards a sense of national awareness. In such outlying regions as the Hijaz and the Persian Gulf, Islamic orthodoxy and traditional absolutism survived.

Turkey's defeat raised new issues. The entire Middle East was now without political and religious cohesion and in some quarters there were well-justified fears that it would fall prey to Britain and France, whose annexationist ambitions were well known. The likelihood of straight-forward partition receded on 7 November when the Allies broadcast a declaration which promised the 'setting up of national governments and administrations that shall derive their authority from the free exercise of the initiative and choice of the indigenous population'. This seemingly open-handed pledge derived from the principles of popular self-determination that had been the keynote of President Woodrow Wilson's plans for post-war Europe. At a stroke, the Sykes–Picot Agreement had been disaffirmed, and the peoples of the Middle East were apparently about to become their own masters. Moreover, a week earlier the Hijaz had been granted the status of a belligerent power, which entitled Faisal to attend the Peace Conference and plead his case for an independent Syria. He sailed from Beirut on 22 November, after suffering the humiliation of having his car stopped by French troops and the Hijazi flag removed.[3]

Notwithstanding this act of French provocation, one of many contrived against the Arabs during the winter of 1918–19, Faisal's departure helped Allenby keep the peace. So long as the prince was engaged in negotiations in Paris the Syrian nationalists would remain comparatively calm, in hopeful anticipation of a favourable outcome. In the meantime, Allenby and his administrative officers turned their attention towards the disorders that inevitably followed the Turkish withdrawal. On 16 November he told General Wilson that 'It looks as if there will be a lot of police work to be done in Europe and Asia before the new little nations settle down, or they will be tearing each other's eyes.'[4]

There were inaccessible parts of the occupied territories where Ottoman control had been fitful or non-existent and banditry was endemic. On 1 December more than 200 brigands attacked Rayak to steal ammunition, but were easily driven off by the garrison. In remote districts of Cilicia isolated and disorganised Turkish resistance persisted until early January and, in the same month, punitive columns had to be sent into the hinterland of Alexandretta to hunt down robber bands. Three months later large bodies of Beduin launched a series of raids on Dera.[5]

More worrying for Allenby than these sporadic outbreaks of traditional lawlessness was the communal violence between Armenians and Muslims which broke out in northern Syria and Cilicia almost immediately the Turks had left. These disturbances were complicated by the activities of Armenian exiles serving with the French Légion d'Orient, who were suspected of various acts of theft and murder in Adana and the assassination in Bozanti of a Turkish officer who had been responsible for the deportation of Armenians from the area in 1916.[6] There was a strong and understandable desire among Armenians to avenge the genocide undertaken against them between 1915 and 1918, in which at least a million and a half had been killed. Racial and religious antipathies remained virulent. Armoured-car patrols which toured the Aintab district at the end of December discovered desecrated Christian churches and a local population which had been armed against the Armenians by the defiant Turkish local authorities. A small detachment of troops was immediately posted in the town to preserve order.[7]

The worst racial disturbances occurred towards the end of February in Aleppo, where tension had increased after the return of local Armenian women and girls who had been forced into Turkish harems. Stirred up by ex-Turkish officers, a Muslim mob attacked an Armenian orphanage; by the time that British and Arab forces had restored order, a hundred Armenians had been murdered and at least fifty rioters shot. Afterwards the ringleaders were tried by court martial and executed.[8]

Most alarming of all for Allenby were Intelligence reports concerning the creation of an underground army in Cilicia, armed and encouraged by the Turks and calling itself the Islamic Union, which was preparing to resist French occupation.[9] Tension increased in the new year as more and more French units, including Armenians, disembarked at Alexandretta. Allenby was forced to act and, on 4 February, he promised the local French commander whatever military assistance he needed to defend his nation's 'legitimate interests' in the region.[10]

This pledge was made reluctantly. For the past four months French high-handedness and intrigues, which even extended to the Hijaz, had been a source of annoyance to Allenby. In November he had expressed the hope that the French would show restraint, conciliate the Arabs and allow Faisal the use of a port.[11] If they did not, then there would be serious disorder. This was also the conclusion of Sir Mark Sykes who, accompanied by Picot, had visited Beirut, Damascus and Aleppo during November to sound out local opinion. Like Allenby, he concluded that any attempt to foist a French administration on Syria would be violently opposed by the majority of Muslims and Orthodox Christians. There were no objections to Allenby's occupying army, which, as he repeatedly stated, was an Allied force, but Sykes warned that 'Any attempt to replace British by French troops in areas where the Arab flag has been recognised invites trouble.'[12] Allenby was well aware of all this; the Arabs mistrusted French liaison officers and wherever he went he found hostility towards the French administrative officers he had appointed. Faisal had been tractable despite his apprehension of the French. He had been persuaded by Allenby to relinquish Beirut on the understanding that it would be occupied by an Allied force. In return, Allenby had promised him that 'the League of Nations intended to give the small nations the right of self-determination'. Faisal was not completely convinced, and told Allenby that he would lead the Arabs in a war to resist any form of French control in Syria.[13] Since there was no answer to this, Allenby pinned his hopes on Faisal procuring an equitable settlement in Paris.

The alternative was unthinkable. Rather than submit to France, the Arabs would fight and, if Faisal led them, Allenby believed the war would spread to Palestine, the Hijaz and possibly Egypt. If events were to take this course, then there was no way in which Allenby's forces could avoid being drawn into the conflict.[14]

The odds against this happening were, however, still remote at the end of 1918. Allenby would have known from his contacts with Sykes that in London the Sykes–Picot Agreement was considered a dead letter. With Germany and Turkey beaten, the Tory Imperialists in the coalition were taking heart and talking in terms of future British dominance of the entire Middle East. Allenby's recent victories had made Britain the paramount power in the region; in purely Imperial terms his final campaign had been as decisive as Clive's in India or Wolfe's in Canada. It would therefore have been imprudent to the point of folly to deliver a substantial chunk of the conquered territory to France, a nation which less than twenty years before that been Britain's rival in the area. A report prepared by Allenby's HQ staff in December expressed fears that Beirut might be transformed into a French naval base and thus a permanent threat to the Suez Canal.[15] It therefore made political and strategic sense to preserve as much of what Allenby had won and exploit current Arab Anglophilia. 'For the safety of our Eastern Empire', wrote Lord Curzon, the Foreign Secretary, 'I would sooner come to a satisfactory agreement with the Arabs than I would the French.'[16]

This was more easily said than done. Lloyd George would not allow Imperial interests to override all others, and he needed the close co-operation of France during the Peace Conference. When Clemenceau visited London in December 1918, Lloyd George tackled him about Sykes–Picot and offered what was in effect a private bargain. Britain would take Palestine, which would satisfy those concerned with the safety of the Canal, and Mosul in northern Iraq, which was already in British hands and was known to contain considerable oil deposits. In return. France got the Lebanon, Cilicia and Syria, the last under direct, and not joint Franco-Arab, government. The enforcement of these arrangements would, presumably, rest with Allenby's army of occupation.

There were signs throughout the winter of 1918–19 that many of the troops under Allenby's command were becoming increasingly discontented with their lot. The first outbreak of mass disobedience began on the night of 11/12 November at the al Qantara base camp, where celebrations of the armistice in Europe ended in a riot in which canteens and a sergeants' mess were ransacked. One cause of the rumpus was a rumour that all men undergoing field punishment were about to be released, and when this was discovered to be untrue a mob of 400 stormed the penal compound.[17] There was more hooliganism between 7 and 11 December when bands of Scottish, New Zealand and Rarotongan troops smashed Egyptian shops.[18]

Far graver was the Surafend incident later in December. Relations between Anzac units and the Beduin had worsened after the recent fighting near Amman, when tribesmen had threatened Turkish POWs and plundered British lines. What particularly angered the Australians and New Zealanders was the refusal of the military authorities to take any preventive or punitive action.[19] Matters came to a head when a New Zealand soldier was shot dead by an Arab thief and the murderer was tracked to the village of Surafend, a short distance from GHQ at Bar Salem. Anzacs surrounded the village while their commander, Chaytor, sent an officer to GHQ with a request for action. None was forthcoming and the Anzacs were ordered to disperse. They returned in vengeful mood at nightfall in the company of some 'bad hats' from adjacent camps and GHQ, and surrounded and entered the village.[20] Women and children were driven out and the men were then given a thrashing which left at least thirty dead or wounded. The vigilantes then set fire to the village, and afterwards vented what was left of their spleen on a neighbouring Beduin camp which they also burned. Just as no official effort had been made to capture the murderer, none was made to interfere with the avengers, even though the glow of the fires could be seen from GHQ.

Allenby was furious. An investigation came up against an impenetrable wall of silence, and so he called a parade of all Anzac units suspected of involvement. Dressed in full kit, the Australians and New Zealanders were formed up in hollow square and faced by Allenby mounted on his massive black stallion, Hindenburg. He delivered an excoriating harangue; his listeners 'were murderers and cowards and by killing the Beduin had taken away the good name of Anzac – in fact [it was] a worse atrocity than any the Turks had committed'. As he bellowed out that he no longer felt any pride in them, there was laughter in the ranks and, probably sensing that his audience was uncowed and on the verge of grosser insubordination, he prudently rode away.[21] Afterwards rumours buzzed about to the effect that he had been jeered and barracked, but these were denied by eyewitnesses.[22]

His fury did not subside. While the defiant Anzacs kicked their heels at Rafah and waited for demobilisation, Allenby sulked. Anzac units were deliberately omitted from his official despatches, and recommendations for gallantry decorations were withdrawn. Pressed by Henry Gullett, the Australian war correspondent, Allenby relented a little and in May 1919 issued a public encomium which praised the Australians' and New Zealanders' bravery and fortitude. At Chauvel's prompting he gave way on the medals, but too late, since in January 1921 the War Office declared that no further awards for the war would be considered.[23]

No one involved in the Surafend incident came out of it well. Allenby was genuinely distressed by an act of monstrous indiscipline which could have damaged relations with the Arabs. He was also inwardly discomposed by his inability to overawe the Anzacs, who had publicly humiliated him. Hurt pride as much as a concern for military law probably contributed to his vindictive treatment of them. It did, however, have an ironic appropriateness, since they too had punished indiscriminately.

Other acts of mass insubordination followed in the new year. On 11 January there was a protest about delays in demobilisation and pay by men of the Gloucestershire Hussars, who were stationed in Aleppo and who had, a few days before, been Allenby's escort during his stay there. Similar complaints were made by troopers of another crack unit, the Middlesex Yeomanry, at Damascus.[24] 'Dissatisfaction with the show' was the official explanation of a riot at the Sidi Bishr base camp, where men from the 53rd and 60th Divisions wrecked a cinema. Australians fought a number of brawls with Arabs and Italians in Port Said in which shots were fired.[25] Less spontaneous but, from the Army's point of view, more menacing disturbances occurred during February at the Ordnance workshops at al Qantara and Haifa, where there were strikes over pay and hours by technicians who were under the illusion that the Army accepted the practices of domestic trade unionism. Underlying this restlessness was a general frustration with the process of demobilisation, which to the troops seemed slow and, at first, highly unfair.[26]

These were all isolated incidents and, save at Surafend, Allenby left his subordinates to deal with them. As later events showed, he sympathised with the predicament of civilians-turned-soldiers, some of whom had been in the Middle East since 1915, who were anxious to return home and find work in what was widely feared to be a shrinking job market. All that he and his staff could do was to balance the wishes of the men with the demands of military security. They managed quite well, which explains why the army in Egypt and Palestine did not suffer mutinous disorders on the scale of those in Britain and northern France during the second half of January 1919. In that month, 17,000 men were demobilised from the al Qantara camp, followed by 23,000 in February and 20,300 in the first three weeks of March.[27]

For the moment, his troops' welfare was a secondary consideration in Allenby's life. He continued to be preoccupied with the future of Palestine, Syria and the Lebanon. On 12 March he was summoned to Paris to give his opinions on local conditions in these provinces to the 'Big Four': Woodrow Wilson, Clemenceau, President Orlando of Italy, and Lloyd George. His arrival on the 19th was spectacular, for the conqueror of Palestine and Syria had become an international celebrity. He was that rare creature, an Allied general who had won great battles without the near extermination of his own forces, and his campaigns in the Holy Land had a glamour that could never attach to the Western Front. Allenby was agreeably astonished by his fame. 'I have been interviewed, snapshotted, cinematographed and stared at continually,' he told his mother.[28] An old friend, Meinertzhagen, thought he had struck Paris 'like desert air pouring through London fog'.

Equally refreshing was his bluffness of manner and candour. Asked during a closed session of the conference to explain what French diplomats considered his lack of accommodation to their country's interests and his partiality towards the Arabs, he remarked, 'When I was at school, if I saw two boys fighting, the one big and the other small, I first kicked the big boy, not the small one.'[29] This invocation of the manly values of public-school fair play must have perplexed the Frenchmen. They, and some of the British listeners, may have wondered for a moment whether this splendid general approached the governance of the Middle East in the same way as he had done the supervision of a particularly unruly dormitory. Perhaps so, although there were worse ways of handling the region's inhabitants.

This outburst did not find its way into the official minutes of Allenby's evidence. It was heard at Lloyd George's flat in the Rue Nitot on the afternoon of 19 March, during discussions on the possibility of a French mandate for Syria. When President Wilson asked what the consequences of this might be, Lloyd George suggested that Allenby should answer. After an extended outline of the principles he had tried to follow in the administration of Syria and the Lebanon, he concluded on a note of foreboding:

> If the French were given a mandate in Syria, there would be serious trouble and probably war. If Faisal undertook the direction of operations there might be a huge war covering the whole area, and the Arabs of the Hijaz would join. This would necessitate the employment of a very large force. This would probably involve Great Britain also if they were in Palestine. It might even involve them in Egypt, and the consequences would be incalculable.[30]

Next morning, Allenby was called into the presence of Arthur Balfour, who was acting as Foreign Secretary in Paris. Reports had been reaching him from Cairo of a nationwide popular insurrection in Egypt directed against British authority. During the past week there had been extensive rioting and a systematic attempt to dislocate all communications, and the British-controlled administration appeared on the brink of collapse. 'Prompt action' was urgently needed to be taken by a strong man in the Kitchener mould, and Lloyd George considered Allenby best suited for the job. He agreed to accept a 'Special High Commission with Supreme Civil and Military Control', with a brief to suppress all disorders and preserve the British protectorate over Egypt on a 'sure and equal basis'. King George V was immediately telephoned and asked to issue the requisite letters of appointment, which were delivered the following day. On 22 March, Allenby left Paris by train for Marseilles, from where he sailed for Egypt in the appropriately named destroyer HMS *Steadfast*.[31]

Lloyd George had dictated Allenby's appointment as High Commissioner. His reasons were echoed by Balfour, who wrote shortly afterwards that 'As far as Egypt is concerned the somewhat unexpected emergence of violent and widespread *sabotage* would seem to demand the peculiar combination of great military prestige with civilian moderation and firmness which General Allenby possesses in a very rare degree.'[32] He had already displayed these qualities in dealing with the French and the Arabs, but more importantly he possessed an open mind. Hitherto, the country's affairs had been managed by specialist Foreign Office officials of a rigid cast of mind, who, as events had proved, had misjudged the temper of the Egyptians. As ever, Lloyd George was inclined to distrust professionals – with good reason, in this case, since in Egypt they had created an appalling mess. It was left to a relatively inexperienced outsider with a powerful sense of fair play to sort it out.

On the other hand, it had been common ever since the late eighteenth century for the government to employ the services of eminent commanders as proconsuls, especially in areas where strong, decisive action was needed. Allenby was therefore following in a long tradition of warrior-governors which stretched back to Cornwallis, who had held viceregal authority in India and Ireland, and Kitchener, who had been a forceful and effective High Commissioner in Egypt between 1910 and 1914. The tradition continued with the appointment of French as Viceroy of Ireland in 1919, and Wavell and Mountbatten as successive Viceroys of India. In each case, as in Allenby's, it was assumed that former fighting soldiers and sailors knew best how to handle restless natives.

Allenby arrived at the High Commission office in Cairo on 25 March. He inherited a permanent staff whose prevarication and ineptness had been largely responsible for the present crisis. His own knowledge of the internal politics of Egypt was slight compared to that of his officials, but unlike them he was not encumbered with prejudices about the Egyptians, although he soon absorbed some. Not long after his arrival, he received from John Marshall, a judge of the Egyptian Court of Appeal, a memo written seven years before which claimed to sum up the Egyptian character.[33] It was a damning and dismissive catalogue of shortcomings: the police were anti-Christian and incompetent; the education system produced lawyers, doctors and engineers, but could 'never make a man a good citizen'; and there was 'no sense of discipline' among Egypt's youth. There existed a sullen pool of educated unemployed, the ruling classes were 'vain, stubborn and obstinate' intriguers, while the peasantry or fellahin were perpetually restless and religiously bigoted. The greatest source of anti-British feeling was the Islamic university of al Azhar, south of Cairo, which Marshall called 'the home of narrow-minded dogma and fanaticism'.

Allenby also perused a speech made in London in 1910 by the former American President and dyed-in-the-wool imperialist, Theodore Roosevelt, who equated British interests in Egypt with those of 'civilisation'. British rule in the country was the best it had had since the Roman occupation, and he cautioned his audience not to let 'weakness, timidity and sentimentality' override firmness in the government of a backward, fanatical people.[34]

Such views permeated every level of the British administration in Egypt. It had been there since 1882 when a British army invaded the country, ostensibly to overthrow the nationalist government of Urabi Pasha, but in fact to safeguard the Suez Canal. Since then British civil servants had supervised Egypt's government and masterminded various fiscal and legal reforms. In 1914 a full protectorate was declared and Egyptians had been swept, with extreme unwillingness, into a war against their fellow Muslims. Egypt provided the army with transport and food, and with 123,000 conscripted labourers who served in Palestine and France. As a consequence, by 1918 the country was suffering from inflation and food shortages, and there was an inevitable growth in anti-British agitation among all classes.

Allenby had been hardly aware of this, although on 7 November 1918 he had received a letter from Wingate which reported 'murmurings of self-determination' among Egyptians.[35] What particularly worried Wingate was Egyptian reaction to the Allied proclamation that pledged independence to the peoples liberated from Ottoman government.[36] He was correct: on the morning of 8 November he was visited by a deputation of three leading Egyptian politicians, Said Zaghlul, Abd al Aziz Fahmi and Ali Sharwani, with whom he had what he called 'somewhat stormy but entirely friendly' exchanges. The Egyptians demanded equal treatment with the Arabs, arguing that they were 'far more capable of conducting a well-ordered government than the Arabs, Syrians and Mesopotamians'. Wingate disagreed, and rolled out the usual Imperial arguments that the Egyptian masses were illiterate and unfit for political responsibility. Zaghlul, who did most of the talking, refused to accept this reasoning and said he was prepared to place the cause of his nation's independence before the 'liberty-loving British people' or even the United States government.[37]

There, in the late autumn of 1918, the matter rested. The Foreign Office imagined that if nothing was done the difficulty would eventually vanish. Writing from Cairo on 28 November, Walrond vented the general view that the Egyptians were just 'naughty children' who would soon be sorry for their silliness. He thought that the nationalist deputation was a consequence of Wingate's irresolution and predicted that 'the Cairo hobbledehoy sort of student, the café-frequenter type' might easily succumb to rabble-rousing.[38] His opinion of Wingate as a temporiser was shared in the Foreign Office and, in January, Curzon recalled him to London for consultations, a move designed to prevent him from making any precipitate concessions to Egyptian public opinion.

During the next three months, the Egyptian nationalist movement made tremendous headway. It called itself the Wafd, which literally means 'delegation', after the group that had first petitioned Wingate. Zaghlul became its leader and chief spokesman, and it drew support from the *effendiya* class of lawyers and officials as well as wealthy landowners. The motives of these groups were not altruistic; the educated classes resented the monopoly of senior posts enjoyed by better-paid British officials, while the landowners disliked recent land-distribution measures and the lawyers suffered a loss of employment in the wake of legal reforms. The participation of the richer classes gave the Wafd considerable funds with which to produce and disseminate propaganda. It was also able to infiltrate and dominate student groups and Egypt's growing trade union movement.[39]

The first chance for the Wafd to show its power came at the beginning of March. On the first of the month, the Egyptian Prime Minister, Hussain Rushdi, resigned after Curzon refused him permission to visit London and argue the case for self-government. Curzon imagined that this Olympian rebuff would be enough to convince the Egyptians that there was no future in trying to change their lot. He had utterly misunderstood the depth of Egyptian feeling. Riots broke out in the cities and on 6 March, Sir Milne Cheetham, a career diplomat who was running the High Commission in Wingate's absence, cabled for permission to arrest and deport Zaghlul and the rest of the Wafd leadership. Curzon complied and on 8 March the wafdists were in placed in custody and sent to Malta.[40]

Curzon had blundered. His contemptuous treatment of the nationalists was a signal for riots and strikes which spread out from Cairo and Alexandria to encompass the Nile Delta and eventually Upper Egypt. Within a few days all transport and communications came to a halt as railway workers, tramwaymen, taxi-drivers walked out. Junior civil servants stopped work and in the countryside telegraph lines were cut and mobs besieged stations and tore up railway track. There were anti-British riots in Cairo, Alexandria and the larger towns and, from the 11th, attacks on British servicemen. Everywhere the demands were the same: at Tanta students of the Islamic Theological College shouted 'Down with the British! Hurrah for Turkey!' and 'We want our independence and our ministers to be free!' and at Wasta, 'Long live Zaghlul!' and 'Long live Egypt!'

The most terrifying incident occurred on 15 March, when a train going from Luxor to Assuit was intercepted and nine British soldiers were cruelly beaten to death by mobs urged on by Egyptian soldiers and 'maniacal' women 'lu-luing'.[41] Bulfin, who was acting supreme commander, heard the first reports of unrest on the 14th at Ramlah and immediately set off for Cairo. His train was stopped outside Minah al Qamh, where a mob of 3,000 people armed with hatchets, sticks and stones were trying to fire the station. They were dispersed after a minute's rapid fire by a dismounted Australian unit which killed at least fifty.[42] Bulfin, shaken by what he had seen, continued his journey by motor with an armoured-car escort, reaching Cairo on the 16th.

Urgent reports from across the country told of blocked rail lines, riots and arson, all part of the Wafd's plan to make Egypt ungovernable and hinder the movement of food, which in turn would provoke further disorders in Cairo. Bulfin decided that swift and condign measures were needed. In grim vein he warned the Egyptian Sultan, Fuad (he took the title King in 1923), that 'no repression could be effective which was not of the severest'.[43] The general kept his word; eighteen well-armed mobile columns, backed by a hundred aircraft, were ordered into the disaffected districts to restore communications, rescue isolated Europeans, hunt down agitators, chastise rioters and uncover hidden arms.[44] Martial law was to be enforced with the utmost rigour. Officers were given summary powers of justice which allowed them to sentence offenders to up to six months in gaol or twenty lashes. On his arrival, Allenby approved all that Bulfin had done.

No time was wasted in executing Bulfin's orders. Although nowadays forgotten, the four-week suppression of the Egyptian uprising matched in ferocity the campaigns of the Indian Mutiny. For the first time aircraft were widely used as instruments of coercion and crowds attacking railways were bombed and machine-gunned.[45] Despite an official order that 'For the Egyptian the cane must be regarded as a more suitable weapon than the rifle', embattled troops frequently opened fire. There was much relish for the work, especially among Australians, who like the rest of the Army had been enraged by the murders of servicemen; there was also a widespread feeling that the chance had come to get back at dishonest tradesmen and punish a race that was universally despised.[46]

Plenty of rough treatment was handed out, particularly during the cordons and searches of villages. The Wafd later produced a catalogue of alleged atrocities, including murder, rape, robbery, and assault, which was circulated during the Paris Peace Conference. Just how much of this was propaganda is difficult to say, but the official British refutation included a note that a major had been reprimanded for a 'lamentable lack of judgement' when, at Naslat Slobek on 30 March, he shot five suspects without a court martial.[47] To restrain the trigger-happy, every eleventh round was officially removed from machine-gun belts to prevent spraying mobs with fire. There was also evidence that in at least one case suspected agitators were flogged to extract confessions.[48]

Allenby believed that his appearance in Cairo would have a 'calming effect' on the Egyptians, while an embattled Cheetham hoped that the new High Commissioner's 'vigorous language and action' would bring them down to earth with a bump.[49] So too did Curzon, who feared that Allenby might be 'too fierce'.[50] Both were mistaken – there was no spectacular display of bullishness from Allenby. In the few days after his arrival in the Residency, he invited Egyptians of all political persuasions, including wafdists, to talk with him. He listened also to the views of Clayton, who favoured some conciliatory gesture towards public opinion, and Bulfin, who was worried about the mood of his men and whether there were enough of them to break the rebellion.[51]

Reports reaching Allenby's desk indicated that Bulfin's measures were working and that order would eventually be restored. But could it be maintained for long? The Wafd had shown that it could command an overwhelming following among Egyptians, and even moderate politicians advised Allenby that he would be wise to release its leaders.[52] He was also aware that since 23 March, when demobilisation had been frozen, there had been a revival of grumbling among his soldiers. A report on morale, presented on 31 March and compiled by military censors from soldiers' letters, indicated a delicate balance between 'bitter disappointment' about the halt to demobilisation and a 'cheerful and sensible spirit'. Much anger was channelled towards the Egyptians, and a 'John Bull' spirit was abroad.[53] At the same time there was a powerful urge to get home: a junior officer wrote, ominously, 'I'll be here for years yet. I'm just about ready to mutiny.'

The only way out of Allenby's difficulties, both political and military, was a concession that would placate the Egyptians. On 31 March he cabled the Foreign Office asking permission to release Zaghlul and the wafdist exiles. Curzon was horrified and, in alliance with Wingate, objected strenuously to what he regarded as an act of weakness that would damage British prestige. His protests were overruled by Balfour, Bonar Law and Lloyd George, whom Allenby approached directly on 5 March.[54]

Two days later, and with the Prime Minister's backing, Allenby announced the return of the wafdist leadership and the British government's willingness to allow them to visit Paris. Soon after he stated that Britain would go further and send a mission to Egypt, headed by Lord Milner, to collect information about local opinion.

Allenby's declarations were greeted with general rejoicing by Egyptians, and with dismay by Europeans who shared Curzon's view that they represented an abject surrender to mob violence. The Army took the news very badly, feeling that its efforts had been dissipated. 'Demonstrations of exultation' by flag-waving crowds in front of the Alexandria Hotel in Cairo incensed some British and Australian soldiers. 'For the vindication of British prestige, as the Higher Authorities appear unwilling to do anything in the matter', they decided to take independent action and attacked the crowd, killing six.[55] In another incident in Cairo, British and Egyptian troops exchanged fire and a military policeman who rashly intervened was wounded in the buttock.[56] Egyptian effendis in the Rameses Club watched with horror as what they described as 'a peaceful demonstration of joy' was ambushed by soldiers, who hurled café furniture at the marchers.[57] In southern Egypt, where Major-General Hubert Huddlestone's forces were still trying to keep the lid on the unrest, the feeling was that Allenby's proclamation had added to their difficulties. Chauvel was astonished by what he considered a pusillanimous gesture, and believed that Allenby had afterwards regretted it.[58]

And yet, as Allenby expected, his conciliatory moves secured a breathing-space. He needed to get the government of Egypt running, and on 9 April he persuaded Rushdi to become Prime Minister. He resigned on 20 April and the country suffered a second, less severe spasm of disorders with an attempted general strike. It was now clear that the Wafd wished to make Egypt ungovernable and Allenby took rigorous measures against the strikers, who were taking wafdist subsidies, and threatened to sack civil servants who failed to turn up to their offices. Coercion worked, and on 1 May he reported to the War Office that the country was relatively tranquil, although isolated attacks on soldiers continued.[59]

While Allenby was consolidating his position and breaking the strikes, a major mutiny occurred among army technical units at al Qantara. The outbreak occurred on 20 April, in circumstances outlined by Allenby in a letter to Wilson:

> I'm sorry to say that some 3,000 men at the Demobilisation Camp at Kantara have refused to allow men to come as helpers on the [Egyptian] railways. I am working the railways by military personnel and had formed some railway companies for Kantara. Some trade union microbe has got into them; and they are obstinate, though polite, in their refusal. I can't shoot them all for mutiny: so I must carry on as best I can, and I must resume demobilisation. I have wired Troopers [the War Office]; and I hope that you will hasten my promised reinforcements. However the real reason is homesickness, and distrust of the War Office and their promises.[60]

The 'trade union microbe' infected men at the al Qantara base for seven days, during which they refused the orders of their officers and NCOs, but maintained the externals of military discipline such as posting guards. Yeomanrymen, who tended to be from rural or middle-class backgrounds, gunners and Indian troops, whose demobilisation had been halted on 4 April, refused to join in.[61] As Allenby guessed, the urge to get home quickly proved a stronger motive than a reluctance to act as blackleg labour on the Egyptian railways, although an appeal to break a strike may have aroused the passions of men who had been militant trade unionists before the war. Some may have had memories of how, during 1911 and 1912, troops had been extensively deployed during a series of mining, railway and dock strikes in Britain.

All that Allenby could do was to ask the men to show patience, accelerate the process of demobilisation, and pester the government for reinforcements. The alternative, as he warned Wilson, was a massive mutiny which would have made it impossible for him to hold down Egypt. Not that the soldiers were unwilling to undertake policing duties. Quite the contrary – one corporal spoke for many when he complained to a British diplomat:

> What we all want is to go home. We are all due to be demobilised now, and if we are kept other men will get our jobs. If we are allowed to shoot hard for ten minutes we should kill a few thousand gippos and the whole thing would be over. We have had plenty of provocation, and a lot of us have been caught alone unarmed and killed. So that's what we would like to do. But General Allenby has been around to all the barracks and has asked us to go slow and kill as few as possible.[62]

Despite such robust, if brutal, patriotism among his men, Allenby remained uneasy about their humour. 'Owing to the present temper of the troops,' he told the War Office on 4 May, 'I expect serious trouble to ensue very shortly.'[63] It followed a week later with more strikes by troops at al Qantara, Ramlah and Haifa.[64] Again the main sources of contention were the slowness of demobilisation and a general ennui; older men with families and businesses were naturally anxious to restart their lives, and younger men feared that they would be last in the queue when it came to jobs.[65]

Allenby understood and sympathised, although there were fears that agitators, possibly Bolshevik inspired, were spreading trouble.[66] Certainly during the April strike there had been an attempt to form soldiers' committees and negotiate through delegates, procedures which aroused fears of Russian-style soviets.[67] Among the mechanics, craftsmen, drivers and metal-workers who manned the Army's workshops and transport services there were men who had done similar jobs before the war, and who believed that they still enjoyed their former rights as trade union members. For the Army, collective bargaining was quite simply mutiny, which was the most serious of military crimes, punishable by death. Allenby wisely did not take a rigid, legalistic view; the strikes during April and May were handled by subordinate officers who were under orders to tread softly and do whatever they could to satisfy the men's demands. Demobilisation was speeded up, and some units were given lectures which explained the Egyptian crisis and the reasons why some men had to remain under arms until the peace treaties were signed.[68]

Haig, after similar disorders among his forces in northern France in January, blamed 'Bolshevist agitators' and was keen to shoot down riotous troops and execute their leaders, indulgences denied him by Churchill, who was now the Secretary of State for War and for Air. Allenby, always looking over his shoulder to what was happening in Egypt, could not afford to be so strict. His approach had to be propitiatory and temperate although, after the mid-May demonstrations, he showed signs of coming to the end of his tether. There were, he told Wilson, large numbers of men who had volunteered in 1914 and 1915 among the protesters who had they been called upon to serve in France would have been dead by now, 'but they take no comfort in that consideration'.[69] Notwithstanding his views of the men's refusal to recognise their good fortune and his apprehension about the general situation in the Middle East, Allenby reactivated the demobilisation process, and during June 26,000 men were discharged.

By May 1919, Allenby was losing men when he most needed them. Egyptian unrest was still simmering, although he believed that the extension of martial law and the promise of a commission would prevent disturbances on the scale seen during March and April. But these had subsided when the Arab problem resurfaced in a new and threatening form. Allenby had to resort to a combination of stick and carrot in order to buy time and keep what he knew to be a brittle peace.

Faisal had returned from Paris at the end of April, empty-handed but optimistic. The big powers had agreed to postpone a decision on Syria until local opinion had been investigated by the three-man Crane-King Commission, at the instructions of the Peace Conference, which, Faisal wrongly believed, was empowered to settle the region's future. In the meantime he had to woo local nationalists, many of whom wanted an immediate declaration of independence even if this led to war with France. On 9 May, in Damascus, Faisal rallied an assembly of Lebanese, Syrians, Palestinians, Beduin, and Druze with a speech in which he presented the Crane-King Commission as a lifeline that would save them from the clutches of France. He ended on a defiant note: 'It now remains for you to choose to be either slaves or masters of your own destiny.'[70] This was more than bluster; Military Intelligence was uncovering evidence that his agents were secretly putting out feelers towards Egyptian nationalists for a common front.[71]

A widespread nationalist upsurge across the Middle East was something Allenby had already predicted, and he knew that he lacked the means to contain it. All that he could do was use his personal influence and confront Faisal face to face. He hurried to Damascus, and arrived on 12 May to an exuberant reception.

There was a great demonstration in my honour – which practically took the form of a mass meeting. The streets were filled with processions of all sorts, bands and flags, troops and civilians, pell-mell, yelling and singing. Hundreds of the lower class population were around with naked swords, knives and sticks which they brandished round my car, in the wildest way, but in perfect friendliness. My wife was with me, and thoroughly enjoyed the experience. The least hint from Faisal would turn all this mob the other way.

That evening the Allenbys witnessed another display of Faisal's authority. They dined with him and in the company of tribal sheiks from Syria and the Trans-Jordan. Afterwards, Allenby wondered whether his arrival had forestalled a *coup d'état* in which Faisal would have proclaimed a free, independent Syria.[72] During their conversations, Faisal remarked that in Paris Lawrence had passed on President Wilson's advice that the Arabs should follow the example of America in 1776 – 'if you want independence recruit soldiers and be strong'. To this end, Faisal asked permission to raise the Arab Army to 14,000 men, with an additional 6,000 gendarmes for police duties. Allenby refused, and observed in passing that he could not believe that Wilson had been so irresponsible.[73] He urged Faisal to show restraint and wait until the Crane-King Commission had completed its deliberations. Like the prince, Allenby believed that it was coming to arrange a settlement rather than listen to local opinion.

Allenby possessed one, hidden, power over Faisal. The Foreign Office paid him a monthly subsidy of £20,000 (which continued until February 1920), and some of this money was redistributed among the tribal sheiks as the price of their loyalty.[74] In the last resort, Faisal might be bridled by threats to withdraw his allowance, but Allenby knew him to be a man of high principle and responsive to Britain's wishes only so long as they accorded with his own desire to be free of French control.

On this matter, Allenby had to be circumspect. He was aware that plans were already in hand for the evacuation of all British forces to a line between Haifa and Dera, rumours of which were soon circulating in Beirut.[75] These buzzes aroused fears that the French would step in once the British had gone and, on 20 May, a nervous Faisal pleaded for a British or United States mandate in Syria. 'Mandate' was the word the peacemakers in Paris had chosen to signify the supervision of one nation's affairs by another. It masked what was more or less old-fashioned colonial control, as one French politician made clear when he assured Faisal that

France's hand would rest as lightly on the Syrians as it did on the Tunisians and Moroccans.

There was little that Allenby or his staff could do to scotch the rumours that continued to unsettle the Syrian and Palestinian Arabs, and he lacked the official authority to deny that they would at some time he delivered into French hands. At the end of May, Beirut gossip alleged that a massive French army would land shortly and that the Crane-King Commission would never appear.[76] Allenby responded with a stern telegram which ordered Faisal to 'maintain order and discipline and to restrain any action that might endanger the future of your country'.[77] On the next day, 31 May, he wired Balfour and Sir Henry Wilson with a reiteration of the warning he had delivered in Paris, to the effect that unless Faisal got adequate reassurances about the Arabs' future, he would resort to war. All of Syria and Palestine would join him, the 'warlike Beduin' would harry British lines of communications, and the trouble would spill over into Egypt.[78] Insurgency on such a scale would be beyond the power of his forces to contain, let alone suppress. This was perhaps over-pessimistic; although short of men, Allenby possessed a formidable air force, including a squadron of Handley-Page bombers that had been flown out to Egypt in February in expectation of local unrest.[79]

Unleashing air power against the Arabs would have been a drastic step, although some months later Allenby revealed that he was willing to use the aerial deterrent to suppress 'internal disturbances' in Palestine.[80] In the event, force was not needed, for the commissioners disembarked at Jaffa on 10 June and began to collect information for their report. The summer passed without incident, and at the end of August Allenby was summoned home to consult with Lloyd George, to receive the honours given him by his country, and to enjoy a month's leave.

CHAPTER 15

SHIFTING SANDS

SEPTEMBER 1919–MARCH 1922

ALLENBY was given a homecoming fit for a victorious general, and the equal of those arranged for Haig and Admiral Beatty. As he stepped ashore at Dover on 16 September, he was greeted by cheering crowds, a party of senior officers including Haig, and a dismounted guard of honour from the 5th Lancers, spurred and holding pennoned lances. From Victoria Station he and Lady Allenby were driven in an open car through the streets of London, to further public acclamation, before travelling to Felixstowe to visit his mother, then aged eighty-two.

On 7 October, the Allenbys arrived, with two minutes to spare, at London's Guildhall as a military band played 'See the Conquering Hero Comes'. Inside, and in the presence of Lloyd George and Faisal, Allenby was presented with a jewelled sword of honour and the Freedom of the City of London, dignities that had also been accorded to Haig and Beatty. In his address, the city's Chamberlain praised Allenby as 'the latest and greatest of the Crusaders', no doubt reminding his listeners of the current entertainment *With Allenby in Palestine* which was being performed to huge audiences at the Royal Opera House. The general answered this civic encomium with humour and modesty. He began with a minor correction, remarking that he had never been 'lured' from the Indian Civil Service to the Army, but had failed the exam for one and passed that for the other. Turning to his campaigns, he praised the exertions of his men,

197

singling out Shea and Bulfin, and in honour of his hosts and Faisal, he commended the 60th London Division and the Arabs.

In keeping with precedents that stretched back to Marlborough, he had been ennobled as Viscount Allenby of Megiddo and Felixstowe, promoted Field-Marshal and voted £50,000 by Parliament. On the scale of rewards he stood just below Haig (an earldom and £100,000), equal with French (Earl of Ypres and £50,000), and above Byng, Rawlinson and Plumer, all of whom received baronies. Gough, unstuck in March 1918 after the Fifth Army had recoiled before the German attack, got nothing. Allenby chose 'Megiddo' as part of his title since its capture marked, he believed, the turning-point of his final offensive. (There were whimsical suggestions from colleagues that another Biblical location, Bashan, might have been more appropriate, since it was famed for its fierce bulls.) He also received a cascade of freedoms from London livery companies, honorary degrees and foreign decorations. Among these splendid trinkets were the Rumanian Order of St Michael the Brave, the Chinese Order of the Striped Tiger and the American Distinguished Service Order.

Alongside these honours, Allenby achieved a wider public recognition. In London that August, Lowell Thomas, an American academic-turned-journalist, had opened his show *With Allenby in Palestine, including the Capture of Jerusalem and the Liberation of Holy Arabia*, a colourful extravaganza comprising Thomas's narrative, slides, moving film, and background music played by the band of the Welsh Guards. The show was an instant hit, and retitled '*With Allenby in Palestine and Lawrence in Arabia*' it transferred to the Albert Hall. The alteration to the title was a response to the tremendous interest shown in Lawrence, hitherto a virtually unknown figure. Notwithstanding Lawrence's emergence as the hero of Thomas's entertainment, Allenby achieved a glamour not enjoyed by his fellow commanders. No one would have been entranced by *With Haig at Passchendaele*, but a campaign fought for the liberation of the Holy Land ('The Last Crusade', according to Lowell Thomas) and the emancipation of its people from an oppressive tyranny was bound to appeal to the public imagination. Here was a world of near make-believe, with echoes of nursery and schoolroom tales of Richard the Lion Heart and far removed from the killing fields of France and Flanders. The casualties were, by First World War standards, trifling, and so audiences were able to enjoy what was a good adventure story without a sense of guilt or shame.

What London theatre-goers witnessed when they watched Thomas's show was the first stage of the metamorphosis of Lawrence into a national and international hero of a war in which the opportunities for old-style heroic deeds had been few. As Thomas had been quick to appreciate,

Lawrence's story was an exciting and romantic one which enthralled the public. Furthermore, Lawrence possessed exceptional attributes: like Gordon he had the ability to command, and earn the respect of, a wild race of warriors; like Sidney and Raleigh, he was soldier, scholar and writer. A young amateur, possessed of almost virginal looks, Lawrence was ideally cast to become a hero for a country mourning a lost generation of young men, and perhaps already sceptical of the heavy-jowled generals who had been set up as official heroes.

In the next six years Allenby came to be overshadowed by his famous subordinate, at least in the public consciousness. And yet his own record was outstanding. In the space of twelve months he had ejected the Turks from Palestine, the Lebanon and Syria, and had dealt the Ottoman Empire a blow from which it never recovered. He had then, by the force of his own will, managed to keep the peace in the lands he had conquered; suppressed a popular uprising in Egypt and preserved British power there; and had deflected a series of mutinies among his own men.

These were remarkable achievements, although, as he was the first to admit, the overthrow of the Ottoman Empire had not won the war in the way that Lloyd George had anticipated. Germany capitulated because her armies were facing total defeat, a fact fully understood by Allenby. In November he had written to Wilson and listed the war-winners in order of importance. First on his list came Wilson, then Lloyd George, then Clemenceau, and lastly Marshal Foch, the Allied supreme commander.[1] It must have pleased Wilson to have Haig relegated to 'also ran'.

Allenby's quartet had indeed all contributed to the defeat of Germany. The accomplishment of his own grand design of September–October 1918 was a victory for the British Empire rather than the alliance of which it was a part. On 1 November 1918 Britain enjoyed a position of unparalleled power in the Middle East. The Ottoman Empire had fallen apart and Russia, that other player in the old Middle East power game, was prostrate and rent by civil war. British armies occupied Constantinople, Palestine, Syria, the Lebanon, Cilicia and Iraq; the oil fields of Iran were within Britain's grasp, and the Red Sea and the Persian Gulf were British lakes.

But how was Britain to maintain her newly won supremacy? This was now Allenby's business: the talents he had employed to establish British paramountcy in the Middle East were to be used in its preservation. His experience in such affairs was still limited. As an emergency High Commissioner in Egypt he had temporarily pacified the country, although his clemency had dismayed the Foreign Office and hard-line Imperialists within the Cabinet. As a warrior-proconsul in Palestine, Syria and the

Lebanon he had skilfully ordered affairs without upsetting local sensibilities or imperilling British interests. His old patron, Lloyd George, thought that in Allenby he had discovered a man who could both uphold British prestige and handle local opposition firmly but realistically. On 2 October, Allenby was confirmed as permanent High Commissioner in Egypt and Wingate was dismissed. No one else with sufficient authority and experience was available for the post, and Wingate had indelibly blotted his copy-book by his vacillation towards the nationalists. Allenby felt sorry for an able man with whom he had enjoyed a close and friendly relationship in Egypt, and sympathised with his predicament. Wingate held no grudges, congratulated his successor on his appointment, and offered him valuable advice.[2]

There remained the question of whether Allenby would continue to command the Egyptian Expeditionary Force. Plainly he would have his hands full with Egypt and, given his mistrust of the French, his poor relations with Picot, and his personal liking for Faisal, he was not the ideal man to implement the new course of British policy. On 14 October he relinquished his command, which passed to General Sir Walter ('Squibbie') Congreve VC. Both men had lost their only sons in the war, and for the next few years worked easily in harness together.

In between receiving honours and making arrangements for his return to Egypt, Allenby was involved in the unfinished and distasteful business of settling the affairs of Syria. On 9 September he had paused on his journey home to France at Deauville, where Lloyd George was enjoying a working holiday. He delivered a note from Faisal, in which the amir melodramatically promised that in the now unavoidable Franco-Arab war his men would never fire on Allenby's.[3] Lloyd George ignored this, and explained that he had decided to withdraw all British forces from Syria and that Allenby would have to settle the practicalities with Foch and Clemenceau. Allenby asked that Faisal be informed, which he was, and then proceeded to make arrangements with senior French officers. He was present at Cabinet sessions on 13, 19 and 23 October in which Faisal heard that he was to be left in control of the districts of Aleppo, Damascus, Homs and Hama without British assistance. Unwavering in his hostility to France and fearful that the French would employ Catholic and Maronite collaborators to provoke a border incident and invade his state, Faisal remained adamant.[4] He refused to make terms with France and, on 15 October, a worried Allenby reported to Wingate, 'In Syria the danger lies. Faisal still here and unconciliatory.'[5]

The outcome was much as Faisal had predicted and Allenby had feared. By July 1920 Faisal, caught between the French and his own nationalists, chose the latter and declared independence. The French invaded with overwhelming force, ruthlessly crushed all resistance and within a week had occupied Damascus, forcing Faisal to flee into British Palestine. The war had not, as Allenby had imagined it might, encompassed the whole region, although in May, when the crisis began, the British had promised the French aerial assistance.[6]

Allenby returned to the High Commission in Cairo at the end of October 1919. For the next two and a half years he was the servant of a coalition government that had been elected at the end of 1918 and rested on an alliance of Conservatives and Lloyd George Liberals. Allenby was directly answerable to Lord Curzon, a former Viceroy of India who assumed full responsibility at the Foreign Office on 24 October. Aristocratic birth and intellectual attainments made Curzon an aloof, autocratic figure with a reputation for pomposity which he sometimes deliberately embellished. An Imperial visionary, he saw India as the keystone of the Empire and had inherited the mid-Victorian obsession with its security.

The Suez Canal was vital for Indian security, and for the Canal to be safe Egypt had to be firmly under Britain's thumb. A general whose temperament and bearing had earned him the nickname 'the Bull' had seemed eminently suitable to keep the Egyptians docile, but Allenby had shown leniency, which disappointed Curzon. The relationship between Foreign Secretary and High Commissioner remained prickly.

The maintenance of British authority in Egypt was part of a larger grand strategy which aimed to consolidate British power throughout the Middle East. As it evolved between 1919 and 1922, the coalition's policy in this region was directed towards the creation of a network of client governments, armed and financially supported by Britain. The costs of direct rule were unbearable for a country already burdened with war debts and, from 1921, facing a serious recession. At the same time, the coalition was determined to exclude disruptive Pan-Islamic and Bolshevik influences from the region. Turkey was seen as the powerhouse of Pan-Islamic agitation and so British forces occupied Constantinople; in addition, since May the government had encouraged Greece and Italy to invade and occupy large areas of western Turkey. The flow of Bolshevism was stemmed by British detachments at Batum in southern Russia and in northern Persia, and by a squadron of warships in the Black Sea.

Alongside these commitments, troops were needed to man the army of occupation in the Rhineland, stiffen anti-Bolshevists in North Russia, and police Ireland, where a full-scale terrorist campaign by nationalists was under way by the end of the year. Further troops were required to crush unrest in northern India and to repel an Afghan invasion in March.

As Allenby had found when he pleaded with Sir Henry Wilson for men to replace mutinous units in Egypt, British manpower was stretched to its limits. Problems in finding enough British and Indian troops to cover all trouble-spots was one of the reasons behind the withdrawal from Syria, which began in November 1919.

Signs of strain continued to be evident and grandiose policies had to be abandoned, often with embarrassing alacrity. While Allenby was in London, British troops were returning from North Russia, and elsewhere policies of bluff and bluster came unstuck. Challenged by the Bolsheviks on the Caspian, the British retired, as they did in 1921 from northern Persia. There was more desperate back-pedalling in Turkey, where Kemal Atatürk had rallied the nationalists and, during 1921–2, successively expelled the Greeks and Italians from Asia Minor and the French from Cilicia. After some huffing and puffing – from Churchill in particular – the British pulled out from Turkey as well in September 1922, when it became clear that the public was weary of futile foreign adventures in the name of abstract Imperial interests.

While the coalition shored up the façade of British power in the Middle East, Allenby had to contend with a new type of threat: indigenous nationalism. The Egyptian revolt of 1919 was one of three simultaneous challenges to traditional Imperial authority. Like their counterparts in India and Ireland, the Egyptian nationalists wanted to sever Imperial ties and manage their own internal and external affairs free of supervision. The leaders of these movements, Zaghlul in Egypt, Éamon de Valera in Ireland, and Mohandas Gandhi in India, presented the Empire's rulers with a phenomenon that had not been experienced since the American Revolution. Each claimed to represent the popular will, was backed by a well-organised political machine, was willing to court international sympathy and, in the cases of Zaghlul and de Valera, were ready to make their countries ungovernable by violent mass demonstrations and terrorism.

Each nationalist party was deeply interested in the others' progress and activities. The wafdists closely followed events in Ireland, particularly during 1921 when the Southern Irish nationalists were negotiating with the British government. Soon after the signing of the Anglo-Irish Treaty in December 1921, Zaghlul was exploring the possibility of contacts with Sinn Féin, either in Ireland or America, according to a Military Intelligence report delivered to Allenby.[7] Similarly, Indians studied developments in Egypt and were especially interested in the concessions that had been granted after the uprising in March 1919. Not surprisingly, the British government imagined that the three nationalist movements were related, and hardliners like Churchill repeatedly argued that any form of indulgence shown to one would encourage the rest.

British Intelligence agencies were naturally extremely concerned to discover how far these independence movements were interconnected. There were suspicions that the Russian government, which had publicly declared its support for all anti-colonialist insurgents in December 1917, was the sinister co-ordinating force behind the unrest in Egypt, Ireland and India as well as industrial unrest inside Britain. During April 1919 Allenby thought that the campaign of strikes in Egypt had the 'smell of Bolshevism' which also, in his view, tainted the simultaneous industrial disturbances in northern England.[8] Secret Service attempts to uncover the hand of Bolshevism in Egypt failed to come up with anything very convincing, however.[9] Nevertheless, in March 1920 the High Commission thought it prudent to send selected police officers to England for training in 'anti-Bolshevist' methods, which presumably involved the surveillance and penetration of trade unions.[10] Efforts were also undertaken to detect connections between Kemal Atatürk and the Wafd; these revealed the presence of three Kemalist agents at the al Azhar University early in 1923.[11]

The quest for evidence of global, anti-British conspiracies was a peculiar feature of the immediate post-war years. It was most vividly reflected in the thrillers of John Buchan and 'Sapper', and had its most sinister side in the speculation about the *Protocols of the Elders of Zion* and the existence of a vast, underground, and probably related Bolshevik conspiracy aimed at Britain and its empire. Only hidden forces directed by a network of agents could explain the sudden, violent assault on British rule in Egypt, Ireland and India.

Allenby never completely succumbed to the paranoiac view of anti-British nationalism. Not long after his return to Cairo, he told Meinertzhagen that the disintegration of the Empire was inevitable as more and more of its subjects became educated. And yet he doubted whether the new educated élites possessed sufficient 'responsibility, integrity and leadership' to manage their countries' affairs.[12] This judgement was based on his experience of Egypt where, as his position demanded, he was willing to stand back and allow the Egyptians to get on with the day-to-day business of government.[13] This policy of non-interference was difficult to follow because, since the declaration of the Protectorate in 1914, British advisers had become involved in more and more aspects of Egypt's administration.

Inside Egypt, Allenby's *laissez-faire* approach soon prompted angry criticism from members of the European community there, who yearned for the pre-war days when men of the stamp of Kitchener and his predecessor, Lord Cromer, had brought the Egyptians to heel with a sharp pull of the leash. This had been done, with Allenby's approval, in

March and April 1919, but the results had been temporary. After General Shea's tour of the recently pacified Luxor on 15 April it was observed that 'the attitude of the native population was submissive but undemonstrative. It is apparent that their present attitude is only the result of "force majeure".'[14] Allenby was never frightened of applying *force majeure* when all else had failed or when European lives and property were in danger, but he understood it could never provide a permanent basis for the security of the Suez Canal and its garrison. Ultimately this could only rest upon the foundation of a new Anglo-Egyptian accord that would take account of Egyptian pride and aspirations.

On his return to Cairo at the beginning of November 1919, Allenby was confronted with a fresh wave of popular tumults masterminded by the Wafd and aimed at disrupting the investigations of the Milner Commission, which was due in December. He feared they were a prelude to a second mass uprising and so, making full use of martial law, he took immediate preventive measures. Newspapers were banned or censored, curfews imposed, cafés closed, and suspected agitators detained, including members of the Wafd Central Committee. Another fountainhead of propaganda, the al Azhar University, was briefly occupied by British troops, which drew protests of sacrilege from its *ulamas* (religious teachers). Allenby responded on 17 December with an ultimatum to Sultan Fuad that demanded he publicly rebuke the university staff for their political activities.[15]

A new and disturbing feature of the Wafd's activities was a campaign of political murder against ministers, functionaries and off-duty British servicemen. The assassins, usually students, operated in cells (with such melodramatic names as the 'Black Revolver Gang') which were difficult for the police to penetrate. When terrorists were arrested it was hard to secure convictions because of intimidation of witnesses; those informers who did testify had to be well paid and, when the trials were over, shipped abroad with new identities.[16] Success against these gangs was therefore limited, and executions inevitably sparked off riots. In July 1920 Allenby pardoned Rahman Fahmi, a demagogue and Central Committee member who, with twenty-eight others, had been found guilty of complicity in political murders, for fear of unrest, a gesture that infuriated Europeans.[17]

During December 1919 Intelligence sources in Rome uncovered details of a plot to assassinate Allenby and Milner involving Egyptian nationalists, Italian socialists, and a trio of former Turkish intelligence operatives, all well-known to the Secret Service. They were Osman Haidar, a 'notorious spy' identifiable by a 'large aquiline nose, small black piercing eyes, one of which damaged'; Haji Sami, who had undertaken Pan-Islamic subversion missions on the North-West Frontier of India; and his brother Ashraf Bey, whose career included undercover anti-British activities in pre-war Egypt and later on the North-West Frontier. The three, who seem also to have been planning a Beduin revolt in Egypt to coincide with the assassinations, could easily have stepped from some contemporary thriller. They were real enough, however, and their past records demanded immediate action by MI Ic (now MI6), which sent an agent to Italy. In the meantime, it was discovered that Haji Sami was in Shanghai and Ashraf in a POW camp in Malta, which strongly suggested that the conspiracy was the invention of an unknown but imaginative informer who was perhaps short of cash.[18]

What made British Intelligence take this tale seriously was the knowledge that the Wafd leadership was determined to frustrate the Milner mission, which arrived on 7 December and was greeted by a spasm of demonstrations. Milner suddenly discovered that the High Commission's accounts of wafdist violence had not been exaggerated; he and his four colleagues were all but barricaded inside the Semiramis Hotel in Cairo, and many Egyptians were too terrified of intimidation and vilification to come forward and meet him.[19] His hope, like Allenby's, was to use the Commission as a wedge with which to separate the rabble-rousers from the moderate politicians who were ready to temper their nationalism with a consideration for British interests. Such creatures existed, but they ran the risk of being condemned as collaborators and of becoming the targets for terrorist guns and bombs.

Milner had been ordered to Egypt solely to diagnose its problems, but once he had made himself familiar with the symptoms, he felt convinced that he could produce a cure. Allenby, who had always been apprehensive about the Commission's effect on public opinion, decided it was best for him to distance himself from its activities so as not to undermine its independence. His contacts with Milner were few, and on 5 January 1920 he left Cairo for a six-week tour of the Sudan and a brief visit to the Hijaz, where King Hussain was getting out of hand. The king gave Allenby a fulsome welcome, offering to 'kiss him on his intelligent forehead', but was unreceptive to official requests that he settle his disputes with Ibn Saud and refrain from meddling in his son Faisal's affairs in Syria. Two years later, and utterly disillusioned with his old ally, he was sponsoring anti-British propaganda in the Sudan.[20]

Back in Cairo on 27 February, Allenby had a candid exchange with Milner. They were both of the same generation and Milner had, throughout a long career of Imperial service, followed the belief that the British Empire was essentially a benevolent, civilising force. What he had witnessed in post-First World War Egypt was a mass rejection of this ideal and of the empire behind it, which he found disturbing. Somehow, he had to return home and devise a formula which pacified the country, allowed a measure of self-determination, but did not harm British strategic interests. Allenby concurred; he had initially been embarrassed by the timing of the mission, which had forced him to dilute his policy of repression. He confessed to Milner that he had been 'rather reluctant' to release detainees for consultation with Milner since, as he knew to his cost, previous gestures of clemency had been interpreted as weakness.[21]

Milner left Egypt on 28 February 1920 and, after a short tour of another trouble spot, Palestine, set off for England. By mid-May he had finished his report, a radical document which proposed the transformation of Egypt into an Imperial hybrid, neither colony, protectorate nor dominion, but a satellite with a permanent garrison. Internal affairs would be under local control, the influence of British advisers would be severely reduced, and there would be limited supervision of Egyptian foreign policy. In June, with Curzon's and Allenby's approval, Zaghlul was invited to London to discuss Milner's proposals. The exchanges lasted until August when an agreement was reached. The protectorate would cease, and Egypt would be recognised as an independent monarchy in alliance with Britain, which would retain a veto over Egyptian foreign policy. In accordance with the wishes of Allenby and Congreve, British forces would remain in Alexandria and Cairo, from where they could protect the Sweet Water Canal, which was the Canal Zone's source of drinking water.[22]

Allenby had hoped that the agreement would be passed quickly to the Cabinet for approval. In the meantime, and much to his annoyance, copies of the document were leaked to and published in the Egyptian press, which was able to announce that the protectorate might soon be ended. Hopes raised by this news were soon shattered by the intransigence of a knot of ministers, headed by Churchill. When the Cabinet reviewed the Milner–Zaghlul agreement on 1 November, Churchill, the Secretary for War, attacked it with characteristic vigour. In his mind, it added up to a surrender of Imperial power in a strategically vital region, while the slackening of Imperial bonds would give heart to Irish and Indian nationalists. Churchill's views swayed the Cabinet, and the Milner–Zaghlul agreement was dropped. Curzon, despite his unease about bargaining with extemists, still hoped to salvage something from Milner's labours. His way out of the impasse was to reopen negotiations but with moderate – that is, non-wafdist – Egyptian politicians who might prove more tractable than Zaghlul.

Allenby, who had favoured the Milner–Zaghlul agreement, reluctantly concurred. In private, his views ran far ahead of the Cabinet's; he shared Milner's opinion that the unworkable protectorate would have to be jettisoned, the sooner the better, and replaced by an alliance. But the word 'alliance' suggested a partnership between equals, and when Allenby used it in a draft announcement of the new negotiations Curzon had it replaced by 'relationship'.[23]

Inside Egypt, the news of the new talks was seen as a challenge by the Wafd, which threw all its resources into a struggle to discredit the politicians who had agreed to go to London. During March, a new ministry had been formed, under a moderate, Yakan Adli, and including a single wafdist, Ismail Sidqi, who had been exiled in 1919. Adli was also chosen by Sultan Fuad, at Allenby's prompting, to lead the delegation in London for the new talks. If he returned with favourable terms, the Wafd would be upstaged and its popular credibility undermined. Zaghlul, who had been taking the waters at Vichy, was determined to prevent this, and returned to Cairo on 4 April to challenge Adli.

During the next few weeks the Wafd launched a new campaign of disruption along the now familiar pattern. 'Bootblacks, out-of-work Berberin and riff-raff armed with sticks, stones and broken bottles filled with sand' assembled on the Cairo streets, were whipped into a fury by Wafd-paid student agitators, and bawled slogans outside ministers' houses.[24] The worst trouble occurred in Alexandria where, according to Clayton, Zaghlul's arrival sparked off 'uncontrolled frenzy and fanaticism' which led to several days of rioting, murder, looting and arson.[25] As so often, the trigger for the unrest was the Friday preaching in the mosques which, on 20 May, was followed by attacks on police stations and the burning of the Customs House by a mob estimated at 5,000. The police and a detachment of Egyptian cavalry had been ordered to show restraint, but, rather than risk being overwhelmed, some units opened fire.

The corpses of dead rioters were taken from mortuaries for vast public funerals, which kept tension high. On 21–22 May the mob's rage shifted towards the European quarter, particularly Greek and Italian shopkeepers, whose persons and property were attacked and plundered. These outrages were religiously and racially motived; some of the rioters carried portraits of Kemal Atatürk, whose forces were currently driving Greek and Italian armies out of Asia Minor. Any breakdown in law and order, however brief, was an opportunity for criminal elements, and so pimps, prostitutes and roughs joined in the attacks on Europeans.

During the early stages of the disorders, Allenby had hoped that they would be contained by Egyptian police and soldiers. Clayton, who was on the spot, soon concluded this was impossible, since some Egyptian soldiers had already joined the rioters. During the afternoon of 20 May and on the advice of Clayton, Allenby sanctioned the use of British armoured cars, which were later followed by troops. During the next few days British forces moved through the city and restored order, joined by landing parties from the cruiser HMS *Calypso* which had arrived on the 25th. The European community was grateful to Allenby for action which was generally believed to have averted a massacre. His resolution was warmly applauded by Congreve, in a letter to Sir Henry Wilson which reveals racist sentiments that were common among soldiers at this time:

> Adli, compelled by riots in Alexandria and propped up by Allenby, flourished the big stick and down dropped Zaghlul flat, so once more [it] is proved that the only thing an Oriental respects is force and very little of it suffices. When you talk politics to an Eastern you may be sure you will get the worst of it, kick him and he loves and respects you.[26]

Zaghlul unconvincingly attempted to distance himself from these disorders. Allenby issued an appeal for calm on 25 May in which he stated that his government was ready to discuss the termination of the protectorate and Egypt's future unfettered by any pre-conditions. This was wishful thinking; the London negotiations between Adli's delegation and the Foreign Office dragged on until November and ended in deadlock. When Adli returned to Cairo, he was cold-shouldered by the upper classes and spat upon and pelted with mud and tomatoes by the mob. On 2 December he resigned.

Allenby was in an impossible predicament. When he had been called to London the previous October, he had bluntly informed the Cabinet that further procrastination would diminish British prestige. He had also predicted that he would be able to maintain order if they came to an unpopular decision.[27] This was indeed possible in the short-term but now, thanks to an adamantine British government, he faced the prospect of coercing Egypt for an unlimited period. This was the solution offered by those rigid Imperialists who had not seriously considered the practical problems involved, although events in Ireland during the past two years should have taught them something about the difficulties of ruling by main force alone. Allenby was a pragmatist first and an Imperialist second, and anyway believed that the Empire would survive a compromise in Egypt.

Once, long before, he had advised a junior officer that doing something was always preferable to doing nothing. More recently, when he encountered a subordinate who constantly complained of 'the difficulties of my position', he had observed, 'What does he mean by the difficulties of his position? I have never been in a *difficult* position in my life. I have sometimes been in an *impossible* one, and then I have got out of it as quickly as I could.'[28] He decided to apply this principle to Egypt.

First he stifled the Wafd. He imposed a gagging order on Zaghlul, which was ignored. So, at Allenby's orders a detachment of British troops appeared at the Wafd leader's Cairo house, the portentously named *Beit al Umma* (Home of the Nation), on 22 December and arrested him. He was immediately taken to Port Suez, where he was joined by several colleagues, was entertained in an officers' mess, played some golf, and was finally shipped to Aden en route for banishment to the Seychelles. British troops took control of Cairo, and all Wafd bank accounts were frozen to halt the flow of funds to agitators. The cruiser HMS *Ceres* and the gunboat HMS *Clematis* were ordered to Egyptian waters (the latter for use on the Nile) and, in response to Allenby's request, other warships of the Mediterranean Fleet were put on standby. In a few days Allenby had temporarily stunned and neutralised the Wafd, although there were some riots in Assuit and a schoolboys' strike in Cairo. Writing to Sir Henry Wilson on 24 December, he felt satisfied with the results. 'I don't expect such big trouble as we had in 1919. One the whole, the country is really glad to get rid of Said Zaghlul, schoolboys, lawyers and profession agitators.'[29]

This was perhaps a little sanguine. Soon afterwards, a gang calling itself the 'Secret Sacrificers' planned to assassinate Allenby as his car crossed the Qasr al Nil bridge but, having lain in wait, they mistook another officer for him and, realising the blunder, abandoned their mission.[30].

Having made himself master of Egypt, Allenby prepared a second coup, this against the Cabinet. He urgently needed a ministry in Egypt, since it ran counter to the terms of the protectorate and earlier treaties for the country to be governed by the High Commissioner, his staff, and British and Egyptian civil servants. He therefore asked Tharwat Pasha, a hardline anti-wafdist who had supported Zaghlul's deportation, to form a government. In return, Allenby promised a termination of the protectorate and limited Egyptian independence.

Neither were his to barter, but he gambled on the Cabinet accepting his *fait accompli* as an alternative to his resignation and to the prospect of direct military rule in Egypt for the indefinite future. There was bound to be opposition, especially from Churchill who was already bitter about Allenby's behaviour in Egypt. The depth of his rancour was revealed during a luncheon party on 24 December attended by Lawrence and Meinertzhagen. Taking Lawrence's observation that all the rumpus in Egypt was created by 'a few political hot heads', Churchill delivered a 'torrent of abuse' against the High Commissioner. 'He referred to

Allenby as a man of no principles, and as a hopelessly weak administrator,' adding for good measure that he had been a 'dud' general who had never made full use of the resources at his disposal.[31]

And yet, as Churchill probably guessed, Allenby held all the high cards. He had, somewhat surprisingly, the backing of Curzon who, although he regretted a proconsul who seemed beyond the Foreign Office's control, appreciated that Allenby was a realist offering a realistic way out of the Egyptian dilemma. Explaining his position to Curzon on 2 February 1922, Allenby argued that by 'satisfying reasonable national aspirations' which had the support of Fuad, the Cabinet would restore stability in the country and win over the moderates. British paramountcy would remain and the new Anglo-Egyptian relations would not imperil the security of the Canal.[32] The uncomfortable alternative for a government that had just been fought to a standstill in a counter-terrorist war in Southern Ireland was to wage a similar campaign in Egypt.

Moreover, public opinion was waking up to what the consequences of a stubborn policy in Egypt might be. In a letter to *The Times* on 29 December 1921 Sir Valentine Chirol, an eminent former diplomat who had recently visited Egypt, argued that it was folly to rule it as 'a conquered country'. It had been an ally during the war, and present policy was driving Egyptians into the arms of Zaghlul. This statement marked the beginning of a minor campaign on Allenby's behalf by *The Times*, whose owner, Lord Northcliffe, felt that the High Commissioner's views, based as they were on local experience, deserved attention.

Summoned home to explain himself to the Cabinet on 15 February 1922, Allenby remained firm and forthright. Backed by Clayton and Sir Sheldon Amos, an experienced official of the Egyptian judiciary, his exchanges with ministers were brusque. He reminded them of how often his advice had been ignored. 'But,' interjected Lloyd George, 'you are now asking me to abandon our entire position in Egypt without guarantee.' 'That, Sir, is not a fair description of Lord Allenby's proposals,' countered Amos, who proceeded to answer ministerial objections. Frustrated with the debate, Allenby finally lost his patience. 'Well, it is no good disputing any longer. I have told you what I think is necessary. You won't have it, and it is none of my business to force you to. I have waited five weeks for a decision, and I can't wait any longer. I shall tell Lady Allenby to come home.' Lloyd George came forward and took his arm, saying 'You have waited five weeks, Lord Allenby, wait five minutes more.' By the afternoon he had what he wanted.[33]

Allenby had staked his career on a victory and had won, despite ministerial fears that another concession to nationalism so soon after the Irish treaty would bring growls from Tory back-benchers. He had shown considerable courage in meeting the Cabinet head-on, and even greater cunning. His unilateral and, in strict terms, insubordinate intervention had forced the Cabinet to face two alternatives. It could impose a British government of Egypt underpinned by troops, aircraft and warships, or else allow the country a special status that would, Allenby believed, both safeguard strategic interests and produce public tranquillity.

This compromise, sometimes called the Allenby Declaration, was published on 28 February 1922. The protectorate was abolished and henceforward an independent Egypt managed its own internal affairs with the minimum of British supervision. The military bases remained, as did local British supremacy, and the High Commission retained a right to interfere with the framing of Egyptian foreign policy if there was any clash of interests between the two countries. Britain also enjoyed special rights in matters relating to public finance and all foreign residents.

Although Egyptian sovereignty was still restricted by these terms, the Allenby Declaration was seen by inflexible Imperialists as an abject surrender to fanaticism and mob violence. Allenby was accordingly regarded as an appeaser although, as he demonstrated during the next two and a half years, Britain still had the loudest and the last say in the affairs of Egypt.

CHAPTER 16

DEATH AND THE NILE

APRIL 1922–JUNE 1925

ALLENBY was an inexplicable and disturbing phenomenon for his political masters. He had been sent to Egypt as 'the Bull', a fearsome creature who would intimidate that country's politicians and rigorously uphold British interests. Instead, he had sought and obtained a compromise which, on the surface at least, suggested a parity between Britain and Egypt and had bullied the Cabinet into agreement. It was a reversal of the Imperial tradition that had obtained in Allenby's youth, when governments had had their work cut out to restrain aggressive warrior-proconsuls who were over-keen to expand and conquer. Of course Allenby had been careful to protect essential national interests; the airfields and the garrisons remained guarding the Canal Zone and its lifeline, the Sweet Water Canal, and were on hand to wave the cudgel in Cairo and Alexandria. And as High Commissioner he still possessed considerable powers, less obvious than they had been during the protectorate, but sufficient to keep Egypt firmly within Britain's orbit.

The art of diplomacy had not come easily to Allenby, although he remained a good listener. At first he had been suspicious of his civilian staff, whom he had once dismissed as 'weak-kneed blackcoats', but in time he came to appreciate their professionalism while they learned to work in harness with an unconventional superior.[1] High Commissioner and officials faced a new, unfamiliar world in which Britain's old right to

212

dictate the public policies of Egypt's governments was challenged by a people who, through the Wafd, were discovering a national identity and spirit of independence. In the past, Allenby had dealt with Imperial subjects with whom it was possible for someone of his background to have some form of empathy. The simple warrior Zulu, the self-reliant, tenacious Boer, the warrior Beduin and the elegant, aristocratic Faisal were all men who could be respected and admired. It was less easy to like the cultivated Egyptian effendis and landowners, who spoke French, dressed as Europeans, and argued with a lawyer's sophistry that their nation had nothing at all to gain from its connection with Britain.

In the 1920s such claims were still a novelty to the men who controlled the Empire, although they had been and were being made with great vehemence in Ireland and India. Equally new and far more repugnant were the shock troops of the nationalists, the young, educated men who stirred crowds to violence and formed shadowy and murderous terrorist gangs which killed the unarmed and unsuspecting as they walked the streets. For these creatures Allenby had only contempt.

As High Commissioner, Allenby was the leader of European society in Egypt and the guardian of its extensive rights. He held court in the British Residency, an impressive, white colonnaded building in the neo-Classical style. Its gardens ran down to the banks of the Nile and contained a tame Maribou stork which was devoted to Allenby. This charming oddity aroused much comment, especially since the bird became intensely jealous if its master was accompanied by ladies or children.

Thanks to Lady Allenby, the many luncheon and dinner parties held at the Residency were both elegant and friendly; she was, according to her husband, a 'perfect hostess'.[2] Both the Allenbys were physically fit and took regular and rigorous exercise. She rode four times around Cairo racecourse each morning, and he enjoyed swimming during the summer hot season when the Residency staff moved to Alexandria. Once, in July 1920, he swam out too far, strained his lungs and heart and broke a blood vessel. Only his stamina saved him, and he managed to get back to the shore.[3]

Now in his early sixties, Allenby was still an impressive figure with a commanding presence. His features remained sharp and strong, with an aquiline nose and piercing eyes that became animated whenever he was in a passion. It was these outward qualities reflecting an inner solidity which so impressed Lawrence: 'His mind is like the prow of the *Mauretania*. There is so much weight behind it that it does need to be sharp like a razor.'

No doubt it was this force which cut through the objections to the new

Egyptian constitution raised by Fuad. Allenby had once characterised the king as 'a weak vessel' but he had considerable difficulties in persuading him to accept a democratic element in Parliamentary elections, an element that would benefit the Wafd. He finally succeeded in January 1923.[4] By now, Allenby had come to terms with the fact that the Wafd could no longer be excluded from Egyptian political life and, in February, he began pressing the Foreign Office for permission to recall Zaghlul, who had recently been shifted to Gibraltar after fears for his health. The Foreign Office attempted to delay the decision by recalling Allenby to London for consultations, but he excused himself on the grounds that he was too busy dealing with terrorism.[5] In the end the Foreign Office caved in; Zaghlul was released on 4 April, and his comrades were also brought back from the Seychelles.

Allenby was indeed preoccupied with measures to stamp out terrorism. Between 1919 and 1924 there were forty-six incidents in which sixty people, mostly British servicemen, were murdered, and many more were wounded. Penetrating the small, Protean terrorist cells and tracking down individual assassins was always extremely difficult. The trouble was that the Egyptian public either favoured the terrorists or were apathetic, so that it was almost impossible to find witnesses even when crimes had been committed in daylight on crowded streets. In these conditions it was repeatedly noticed that no one intervened to seize the criminals. There were also suspicions that wafdists in the police and Ministry of the Interior were guilty of collusion with the gunmen, and of hindering investigations.

The answer, thought Allenby, was to make the Egyptians aware of their responsibilities and, in the spring of 1923, he suggested the imposition of collective fines on districts where incidents had occurred, and compelling the Egyptian government to pay compensation to the kinsfolk of murdered Europeans. On a practical level, he wanted whole areas to be cordoned off and combed for hidden arms.[6] All measures required the close and sympathetic co-operation of the Egyptian authorities, since in July 1923 he had replaced British martial law with Egyptian law. He was also anxious that, on the rare occasions when captured terrorists had been found guilty, the death sentence should be carried out. During the summer of 1923 he accelerated the hangings of four members of the 'Black Revolver Gang' whom he wanted 'scragged soon', that is, before Zaghlul's return, when their case might become the focus for a spate of violent agitation.[7]

Zaghlul returned from a holiday in France on 17 September 1923, and immediately began preparations for the general election which was due in February. He was the only political figure in Egypt who possessed a national following, because of his charisma, passionate oratory and an unbroken record of hostility to Britain. As Allenby later and percipiently recognised, the Egyptian's first need was always to maintain his popularity. At heart Zaghlul was a liberal conservative and his party, with its substantial middle- and upper-class backing, consistently supported the social and economic status quo. What gave it its popular appeal was its fervent nationalism, which was the cement that prevented right- and left-wing sections from breaking away.

Allenby judiciously left Egypt for a tour of the Sudan during the elections. Since the Wafd was the only political party its electoral triumph was inevitable. Wafdists gained 179 of the 211 seats in the Egyptian lower house with just under half of the popular vote. Once in power, Zaghlul, conscious of the overriding need to preserve party unity, began beating the nationalist drum and demanded total independence. The chances appeared good, for his own election victory had coincided with that of the British Labour Party, which had in the past showed itself friendly towards Egyptian nationalism.

Like many other nationalists who came after him, Zaghlul quickly discovered that, once in power, Labour quickly shed its sentimental attachment to colonial liberation movements. Heading a minority government dependent on Liberal support, the new Prime Minister, Ramsay MacDonald, was anxious to show voters that his party upheld Imperial interests with a vigour equal to that of its opponents. Zaghlul therefore heard that the questions of British bases in Egypt and the future of the Sudan were not negotiable. His discussions with MacDonald, whom he had hitherto counted an ally, ended inconclusively, and he returned to Egypt in October with nothing gained.

Since 1922, nationalist passions had been concentrated on the Sudan. It had been an Egyptian province until the Mahdi's rebellion in 1883, and was abandoned two years later. An Anglo-Egyptian army, commanded by Kitchener, reconquered the Sudan between 1896 and 1898, when it became a British and Egyptian condominium. From the start it had been an unequal partnership: senior civil servants and district commissioners were British; Egyptian Coptic Christians and Lebanese held junior posts; and the Governor-General of the Sudan, who also held the post of Commander-in-Chief (Sirdar) of the Egyptian Army, was always a British officer. This monopoly of power was justified in strategic terms, since whoever ruled the Sudan controlled Egypt's lifeline, the Nile.

For the Wafd Egypt and the Sudan were indivisible. 'The Egyptian nation will never give up the Sudan,' Zaghlul proclaimed at the end of June 1924. The British government was equally adamant, and refused even to consider discussions on the province's future. Allenby thought there might be room for bargaining, but MacDonald wanted no equivocation on the matter.[8] Inside the Sudan, the Governor-General, Sir Lee Stack, favoured a diminution of Egyptian influence and the possible detachment of the southern region, with its predominantly Negro and animist population, from the Muslim, Arab north.[9] With Allenby's backing, he hoped eventually to pull the Sudan from Egypt's orbit and strengthen links with the Empire, with Britain posing as the protector of the Sudanese against the Egyptians.

During 1923–4, the Wafd had been canvassing support in the Sudan for amalgamation with Egypt. It used the pro-Egyptian White Flag League, founded in 1920, which was reborn and provocatively renamed 'The Party of Egypt and the Sudan' in February 1924. From then on, Khartoum's Intelligence Department received a stream of reports which revealed a campaign of Wafd-inspired subversion. Egyptian Army officers and officials were holding meetings in which speakers praised Zaghlul and claimed that Egypt had rights over the entire Nile valley, statements that reduced some listeners to tears.[10] Evidence of direct wafdist involvement in such activities could not be found, but officials noticed similarities between wafdist methods of agitation and those used by anti-British elements in the Sudan; both, for instance, recruited and paid street urchins to break the windows of European-owned cafés.[11]

The first outbreaks of violence occurred on 19 June 1924 with anti-British riots in Khartoum. There were rumours of an imminent wave of assassinations and the agitation was renewed in July, spreading to Port Sudan and Atbara. Here there was a small demonstration of sympathy on 9 August following the arrest of a suspected agitator, an Egyptian employed by the Posts and Telegraphs Department. There were simultaneous demonstrations in Khartoum by cadets of the Military School, and on the following day an Egyptian Railway Battalion, stationed at Atbara, mutinied. Preventive measures were swiftly taken: British and Arab troops were rushed to Atbara where the mutineers were overcome after a brief struggle in which four were killed and sixteen wounded, while the cadets were rounded up and imprisoned on Nile gunboats.[12]

Reinforcements were hurried to the province. A battalion of the Argyll and Sutherland Highlanders was sent from Egypt; the cruiser HMS *Weymouth* was ordered to Port Sudan; and a flight of aircraft was flown to Khartoum from Egypt. The Atbara disturbances continued until 17 August, when the defiant battalion was sent back to Egypt. Four days later, fifty-four Egyptian officers protested against the repressive measures and the arrival of additional British troops.

The British response had been overwhelming, and a reminder to all concerned of what could be done in an emergency. Stack was convinced that Egyptian propaganda had been at the root of the rioting and mutinies. He also noticed an ominous, sullen defiance among the Sudanese officer cadets.[13] By 23–24 September reports were reaching Cairo of the spread of sedition among black troops and the mutiny of the 12th Sudanese Battalion at Malakal on the Upper Nile.[14] This was promptly dealt with by a company of the Leicesters, and subsequent investigation uncovered the cause as agitation by Egyptian officials and clerks.

The August emergency and the likelihood of further unrest among Sudanese forces convinced Stack and Allenby that it would be necessary to withdraw all Egyptian units from the Sudan. This decision, justifiable on purely military grounds, was, in political terms, a dramatic assertion of British control over the Sudan and a reminder to Egyptians that a British officer commanded their army. Details of the planned evacuation were leaked to the Wafd.

Zaghlul had been closely watching events in the Sudan and had strenuously denied any wafdist involvement in the disturbances there, which he blamed on the high-handedness of British officials. His party made much capital out of the shooting of the mutineers at Atbara, which was incorrectly attributed to British troops. At the same time there was a spate of Parliamentary criticism of Stack, who personified Britain's continuing grip on the Sudan and who, as Sirdar, was about to pull Egyptian troops out of that province. For Zaghlul, the crisis in the Sudan coincided with a period when his own political position was precarious. He was both the victim of King Fuad's intrigues and under pressure from extremists inside his own party, who were disappointed by his lack of success in London. He staged a theatrical resignation on 15 November which brought his followers to their senses and to his side, and returned to power the next day, publicly resolved to continue the struggle with Britain. Others were preparing to go further and strike at the man who, next to Allenby, represented British power over Egypt: Stack.

At just after 1.30 pm on 19 November, Stack was being driven from the War Ministry when his car was ambushed by a gang of terrorists, who sprayed it with twenty rounds of dum-dum bullets fired from ·32 automatic pistols at close range. They also threw a bomb, which failed to explode.[15] Chased by an Egyptian policeman, whom they wounded, the assassins ran through the passive bystanders, hailed a taxi, and escaped. All wore European-style suits and fezzes, which marked them as members of the *effendiya* class. Although wounded and in great pain, Stack's Australian driver steered the car through the crowds and reached the High Commission a few minutes later. He, Stack and Stack's injured

ADC, Captain P. K. Campbell, were carried into the building by servants whose starched white uniforms were soon bloodied.

Allenby was holding a luncheon party for guests, who included Lord Asquith, the former Prime Minister, and immediately supervised the moving of the wounded men. They were attended by Dr Madden, the High Commission doctor. Stack, who had three wounds one of which was diagnosed as dangerous, was given morphine by the doctor; Campbell and the chauffeur, although in agony, had less serious injuries. At two-thirty Zaghlul arrived at the High Commission 'waving his arms in the air' and was confronted by Allenby, who showed signs of 'considerable emotion'. He took the Egyptian by the shoulder and said, 'Come and see what you have done.' He conducted him to the wounded driver and then Campbell. Then, according to Campbell, in 'great agitation' he invited Zaghlul to see Stack, who had been joined by his wife, summoned by Lady Allenby. The suggestion brought angry protests from the High Commission staff who were nearby, and Zaghlul was ushered out.[16] 'He had every appearance of being horror-struck and seemed unable to express himself coherently,' Allenby reported soon afterwards in a cable to the Foreign Office.[17]

In the meantime Stack had been taken to the Anglo-American Hospital for a blood transfusion and an operation to remove a bullet from his abdomen. This was performed soon before midnight but he died at 11.45 pm the following day.[18]

Allenby was deeply shocked. Stack had been a close friend as well as a colleague, and his murder was both a challenge to British authority in Egypt and an affront to the whole European community. In his anger, Allenby may have recollected a similar assassination in June 1922 when another friend, Sir Henry Wilson, had been murdered outside his London house by IRA gunmen. As he made forcefully clear to Zaghlul, he was convinced that the Egyptian leader and the Wafd were responsible for the attack. Wafdist propaganda had singled out Stack, and so those who had contrived it were as guilty as the youths who had fired the shots.

The eminence of their victims demanded a severe response. The British lion had growled, sometimes roared, in Egypt during the past five years; now it was time for it to pounce. At eight in the evening of the 19th, Allenby wired the Foreign Office and announced his readiness to cow the Egyptians once and for all with 'a signal act of assertion'.[19] Three hours later he outlined the 'rigorous and immediate action' he had in mind. The government of Egypt would formally apologise for the murder; catch and punish the assassins; pay an indemnity of £250,000; allow Britain to frame its foreign policy and continue supervision of its judiciary; and cede control of the Sudan. Moreover, the Egyptians would have to accept a

British finger on their country's jugular vein, for Allenby demanded the right to divert unlimited amounts of Nile water for Sudanese irrigation schemes.[20]

A copy of this ultimatum was wired to the Foreign Office shortly before midnight on the 19th. There was now a Conservative government in Britain, which had taken power in October after the 'Zinoniev Letter' election. The new Foreign Secretary, Austen Chamberlain, was a politician of unremarkable talents but with a timeserver's knack of distancing himself from those of his decisions which proved mistaken. His first reaction to the news of the shooting had been similar to Allenby's, and when the report of Stack's death arrived he suggested that the indemnity should be quadrupled to a million pounds.[21] Allenby thought half a million was enough when he sent a slightly revised list of demands to the Foreign Office on the 21st. In sum, he believed that his demands of the Egyptian government constituted 'the sort of humiliation which is understood here'.[22] This telegram was received in London at midnight and Chamberlain promised to send details of the Cabinet's decision at 9.40 on the 22nd, about midday Cairo time.[23]

In the meantime Allenby, who thought that Zaghlul's official apology had been utterly inadequate and close to flippancy, had an audience with Fuad in an attempt to persuade him to issue a statement as titular head of the Egyptian Army. The king refused, saying 'No. My hands are tied and you bound them,' a reference to the constitution which Allenby had forced on him eighteen months earlier. Allenby replied, 'I regret that Your Majesty refuses, and I shall inform my government,' which upset the king who began to rail against Zaghlul and his ministry. 'They were a crowd of revolutionaries and cads while he (His Majesty) was a gentleman; and now I (Allenby) too, his friend was pushing him to the sacrifice.'[24] Afterwards Fuad recovered his equanimity, spoke to the hated Zaghlul, and issued the apology Allenby had requested.

Zaghlul, in his capacity as head of the Egyptian government, was present at Stack's funeral on 22 November, much to the disgust of many Europeans. It was a tense, sombre occasion and Allenby, in uniform, was noticeably distressed, standing for some time beside his friend's coffin. On his return to the High Commission he found that the telegram from Chamberlain had not arrived. He faced a dilemma, for he knew that Zaghlul intended to sidestep the ultimatum by offering his resignation to the Egyptian Parliament, which was due to convene at five in the afternoon, leaving the country without a government. Allenby faced two choices. He could play the part of a dispassionate and dutiful servant and wait for his orders from London, even though, in all likelihood, this would allow Zaghlul to outwit him and outmanoeuvre the British government.

On the other hand, he could, as he had done in the past, go ahead and do what he thought was right without the approval of his masters. There was a good case for such a course of action, but for Allenby passion rather than reason was his guide. The funeral had rekindled the emotions he had felt the day that Stack had been brought to the High Commission. Then, his instinct had told him that the words and actions of Zaghlul lay behind Stack's murder, and many others. He would not let Zaghlul avoid that responsibility.

At a quarter to five, Allenby was driven to Zaghlul's house with an impressive escort of the 16th/5th Lancers. He was dressed casually in a lounge suit and felt hat as a gesture of contempt: upper-class Egyptians were very punctilious in such matters, and convention demanded that Allenby appear before Zaghlul in frock coat and silk hat. (A report of Allenby's sartorial insult upset King George V, who was also pernickety about correctness of dress.) As Allenby's car pulled away from the High Commission, the expected telegram arrived from the Foreign Office, but it was too late given the time it would take to decipher it. Allenby reached Zaghlul a few minutes later, just as the Egyptian was about to leave for Parliament. He read the ultimatum in English, which his host did not understand, delivered a French translation, and departed. On his return to the High Commission, he discovered that the Cabinet had considerably diluted his demands.

This confrontation had been the diplomatic equivalent of a cavalry charge. Chamberlain was horrified that Allenby had acted without proper authorisation, but admitted that the government would, with deep misgivings, support him. Zaghlul, ignorant of Allenby's insubordination, called a meeting of his cabinet and agreed to concede all the terms saving those concerned with the Sudan and the Nile waters. Allenby was not satisfied, and on 24 November ordered the immediate evacuation of all Egyptian servicemen in the Sudan.

Allenby now had the bit between his teeth. He was a soldier again and free from the restraining codes of diplomacy. Having stunned Zaghlul with his ultimatum, he followed up the offensive with a series of measures designed to keep the Wafd and its leader in a state of terror and confusion. On 23 November he asked for units of the Mediterranean Fleet to proceed to Egyptian waters as an earnest of Britain's determination. It was gunboat diplomacy on a grand scale: a day later the battleships HMS *Iron Duke* and HMS *Malaya* dropped anchor off Alexandria, and the cruiser HMS *Caradon* hove to off Port Said. At Allenby's orders, bluejackets and marines came ashore and occupied the Alexandria Customs House, in case the Egyptian government failed to pay the indemnity. Furthermore, some Alexandrians had staged an anti-British demonstration on the day of Stack's funeral, and so Allenby arranged for them to see a demonstration of British power. On 1 December landing-parties from the *Iron Duke* and the recently arrived battleships *Benbow* and *Valiant* marched through the city's streets. As they watched, older Alexandrians may have remembered a similar show of muscle over forty years before, when British ironclads had shelled the city's fort prior to its occupation by marines and sailors.

The Cairenes were also given a display of Imperial might. On 26 November the Highland Light Infantry, the Duke of Wellington's Regiment and the Hampshire Regiment paraded through the streets; two more infantry battalions were on their way from Gibraltar, summoned by Allenby. It was all part of a carefully contrived object lesson for all Egyptians. The British lion was still a strong, awesome beast with sharp teeth, and was not to be trifled with.

The battleships and battalions had the desired effect. There were no major demonstrations, and the Egyptians accepted a new government headed by the pro-British Ziwer Pasha. On 27 November three leading wafdists, Makram Ubayd, al Rahman Fahmi and Mahmund Nuqrashi (who had been Under-Secretary of State in Zaghlul's ministry), were arrested for alleged complicity in the plot to kill Stack. There were suspicions, too, about Fath Allah Barakat, the Minister of the Interior, but as with the other three it proved impossible to find enough evidence for convictions.[25]

Allenby's strong line was less easily enforced in the Sudan. As expected, the showdown with the Egyptians there led to some disturbances, but by and large the Egyptian Army's withdrawal proceeded peacefully. Cadets and artillerymen in Khartoum objected, however, and on 27 November mutinied and occupied a military hospital. They surrendered the following day after a night-long bombardment, and the ringleaders were subsequently executed. There were also mutinies, anti-British rather than pro-Egyptian, by the askaris of the 10th and 11th Sudanese Battalions, which were suppressed by local British forces. As a precaution against further unrest, aircraft and armoured cars were sent from Egypt to Khartoum.

Within a fortnight Allenby had demonstrated that British power in Egypt was firm and immovable. He was publicly congratulated for his boldness and resolution, particularly by the local European communities, who were delighted to see the Egyptians put in their place. Behind the scenes, however, and completely hidden from the Egyptians, he was engaged in a furious row with the British government. It had erupted on 24 November, when Allenby had wired the Foreign Office with proposals for security measures which included the taking of hostages against future assassinations. Austen Chamberlain was dumbfounded, and replied, 'His Majesty's Government disapprove [of] the shooting of hostages. This measure must not be adopted in any circumstances.'[26] Allenby seemed to be completely out of control, and was riding roughshod over all the conventions that normally bound proconsuls. Moreover, he was unrepentant: when reminded of the illegality of one of his measures, he remarked, 'I suppose one more anomaly does not matter.'[27]

It was too much for Chamberlain. On 24 November he cabled Allenby that he was sending an experienced diplomat, Nevile Henderson, to Cairo to explain 'the objects at which His Majesty's government is aiming and the difficulties they wish to avoid'. Allenby was asked to bear in mind that the views expressed by foreign residents in Egypt were not those of their governments, and that while he was correct to force the Egyptians to do their duty, it was not for him to do it for them. Chamberlain hoped, vainly as it turned out, that Allenby had not declared martial law or seized the Alexandria Customs House.[28]

Allenby was enraged by what he saw as an encroachment on his powers. On 26 November he complained to Chamberlain of the 'lamentably bad effect' of Henderson's appointment, which was bound to undermine his authority and would be interpreted as a token of official disapproval, which of course it was. He concluded with an offer of resignation, 'seeing I no longer have the confidence of His Majesty's Government'.[29] Rather than face the political repercussions of Allenby's recall in the middle of a crisis, Chamberlain back-pedalled and assured him that Henderson would 'strengthen' his position in Egypt. Allenby was unmoved, and in a telegram of 29 November drew Chamberlain's attention to his 'long experience' of Egyptian affairs, warned of the dangers that might follow if his advice was overridden, and accused the Cabinet of an 'infirmity of purpose'.[30]

Tempers cooled, Allenby's more slowly than Chamberlain's. He found it easy to work in concert with Henderson although, on 4 January 1925, he packed the diplomat off to the Sudan to assess the situation there.[31] A fortnight earlier Chamberlain had offered Allenby an olive branch by congratulating him on the success of his measures and hoping that their 'momentary' misunderstanding would be forgotten.[32] Allenby replied with a justification of his actions: they had been the only possible response to the Stack murder, which had been part of a 'carefully prepared' programme of violence directed against the condominium in the Sudan. A 'sharp lesson' had been given, and the Egyptians were now reflecting on its implications.[33]

By 1 January 1925 Allenby was prepared to make his peace with

Chamberlain, although he insisted that he should be allowed to resign at the earliest convenient moment.[34] He suggested that he should go at some time after the Egyptian general elections in March, but after the arrest of Stack's assassins in February he proposed a date after their trial. Since police evidence appeared to confirm that he had been right in his assumption that leading wafdists had been party to the conspiracy, his pride demanded that he should stay in Egypt to see himself vindicated.[35]

The elections resulted in a wafdist majority, but Fuad dissolved Parliament, leaving Ziwer in power while adjustments were made to the electoral laws. Shaken by the events of the past five months, Zaghlul bowed to royal authority and, perhaps cowed by the recent displays of British might, his followers stayed inactive and mute. The trials in May ended in the convictions and execution of the principals involved in Stack's murder, thanks to the evidence of an informer, Shafiq Mansur, himself a former terrorist. Attempts to implicate the senior wafdists came to nothing, although one minor official was found guilty of collusion and was hanged.[36]

Allenby had asked to leave in June and the Foreign Office agreed. His successor was George Lloyd, who had been one of his Intelligence staff in 1917 and a colleague of Lawrence. Lloyd was an old-style Imperialist with an impeccable bureaucratic and political background, and was therefore unlikely to kick over the traces. Allenby heard of his appointment by way of Reuter's press release, a tactless reminder that the government still bore a grudge against its wayward proconsul.

And yet he and Lady Allenby had plenty of friends in Egypt, and during the months before their departure on 14 June they were widely and warmly entertained by leading Egyptians – wafdists excepted – and the European communities. They had something to be grateful for: Allenby had recognised the new mood of the Egyptians and had done what he could to satisfy it, but, as recent events had dramatically shown, he had always placed his own country's interests first.

PART 5

FINAL YEARS

JULY 1925–MAY 1936

CHAPTER 17

FINAL YEARS

1925–1936

THE Allenbys returned to England in June 1925, he apparently unruffled by the events of the past seven months. The *Spectator* hailed him as a 'warrior statesman' who 'suffers fools nor red tape gladly', and who had completed a longer period of continuous public service than any other comparable figure. He was sixty-four, still in excellent health and with a strong constitution, but the government declined to offer him any responsible post. 'Poor Allenby!' wrote Lawrence. 'It was sad to see a big man in retirement and not knowing what to do. I wish we could all die in harness.' The trouble was that Allenby, like Lawrence, was out of sympathy with the bureaucratic mind, and for the past six years had chafed at the restrictions imposed upon him by his superiors.

So Allenby withdrew from official life and public controversy. Public speaking was an ordeal for him, but there were three issues about which he felt strongly enough to address the House of Lords during the winter and spring of 1929–30. On 14 November he challenged the cuts made in the military budget. He confessed to a general ignorance of present technical developments and political and financial circumstances but, speaking as a fighting soldier, he observed: 'I do know the difficulty in meeting with ten thousand one who comes against you with twenty thousand.' He reminded his listeners how an under-strength British army had had to improvise to escape disaster in August 1914. A week later he spoke again, this time as a naturalist, in favour of a wildlife preservation bill.[1]

On 1 April he rallied to the defence of the British National Cadet Association, which was in danger of losing its small official grant. As the Association's President, he pointed out that it introduced working-class youths to the 'virtues of citizenship', and he repudiated charges that he was a militarist for supporting it. Remembering the allegations that had been levelled against him when he had been in Egypt, he added, 'I have also been called at various times a pacifist and a defeatist.' Again on a military matter, he supported Lord Plumer's objections to the Labour government's proposed abolition of the death penalty for the military offences of deserting a post in action and cowardice in the face of the enemy. Allenby argued that the strongest penalty was needed to deter men from crimes which imperilled their brothers-in-arms.[2] The measure was passed: during and after the war there had been disquiet about a number of miscarriages of justice, and about the willingness of too many courts martial to sentence to death soldiers, often with fine records, for momentary lapses. This rearguard action, in defence of a scarcely tenable position, was Allenby's final essay into public affairs.

His retirement was restless, in so far as he and his wife spent many winters on extended tours abroad. In 1925 the government had given for his lifetime Deal Castle as a home, but this 'funny little Tudor fort' was unsuitable since he was no longer attracted by golf or the seaside.[3] The Allenbys moved to Kensington where he installed an aviary in the garden. Free from the money worries that had troubled him just after the war, when he had been in debt (he left £29,000 in his will), he and Lady Allenby decided to travel as they had done before the war.[4]

During the winter of 1925–6 and at the invitation of Chauvel they toured Australia. At a reception in Melbourne Town Hall, Allenby was introduced as the greatest soldier since Wellington, which prompted an Anzac to object, 'Since Hannibal!'[5] Memories of Surafend and its aftermath had clearly evaporated. During 1928–9 the Allenbys visited the United States, where General Pershing invited them to an ex-servicemen's rally at San Antonio. Later, they progressed to Hollywood and watched, unimpressed, the making of an early talkie. There were other excursions to South Africa, Rhodesia, India, South America and the West Indies. In 1935 he followed an impulse to test the truth of an article in the *Field*, which claimed that the salmon fishing off Patagonia matched if not surpassed his beloved River Tay. It was a formidable expedition for a sixty-nine-year-old, but with the assistance of the British Ambassador in Buenos Aires and his former colleague Nevile Henderson, he accomplished the trip.

On 14 May of the following year Allenby died, unexpectedly and suddenly, from a blood tumour on the brain. He was cremated and his remains placed beneath a slab in Westminster Abbey; at his funeral the new King, Edward VIII, was represented by Allenby's old comrade, Field-Marshal Lord Chetwode. His death and burial made little impression in the newspapers, which were filled with ominous news of an Arab uprising in Palestine, Mussolini's invasion of Ethiopia, and Japanese incursions into Manchuria. Allenby had read and been disturbed by these portents of a disintegrating world order and during his final public act, installation as Rector of Edinburgh University, had appealed for an international peacekeeping force directed by the League of Nations.

The Times alone gave Allenby an extended and fulsome obituary which traced the outline of his career and achievements. He had been 'A man of powerful physique and of determined will, a bold sportsman and a fearless rider', who possessed extensive reserves of moral and physical courage coupled with a 'straightforwardness' of address. His title, according to his wish, passed to his brother's son.

PART 6

THE MAN
AND HIS TIMES

CHAPTER 18

THE MAN
AND HIS TIMES

THE qualities that had made Allenby a great commander were not apparent before he left England for the Middle East. Until June 1917 he had been a conventional general whom fate had thrust into a position for which he seemed mentally unfitted and in which he floundered. All that could be said in his favour was that during the nerve-racking weeks of August and September 1914 his presence of mind and capacity for improvisation had held the cavalry together. For the next three years he survived by doing what he was told and sticking to the aggressive doctrines handed down by French and Haig. These accorded well with the 'cavalry spirit' cultivated by Allenby, but their value in trench warfare was questionable.

Arguably, Allenby was miscast as a Western Front commander, even though his qualifications – colonial campaigns and Staff College – were no better or worse than those of others similarly placed. He had risen steadily since 1902 without manifesting any signs of ambition or calculation, and had carefully avoided intrigue or attachment to cliques. His political neutrality was invaluable in terms of his career, for it enabled him to remain on easy and cordial terms with Robertson, Sir Henry Wilson, Lloyd George and, despite undercurrents of misunderstanding and jealousy, Haig.

There were no doubts about Allenby's professionalism. He was not an original thinker, but his advocacy of machine-guns for his cavalry and insistence that they received training as mounted infantry revealed a flexible mind, although it fell into abeyance the moment he took up his command at Ypres in 1915. For the next two years he followed the directions of superiors who, like him, were stumbling towards a strategic formula that would end the deadlock in the trenches.

Political circumstances and a stroke of good fortune released Allenby from the imbroglio of the Western Front. Whatever he may have said about the virtues of 'cheerful obedience', Allenby had great difficulty in submitting to the will of Haig. Perhaps, and this is only conjecture, his frequent and vividly remembered rages in France stemmed from an inner frustration at having to carry out orders that he believed to be pointless or mistaken. Certainly these outbursts were less common in the Middle East, where he was his own master.

In the Middle East Allenby was a new man, free and brimming with energy and ideas, and many who knew him then were amazed by the transformation.[1] What was most striking was the power of his personal magnetism, which inspired those with whom he came in contact. It was felt by Nevile Henderson, who must have approached Allenby with some trepidation when they first met in Cairo in December 1924. Soon afterwards he wrote, 'I like him and his personality. He has the gift of winning the admiration and affection of his subordinates.'[2] Such testimony was as common from those who served with him after 1917 as it had been rare before.

As a general, Allenby had inherited a favourable situation in southern Palestine. In terms of numbers, morale and resources he had a permanent advantage over his opponents. His strategy for the Gaza breakthrough had been devised by Chetwode, to whom he was publicly grateful, but Allenby was the driving force behind its execution. In August 1917 he adapted and refined Chetwode's scheme for his own offensive, which revealed how much he had learned in France. Of course the conditions in Palestine were very different and gave Allenby the scope for a classic cavalry campaign. It was the last opportunity for the sort of action which cavalrymen had dreamed about before the war, and Allenby was the best man to exploit it.

The battle of Armageddon and the advances to Damascus and Aleppo were a token vindication of the value of cavalry in modern warfare, and the swan-song of the mounted soldier. In terms of the history of warfare, the campaign was a hybrid of old and new methods. Before the cavalry could advance, the Turkish line had been fractured by a pin-point, wireless-directed bombardment and Turkish bases and lines of communication had been hammered by round-the-clock bombing. As the columns of horsemen encircled the enemy, aircraft harried his retreating formations. If tanks had been substituted for horsemen the campaign would have mirrored the blitzkrieg attacks by the German Army in 1939–40. Of course there were other factors that favoured Allenby's audacious campaign of manoeuvre which were not reproduced on other fronts. He outnumbered his adversary, and the Turco-German armies were debilitated and war-weary. Moreover, as he generously stated afterwards, Faisal's Arab contingent provided a valuable diversion, and by harassing the Turks helped keep up the momentun of their retreat.

Having won the last major campaign in which cavalry played a vital role, Allenby was unsentimental about the future of his arm of the service. He was essentially a practical soldier and, in 1919–20, when faced with the possibilities of a Franco-Arab war in Syria and disturbances in adjacent British territory, his exigency plans were based on the use of aircraft and motorised infantry.[3] The techniques he had in mind became official policy after the 1921 Cairo Conference when, with the backing of Churchill and Lawrence, units which combined armoured cars and bombers were designated as the police force for Britain's Middle Eastern mandates.

Allenby's victories were the springboard for a new career as a proconsul. From the start, he was an awkward subordinate who used his prestige and authority to back his own views. He interpreted his task as one of preserving British strategic interests at the same time as extricating Britain from the internal affairs of Egypt, where her involvement was plainly unwelcome. The result was a sequence of tussles between him and the Cabinet which he won by a mixture of coercion and cajolement. It was bewildering for a government which had appointed him as a strong man to find him advocating policies that looked very much like appeasement.

It was equally puzzling, and sometimes frightening, for the Egyptians to have a High Commissioner who alternately proffered the velvet glove of conciliation and then threatened them with a mailed fist. And yet a more patient and less volatile man could have done no better in the circumstances. Allenby was the servant of governments which were divided over what line to take towards Egypt, and so it was left to him to react to events as they occurred.

Matters were made worse for him by the British community inside Egypt who embodied the racial attitudes of the time. They lived in the isolation of their hotels, clubs and messes, and devoted a greater part of their time to preserving their national identity and indulging in those sporting pastimes which contributed to it. Egyptians shared none of their interests and were widely seen as a sly, weak and decadent race who could be treated with contempt. One case, which arrived on Allenby's desk in

August 1924, summed up the attitude of many of his countrymen towards the Egyptians. After the end of a dance at the Heliopolis House Hotel the band played '*Salaam es Sultan*', the Egyptian national anthem, which prompted an RAF officer to shout 'What the hell is this for?' In the ensuing rumpus Allenby demanded the playing of the British national anthem, and no further performances of the Egyptian.[4]

Those who would have approved the airman's behaviour looked askance at Allenby's efforts to accommodate Egyptian political aspirations. His proclamations on public order were ridiculed as 'windy pie-crust' or puff pastries.[5] How far such pressure contributed towards his actions after the Stack assassination cannot be judged, but he was certainly aware that the European community was growing increasingly disturbed by what it regarded as Egyptian insolence, particularly from Zaghlul.

Allenby's own racial attitudes remained his own affair. Once, in 1920, he was accused of anti-Semitism after he had become involved in an attempt by senior officers in Palestine to veto the appointment of Sir Herbert Samuel as High Commissioner there. Bols, then in charge of the administration, backed by Congreve, got Allenby to approve a protest which alleged that the Arabs would consider Samuel as Jewish and not British, and therefore not a disinterested administrator. What was a misjudgement on Allenby's part provoked Meinertzhagen, in a report to the War Office, to brand all British officers as anti-Semitic. 'I believe that most Englishmen have inherited a dislike of the Jew,' he wrote, adding, 'I do not think any normal body of British officers could both hold the scales equally between Jew and Moslem.'[6] Allenby was displeased and had Meinertzhagen dismissed, although the two parted on good terms and remained friends. The nub of the problem in 1920 and afterwards had been the tension in Palestine created by Jewish immigration, and Arab fears that their country was on the verge of becoming a Jewish colony. The overbearing attitude of some Zionists did not help matters, and materially contributed to the hostility felt towards their cause by British officers. In many cases what appeared to be anti-Semitism was in fact a concern for the rights of Arabs, who then made up 90 per cent of Palestine's population. This probably lay behind Allenby's intervention against Samuel. Certainly Weizmann found that Allenby approved strongly of Jewish settlements in Palestine, which he hoped would become a valuable part of the Empire and a bulwark for the defence of the Suez Canal.[7]

Allenby's personal feelings did intrude, however, into his dealings with the French and the Arabs immediately after the war. He found Picot unbearable on account of his arrogance, and liked Faisal, who had the qualities of a gentleman and whose forces had been so useful during a campaign in which the French contribution had been minimal. And yet, having spoken forcefully in favour of an Arab Syria, Allenby submitted in the autumn of 1919 to the government's decision to abandon the country to France. By contrast, Lawrence fought the government tooth and nail and his protests and machinations, the latter abetted by Churchill, secured Faisal the throne of Iraq in 1921.

By then, the name of Lawrence was already celebrated, and his fame grew in the wake of a stream of press articles, biographies by Lowell Thomas, Robert Graves and Liddell Hart, and his own *Revolt in the Desert*, which appeared in 1927. Allenby viewed the unstoppable expansion of the Lawrence legend with a tolerant good humour. He had always cherished unconventional men who offered him diversion and stimulation. In South Africa he had enjoyed the company of 'Banjo' Paterson and Father Knapp, and in Egypt that of his fellow naturalist Meinertzhagen. Lawrence was also an engaging companion and conversationalist, and Allenby was happy to allow their discussions to wander away from politics and strategy to more congenial subjects like poetry, birds and castles.

Lawrence was more than an entertainer, however, he was a capable commander of guerrillas who knew how to handle Arab irregulars, a task that was often beyond the patience of professional soldiers. Allenby, with his South African experience, was a good judge in such matters, and he never wavered from his view that Lawrence was eminently suited to lead the Arabs. In June 1919, when Ibn Saud's Wahabbi warriors were poised to invade the Hijaz, Allenby sent an urgent request for Lawrence to be rushed from Paris to take command of the Hijazi forces.[8]

And yet some years later, when Edmonds asked him for his views on Lawrence, Allenby answered, 'I had a dozen chaps who would have done the job better.'[9] This was Allenby's only direct criticism of his protégé, but it is worth mentioning that in March 1918 he had been anxious to have George Lloyd posted as liaison officer with the Arabs east of the Jordan, an area where Lawrence had been active.[10] There was a pool of daring and talented officers working alongside Lawrence, including Newcombe, Pierce Joyce, Hubert Young and (briefly) Alan Dawnay, all of whom admired and stayed loyal to him after the war. The difference between them and him was that he had the literary skills to transform their campaign into an epic and himself into its hero.

The hyperbole which Lawrence inspired and sometimes invited upset many professional officers, including some who had worked with him. Chauvel, with whom Lawrence's misrepresentation of the fall of Damascus rankled, sent Allenby a letter listing all the factual errors in *The Seven Pillars of Wisdom*. He concluded that Joyce, the commander of

Aqaba, had been the 'organiser of the only real fighting force in the whole of the Arab army'.[11] In 1955, when asked to add his voice to the protest being organised against Richard Aldington's hostile biography of Lawrence, General Bartholomew refused. Lawrence, he said, had been 'useful' and had 'made it easier' for Allenby to win in 1918, but he and his role had been exaggerated by the 'extravagant' claims of Churchill and others. Bartholomew had persuaded Lawrence to 'modify' some of *The Seven Pillars of Wisdom*, but he believed that the book was evidence that the author had 'lost a sense of proportion'.[12]

Allenby's response to the book had been generous and measured. 'I congratulate you on a great work; fit record of your splendid achievements in the war,' he wrote to Lawrence in January 1927. He added, 'I am grateful for the kind way in which you refer to my part in our collaboration, and am happy to think that to our unity of thought and intention can be attributed, in great measure, the success obtained.'[13] In the same vein, Allenby delivered an obituary of Lawrence after the BBC's 9 o'clock evening news on 19 May 1935. He spoke of him as 'a good friend and a valued comrade', and concluded:

> Such men win friends – such also find critics and detractors. But the highest reward for success is the inward knowledge that it has been rightly won. Praise or blame was regarded with indifference by Lawrence. He did his duty as he saw it before him. He has left, to us who knew him and admired him, a beloved memory.

All this was sincere, but Allenby had some inner misgivings, not so much about the man, but what he had become as a consequence of his own vanity and public adulation. Some time after copies of *The Seven Pillars of Wisdom* had been in circulation, Allenby was visited by Barrow. He remarked, 'Lawrence goes for you in the book, George,' referring to a distorted account of their meeting at Dera in September 1918. Barrow agreed, but said he would take no action against the author. 'No, that would be a mug's game,' answered Allenby. 'Besides we know Lawrence. He thinks himself a hell of a soldier and loves posturing in the limelight.'[14]

These remarks do not detract from the sincerity of Allenby's other utterances about Lawrence, which were based upon wartime memories –the two men had last met briefly in June 1919. Afterwards Lawrence had played the maverick: he had, and this offended Allenby, rejected his decorations from King George V; he had thrown over a post with the Colonial Office; and had afterwards enlisted as an aircraftman in the RAF and a private soldier in the Tank Corps. For many senior officers this amounted to the worst sort of unsteadiness, and a betrayal of his social position. In a letter of August 1921, Sir Henry Wilson agreed with Congreve that Lawrence was a 'dangerous little fellow', adding, 'but if you have poor Winston at the top [Churchill was then Colonial Secretary] he naturally surrounds himself with men of like kidney'.[15] Furthermore, as Allenby observed to Barrow, Lawrence the amateur soldier considered himself the equal of professionals.

It seems paradoxical that admirers of Lawrence and Allenby considered both men as embodiments of national virtues. Wavell saw Allenby as possessing in an exceptional degree all the finest qualities of Englishness: integrity, courage, trustworthiness, frankness, good humour, and a sense of justice. Lawrence too wrote about Allenby in similar terms, and paid high tribute to his omniscience and compelling powers of leadership, in fact all the characteristics of the great general.

What Allenby thought or would have thought of such compliments cannot be guessed. He was not a notably vain man, although he was quickly roused to anger if his judgements were challenged. Nor was he introspective, which was not surprising, since his upbringing and education had occurred at a time when a man was expected to keep his interior emotions to himself. He gave a glimpse of the values he lived by in the letters he wrote after his son's death, and they accord closely with the qualities praised by Wavell and Lawrence.

And yet Allenby was manifestly not the paragon they presented. Throughout his life he struggled with varying success to overcome the passion of the moment. When he failed he became 'the Bull', a bombastic, self-centred creature who bullied junior officers and cabinet ministers and seemed unaware of the distress he caused. His frenzies often had a peculiar grotesqueness, since many of those who witnessed them knew another man who enjoyed fine literature, conversation, wild flowers and birds. He was also a humane man; as High Commissioner he and Lady Allenby had supported and facilitated the work of the Cairo branch of the Association Internationale pour la Répression de la Traite des Blanches, which endeavoured to fight the white-slave trade. This involved enticing and sometimes kidnapping European girls for brothels in Egypt and elsewhere in the Orient; much to the Allenbys' satisfaction, the organisation changed its name to one which was less easily identifiable with prostitution, the Ligue Internationale pour le Protéction de la Femme, in December 1920.[16]

In psychological terms the more familiar, public Allenby could be diagnosed as an extrovert guided by his own intuition, an apparently unsafe combination in a commanding officer. Nevertheless, according to Jung, these characteristics give their possessor an unequalled 'capacity to inspire his fellow-men with courage, or to kindle enthusiasm for something new'. To this capacity might be added, in Allenby's case, a large amount of good luck.

NOTES AND SOURCES

ABBREVIATIONS

Adm.	Admiralty
BL	Bodleian Library
Cab.	Cabinet
EEF	Egyptian Expeditionary Force
IWM	Imperial War Museum
FO	Foreign Office
LHC	Liddell Hart Centre
NAM	National Army Museum
NLS	National Library of Scotland
OH	Official History
PRO	Public Record Office
RHL	Rhodes House Library
WO	War Office

SOURCES

This list includes the material referred to in the notes. All books are published in London unless otherwise stated.

UNPUBLISHED WORKS

London, Imperial War Museum
Letters, papers etc. of Major-General Guy Dawnay.

London, Liddell Hart Centre for Military Archives
Papers of Field-Marshal Viscount Allenby, Sir Basil Liddell Hart and Brigadier-General Sir James Edmonds.

London, National Army Museum
Diaries of Sergeant A. G. Beer and Field-Marshal Lord Rawlinson.

London, Public Record Office
Adm. 137; Air 1, 5; Cab. 45, 103; FO 141, 371, 800, 848; WO 32, 33, 76, 95, 106, 108, 154, 157, 158, 159.

Edinburgh, National Library of Scotland
Diary of Field-Marshal Earl Haig; diary and letters of General Sir Aylmer Haldane.

Oxford, Bodleian Library
Papers of Viscount Milner.

Oxford, Rhodes House Library
Diary of Colonel Richard Meinertzhagen.

PUBLISHED WORKS

L. S. Amery, ed., *The Times History of the War in South Africa*, 7 volumes (1900–1909)

Marquess of Anglesey, *A History of the British Cavalry 1816–1919*, IV (1899–1913) (1986)

Anon., 'About Soldiers by a Soldier', *Blackwood's Magazine*, 151 (June 1892)

Anon., 'The War Crisis in South Africa', *Blackwood's Magazine*, 166 (December 1899)

Anon. (A Military Correspondent), 'The War Operations in South Africa', *Blackwoods Magazine*, 166 (December 1899)

Anon., 'Shot, Shell and Bullets', *Blackwood's Magazine*, 167 (February 1900)

Anon., 'Concerning our Cavalry', *Blackwood's Magazine*, 167 (June 1900)

Anon., 'Our Officers', *Blackwood's Magazine*, 167 (July 1900)

Anon., 'The Turkish Operations in Palestine', *Journal of the Royal United Services Institute*, 66, (1921)

Anon. (Ex-ADC), 'Aleppo during the Armistice', *Cavalry Journal*, 14 (1924)

Anon., 'Lord Allenby's Return', *Spectator*, (20 June 1925)

Anon. (Officer of Buckinghamshire Yeomanry), 'Beersheba, Beitunia, Bethoron, stopping at Bishop's Stortford', *Cavalry Journal*, 28 (1937)

G. Antonius, *The Arab Awakening* (1938)

A. H. Atteridge, *History of the 17th (Northern) Division* (Glasgow, 1929)

A. Babington, *For the Sake of Example: Capital Courts-Martials 1914–1918* (1983)

J. W. Barrett and P. E. Deane, *The Australian Army Medical Corps in Egypt* (1918)

G. W. Barrow, 'Cavalry Episodes in the Palestine Campaign 1917–1918', *Cavalry Journal*, 28 (1937)

——, *The Fire of Life* (1943)

I. F. W. Beckett, ed., *The Army and the Curragh Incident* (Army Records Society, 1986)

S. Bidwell and D. Graham, *Firepower: British Army Weapons and Theories of War, 1904–1945* (1982)

M. B. Bishku, *The British Empire and the Question of Egypt's Future, 1919–1922* (University Microfilms International, Ann Arbor, 1988)

B. Bond, *The Victorian Army and the Staff College, 1854–1914* (1972)

R. C. Boyle, *A Record of the West Somerset Yeomanry, 1914–1919* (n.d.)

G. Brenan, *A Life of One's Own* (1962)

S. Brugger, *The Australians in Egypt, 1914–1919* (Melbourne, 1980)

J. Charmley, *Lord Lloyd and the Decline of the British Empire* (1987)

J. Charteris, *Field-Marshal Earl Haig* (1929)

——, *At G.H.Q.* (1931)

P. Chetwode, 'The Employment of Cavalry', *Army Review* (July 1912)

J. Connell, *Wavell: Scholar and Soldier* (1964)

J. W. and P. F. Coogan, 'The British Cabinet, the Anglo-French Staff Talks 1904–1914: who knew what and when did they know?' (*Journal of British Studies*, 23 (1985)

F. P. Crozier, *The Men I Killed* (1937)

Daily Review of the Foreign Press (1917–1920)

G. Dallas and D. Gill, *The Unknown Army* (1985)

J. Darwin, *Britain, Egypt and the Middle East: Imperial Policy in the aftermath of war, 1918–1922* (New York, 1981)

G. de Groot, *Douglas Haig, 1861–1928* (1988)

Documents on British Foreign Policy 1919–1939, ed. E. L. Woodward and R. Butler, First Series, IV (1952)

J. C. Dunn, *The War the Infantry Knew: 1914–1919* (1987 edn)

A. F. Duguid, *Official History of the Canadian Forces in the Great War, 1914–1919* Volumes I and II (Ottowa, 1938)

M. Earle, 'The Army and Public Schools', *Army Review* (October, 1911)

J. Edmonds, *A Short History of World War I* (Oxford, 1951)

A. Emin, *Turkey in the World War* (New Haven, 1930)

C. Falls, *Armageddon* (1964)

Foreign Relations of the United States: 1919 Paris Peace Conference, V (Washington, 1944)

D. French, *British Strategy and War Aims 1914–1916* (1986)

E. G. French, *The Life of Field-Marshal Sir John French, Earl French of Ypres* (1931)

J. F. C. Fuller, *The Last of the Gentleman's Wars* (1937)

B. Gardner, *Allenby* (1965)

P. Gibbs, *The Battles of the Somme* (1917)

G. S. Goldman, *With General French and the Cavalry in South Africa* (1902)

H. Gough, *The Fifth Army* (1931)

——, *Soldiering On* (1954)

H. S. Gullett, C. Barrett and D. Barker, *Australia in Palestine* (Sydney, 1919)

H. S. Gullett, *The Australian Imperial Force in Sinai and Palestine* (Sydney, 1939: the seventh volume of the Australian Official History, edited by C. E. W. Bean)

C. Guy Powles, *The New Zealanders in Sinai and Palestine* (Auckland, 1922)

C. W. Gwynn, *Imperial Policing* (1936)

Haileybury Register, ed. L. S. Milford (1900)

C. Harrington, *Plumer of Messines* (1938 edn)

G. F. R. Henderson, *The Science of War: a collection of essays and lectures, 1892–1903* (1905)

A. J. Hill, *Chauvel of the Light Horse* (Melbourne, 1978)

R. A. Hinnebusch, 'The Re-emergence of the Wafd Party: a glimpse of the liberal opposition in Egypt', *International Journal of Middle East Studies*, 16 (1984)

G. B. Hurst, 'The Administration of Military Law', *Contemporary Review*, CXV March 1919)

I. L. Idriess, *The Desert Column* (Sydney, 1933 edn)
D. Ingrams, *Palestine Papers* (1972)

L. James, *The Golden Warrior: The Life and Legend of Lawrence of Arabia* (1990)
H. A. Jones, *The War in the Air*, Volumes II–VI. (Oxford, 1928–37)

D. Kahn, *The Codebreakers* (1966)
E. Kedourie, *The Chatham House Version* (1970)
——, *England and the Middle East* (1978 edn)
M. Kent, ed., *The Great Powers and the Ottoman Empire* (1984)
P. S. Khoury, 'The Tribal Shaykh, French Policy and the Nationalist Movement in Syria between the wars', *Middle East Studies*, 18 (1982)
V. J. Kiernan, *European Empires from Conquest to Collapse* (1982)
The Memoirs of Paul Kruger, 2 volumes (1902)

V. J. Lambert, 'The Fight near Aleppo A, October 26 1918', *Cavalry Journal*, 14 (1924)
T. E. Lawrence, *The Seven Pillars of Wisdom* (1935)
B. H. Liddell Hart, *A History of the First World War* (1970 edn)
Liman von Sanders, F., *Five Years in Turkey* (US Navy Institute, Annapolis, 1927)
D. Lloyd George, *Memoirs of the Paris Peace Conference*, 2 volumes (New Haven, 1939)
Z. Lockman, 'British Policy towards Egyptian Labor Activity, 1882–1936, *International Journal of Middle East Studies*, 20 (1988)

L. Macdonald, *Somme* (1983)
W. G. Macpherson, *Official History of the Great War: Medical Services*, 4 volumes (1924)
——, W. H. Horrocks and W. W. O. Beveridge, *Official History of the Great War: Medical Services, Hygiene at War*, 3 volumes (1923)
F. Manning, *The Middle Parts of Fortune* (1977 edn)
W. T. Massey, *How Jerusalem was won: being a record of Allenby's campaigns in Palestine* (1919)
——, *Allenby's Final Triumph* (1920)
F. Maurice and M. H. Grant, *Official History of the War in South Africa*, 4 volumes (1906–1910)

E. May, *Chances and Changes in a Soldier's Life* (1925)

B. L. Montgomery, *Memoirs* (1958)

S. Morewood, 'Protecting the jugular vein of empire: the Suez Canal in British defence', *War and Society*, 10 (1992)

Official History of the Great War: Military Operations, France and Flanders, 1914, compiled by J. Edmonds, 2 volumes (1922 and 1923)

Official History of the Great War: Military Operations, France and Flanders, 1915, compiled by J. Edmonds, 4 volumes including maps (1927 and 1928)

Official History of the Great War: Military Operations, France and Flanders, 1916, compiled by J. Edmonds, 4 volumes including maps (1932 and 1938)

Official History of the Great War: Military Operations, France and Flanders, 1917, compiled by C. Falls, 4 volumes including maps (1940 and 1948)

Official History of the Great War: Military Operations, Egypt and Palestine, 1917–1918, compiled by C. Falls, 4 volumes including maps (1930)

T. Pakenham, *The Boer War* (1979)

J. Parker, *The Old Lie* (1987)

W. P. Pick, 'Meissner Pasha and the construction of railways in Palestine and neighbouring countries', in G. G. Gilbar, ed., *Ottoman Palestine* (The Hague, 1990)

[H. Pirie Gordon], *A Brief Record of the Advance of the Egyptian Expeditionary Force* (Cairo, 1919)

R. M. P. Preston, *The Desert Mounted Corps: an account of the Cavalry Operations in Palestine and Syria, 1917–1918* (1921)

W. J. Reader, *At Duty's Call: a Study in Obsolete Patriotism* (Manchester, 1988)

C. à C. Repington, *The First World War*, 2 volumes (1920)

The Military Correspondence of Field-Marshal Sir William Robertson, Chief of the Imperial General Staff, December 1915–February 1918, ed. D. R. Woodward (Army Records Society, 1989)

Royal Commission on the War in South Africa (1903)

G. St Aubyn, *The Royal George: The Life of Prince George, Duke of Cambridge, 1819–1904* (1963)

R. Savage, *Allenby of Armageddon* (1925)

D. M. Schreuder, *The Scramble for Southern Africa, 1877–1895* (Cambridge, 1980)

A. Sillery, *Founding a Protectorate: the History of Bechuanaland, 1885–1895* (The Hague, 1965)

E. Spears, *Liaison, 1914* (1968 edn)

E. M. Spiers, *The Army and Society, 1815–1914* (1980)

O. Teichman, *Diary of a Yeomanry M.O.* (1921)

J. Terraine, *Douglas Haig: The Educated Soldier* (1963)

——, *Mons* (1972 edn)

J. J. Terry, *The Wafd* (Beirut, 1982)

L. Thomas, *With Allenby in the Holy Land* (1938)

T. Travers, *The Killing Ground: The British Army of the Western Front and the Emergence of Modern Warfare, 1900–1918* (1987)

U. Trumpener, *Germany and the Ottoman Empire* (Princeton, 1968)

J. Turner, *British Politics and the Great War, Coalitions and Cabinets, 1915–1918* (1992)

E. C. Vaughan, *Some Desperate Glory: The Diary of a Young Officer, 1917* (1981)

B. S. Vester, *Our Jerusalem* (Beirut, 1950)

G. R. Warburg, *Egypt and the Sudan* (1985)

(C. Warren), *Report of the Proceedings of the Bechuanaland Field Force* (War Office, 1885)

P. Warwick, ed., *The South Africa War* (1980)

B. Wasserstein, *The British in Palestine: The Mandatory Government and the Anti-Jewish Contest, 1917–1929* (1978)

W. H. H. Waters and H. du Crane, *The War in South Africa* (translation of the official German account), 2 volumes (1904 and 1906)

A. P. Wavell, *The Palestine Campaigns* (1931 edn)

——, *Allenby: A Study in Greatness* (1940)

——, *Allenby in Egypt* (1943)

F. J. Weber, *Eagles on the Crescent* (Ithaca, 1970)

C. Weizmann, *Trial and Error* (1949)

W. W. Williams, *The Life of General Sir Charles Warren* (Oxford, 1941)

Field-Marshal Sir Henry Wilson, his life and diaries, ed. C. E. Caudwell, 2 volumes (1927)

The Military Correspondence of Field-Marshal Sir Henry Wilson, 1918–1922, ed. K. Jeffery (Army Records Society, 1985)

J. Wilson, *Lawrence of Arabia: the authorised biography of T. E. Lawrence* (1989)

D. Winter, *Haig's Command: A Reassessment* (1991)

J. W. Yardley, *With the Inniskilling Dragoons: The Record of a Cavalry Regiment during the Boer War, 1899–1902* (1904)

G. Young, *Egypt* (1927)

M. Y. Zayid, *Egypt's Struggle for Independence* (Beirut, 1965)

NOTES

PART I IMPERIAL WARRIOR: 1861–1902

1 A Victorian Upbringing: 1861–1882

1. LHC, Allenby 6/V, 45
2. LHC, Allenby 1/2, 57
3. LHC, Allenby 1/6/7; 1/2/108
4. LHC, Allenby 6/I, 6, 46, 53
5. Williams, 18
6. LHC, Allenby 6/I, 43, 46
7. Brenan, 126
8. Earle, 254, 259
9. Anon., *Blackwood's*, June 1892, 879
10. Anon., *Blackwood's*, February 1900, 21, 32
11. Gough, *Soldiering On*, 31–2, 36
12. May, 18
13. Reader, 91
14. LHC, Allenby 6/III, 16
15. LHC, Allenby 6/II, 24 (Major-General Sir Thomas O'Donnell)

2 A Soldier of the Queen: 1882–1896

1. LHC, Allenby 6/II, 10
2. LHC, Allenby 6/II, 24; 6/IV, 14
3. LHC, Allenby 1/1,14
4. For the Bechuanaland campaign I have relied on: Williams, 153 ff; PRO, WO 33/44 and WO 106/264 (Report of the Proceedings of the Bechuanaland Field Force)
5. *Report of the Royal Commission on the War in South Africa*, II, 225
6. PRO, WO 106/263, 19, 20
7. *Ibid.*, 17
8. Williams, 169
9. PRO, WO 33/44, 664
10. Kruger, I, 195; PRO, WO 106/263, 13
11. PRO, WO 106/264, 17
12. PRO, WO 33/44, 665–665d
13. LHC, Allenby 6/IV, 48

14. *Ibid.*

3 The Art of War: 1896–1899

1. St Aubyn, 172–3
2. *Ibid.*, 190–1
3. Bond, 131
4. LHC, Allenby 6/III, 3, 4, 9, 12
5. LHC, Liddell Hart 11/1937, 2
6. LHC, Edmonds III, 2, 13–14; Allenby 6/III, 9–10
7. LHC, Allenby 6/III, 9
8. LHC, Allenby 6/III, 6
9. *Ibid.*
10. Charteris, 12–13; Wavell, 61–2; LHC, Allenby 6/VII, 27
11. LHC, Edmonds III/2, 8
12. Henderson, 339–40
13. *Ibid.*, 210–11, 213
14. *Ibid.*, 61–2, 81
15. Chetwode, 41, 42–3
16. NLS, Haig Diary, 11.4.15
17. LHC, Allenby 6/III, 24
18. Wavell, 39 n.; NLS, Haig Diary, 2.2.15; Barrow, 142; Allenby qualified as an Army interpreter in French in 1896 (PRO, WO 76/535, 56, 87); RHL, Meinertzhagen, 21, fo 128d
19. This point is discussed in de Groot, 47–50

4 Fighting Brother Boer: 1899–1902

1. LHC, Allenby 1/2/87
2. Waters and DuCane, I, 130
3. Amery, III, 333–4
4. Anon., 'The War Crisis in South Africa', *Blackwood's*, December 1899, 875
5. *Report of the Royal Commission on the War in South Africa*, II, 212
6. LHC, Allenby, 1/2/17
7. LHC, Allenby, 1/2, 23
8. PRO WO 32/7967, 138
9. Maurice and Grant, I, 402; Yardley, 18; PRO, WO 32/7967, 140
10. LHC, Allenby, 1/2/27
11. Amery, III 351
12. Goldmann, 81; Yardley, 68; LHC, Allenby 1/2/27
13. Waters and Du Cane, I, 176n

14. Maurice, II, 187
15. Yardley, 52, 56–7, 68, 94
16. Amery, IV, 188
17. Yardley, 88; Goldmann, 266–7
18. LHC, Allenby 1/2/33, 35, 36
19. LHC, Allenby 1/2/43
20. LHC, Allenby 1/2/38
21. LHC, Allenby 1/2/28, 63
22. LHC, Allenby 1/2/43
23. LHC, Allenby 1/2/67
24. LHC, Allenby 1/2/50
25. Pakenham, 497; Wavell, 103–4
26. LHC, Allenby 1/2/92
27. Gardner, 38
28. PRO, WO 32/8044, No. 21
29. LHC, Allenby 1/2/119
30. LHC, Allenby 1/2/122
31. Warwick, 201; PRO, WO 32/8029, No. 1
32. Pakenham, 498; LHC, Allenby 1/2, 204, 321
33. PRO, WO 32/8027, 2
34. LHC, Allenby 1/2/87
35. PRO, WO 32/8029, No. 1
36. PRO, WO 32/8029, No. 1; Pakenham, 539
37. *Report of the Royal Commission on the War in South Africa*, II, 225
38. Pakenham, 498

PART II HIGH COMMAND: 1902-JUNE 1917

5 The Road to War: 1902–August 1914

1. LHC, Edmonds III/2, 14
2. LHC, Allenby 6/V, 42
3. LHC, Allenby 6/V, 18
4. LHC, Allenby 6/VI, 1; Wavell, 119–20
5. LHC, Allenby 6/V, 19
6. Gough, *Soldiering On*, 95–6
7. LHC, Allenby 6/VIII, 52; Edmonds III/2, 15–16
8. J. F. C. Fuller, 5, 7–8
9. Spiers, 248
10. LHC, Allenby 6/V, 18
11. *Report of the Royal Commission on the War in South Africa*, II, 306, 403

12. *Ibid.*, 294; PRO, WO 108/263
13. PRO, WO 108/267, 4
14. Wavell, 117n
15. Anglesey, 422
16. PRO, WO 106/50
17. Beckett, 169
18. LHC, Allenby 6/V, 8
19. LHC, Allenby 7/I, 9
20. Beckett, 266
21. *Ibid.*
22. *Ibid.*, 276
23. *Ibid.*, 124
24. LHC, Allenby 6/VII, 36

6 With the Cavalry to the Front: August 1914–April 1915

1. LHC, Allenby 1/5, 5
2. Barrow, 142
3. PRO, WO 95/1; Spears, 138
4. PRO, WO 95/1109 (11th Hussars), 21.8.14
5. PRO, WO 95/1 (GHQ), 21.8.14; WO 33/713, 59
6. Charteris, *Haig* 93–4
7. PRO, WO 95/1109 (11th Hussars), 27.8.14, App. A, 26.8.14
8. NLS, Haldane 27.8.14
9. Barrow, 149
10. LHC, Liddell Hart II/1926, 14.6.26 (interview with General Shea)
11. Gough, *Fifth Army*, 23, 26
12. LHC, Edmonds III/9, 5B
13. LHC, Allenby 6/VI, 10, 45
14. LHC, Allenby 6/VI, 10
15. Terraine, *Mons*, 98–9; PRO, WO 95/1113 (9th Lancers), App. I
16. NLS, Haig, 24.8.14; LHC, Allenby 6/VI, 48; 6/VII, 40; PRO, WO 79/62, Vaughan to Murray, 24.6.19, 27.7.19
17. PRO, WO 95/1 (GHQ) n.n.
18. PRO, WO 33/713, 14
19. NLS, Haldane, 25.8.14 (Smith-Dorrien to Haldane, 3.5.19)
20. PRO, Cab. 103/113, 90 (Edmonds to Acheson, 26.7.50)
21. PRO, WO 33/713, 91, 102
22. PRO, WO 33/713, 136
23. PRO, WO 33/713, 156–7
24. Terraine, *Mons*, 173–5
25. NLS, Haig, 7,9,10.8.14

26. LHC, Allenby 1/5, 6
27. LHC, Allenby 1/5, 6; Allenby 6/VI, 11
28. LHC, Allenby 6/VI, 16
29. LHC, Allenby 6/V, 29
30. LHC, Allenby 1/5, 13
31. PRO, WO 95/1109 (11th Hussars) 30.10.14
32. PRO, WO 33/713, 906
33. LHC, Allenby 1/5, 45
34. PRO, WO 95/575 (Cavalry Divisional HQ), Apps. 100 and 116

7 An Offensive Spirit: April–December 1915

1. LHC, Edmonds III/9, 23
2. D. French, 64–5
3. PRO, WO 158/17, 27; WO 159/4, 12
4. PRO, WO 159/4, 1
5. H. Wilson, *Diaries*, I, 205
6. PRO, WO 158/17, 20
7. OH, *France and Belgium, 1915*, I, 338
8. NLS, Haldane, 20, 22.4.15
9. NLS, Haig, 5.5.15
10. NAM, Beer, 5.8.15
11. NLS, Haldane, 30.5.15
12. Duguid, 401,413; PRO, WO 744 (V Corps HQ), 8–9.5.15
13. LHC, Allenby 6/VI, 27
14. Duguid, 407; PRO, WO 95/744 (V Corps HQ) 23.5.15
15. PRO, WO 95/744 (V Corps HQ), App. GX 1149
16. NLS, Haldane, 10.6.15
17. PRO, WO 95/744 (V Corps HQ), App. GX 1245
18. NLS, Haldane, 4.6.15
19. NLS, Haldane, 4.6.15
20. NLS, Haldane, 6.6.15
21. PRO, WO 95/744 (V Corps HQ), App. GX 1484
22. OH, *France and Belgium, 1915*, II, 78
23. *Ibid.*, II, 101; PRO, WO 95/744 (V Corps HQ), App. GX 1461
24. NLS, Haldane, 16.6.15
25. LHC, Allenby 1/6, 8
26. OH, *France and Belgium*, 1915, I, 102
27. LHC, Allenby 1/6, 9
28. PRO, WO 95/744 (V Corps HQ), App. GX 1456
29. PRO, WO 95/744 (V Corps HQ), App. GX 1475
30. PRO, WO 95/744 (V Corps HQ), Allenby to Milne, 18.6.15

31. Travers, 85
32. PRO, WO 158/17, 286–7; NLS, Haig, 22.12.15, 14.1.16
33. J. G. Fuller, 2, 65; Barrow, 159
34. PRO, WO 95/745 (V Corps HQ), App. GX 2737; Report of Action on 25.9.15, 3–4, 7–9
35. LHC, Allenby 1/6, 16
36. PRO, WO 95/1 (GHQ: Commander-in-Chief's Diary), 19.8.14; NLS, Haldane, 4.9.14
37. Babington, 7; PRO, WO 159/2, 11
38. PRO, Cab. 45/116 (Col. A. D. M. Browne)
39. Travers, 20, 205; LHC, Edmonds III/12, 16–17; Babington 130–2
40. *Ibid.*, 39–40
41. Crozier, 54, 60, 71, 88
42. Hurst, 324–5
43. LHC, Liddell Hart 11/1934, 36
44. Travers, 21–2
45. Montgomery, 35–6
46. Manning, 181–2
47. NLS, Haig, 25.4.17
48. LHC, Allenby 6/VII, 27
49. LHC, Allenby 6/VI, 34; Edmonds III/2, 34
50. LHC, Allenby 6/V, 32
51. NLS, Haldane, 5.6.15
52. NLS, Haldane 16.6.15, 8.11.16
53. Brenan, 202

8 Under Haig's Command: January–December 1916

1. PRO, Cab. 103/113, 94
2. Travers, 101
3. LHC, Liddell Hart 11/1937, 45
4. NLS, Haldane, 7.11.16
5. NLS, Haig, 24.1.16
6. Liddell Hart, *History of the First World War*, 411–12; Charteris, *At GHQ*, 10–11, 210–11
7. Terraine, *Haig*, 308
8. Gardner, 93; Haldane, 8.8.16
9. Repington, I, 269, 285; Wavell, 170
10. LHC, Edmonds III/10, 4
11. Repington, I, 573
12. Barrow, 157
13. PRO, WO 159/4, 27

14. NLS, Haig, 18.3.16
15. PRO, WO 33/806, 4105
16. De Groot, 346
17. J. G. French, 187; PRO, WO 33/806, 3990
18. Dallas and Gill, 74
19. NLS, Haig, 21.5.16; de Groot, 251–2
20. PRO, WO 33/806, 3630
21. NLS, Haig, 1.3.16
22. PRO, WO 95/2745 (HQ 48th Division), 6.12.15
23. NAM, Rawlinson, 17, 21 and 24.2.16
24. OH, *France and Flanders, 1916*, I, 455, 450
25. *Ibid.*, 461–2; PRO, WO 95/360 (HQ Third Army) July, App. 3–4, 8–9; Gibbs, 65, 69; MacDonald, *Somme*, 66
26. OH, *France and Flanders, 1916*, I, 474–5
27. Wavell, 169
28. OH, *France and Flanders, 1916*, I, 491
29. *Ibid.*, 491–2
30. NAM, Rawlinson, 1.8.16
31. PRO, WO 95/360 (HQ Third Army), 30.8.16
32. NLS, Haldane, 7,8, and 27.11.16
33. Dunn, 358

9 Unstuck at Arras: January–June 1917

1. LHC, Allenby 1/8, 1
2. PRO, WO 159/2, 11
3. Charteris, *Haig*, 231
4. NLS, Haig, 24.4.17
5. NLS, Haig, 8.4.17 (Haig to Robertson); Repington, I, 535
6. De Groot, 312
7. Bidwell and Graham, 71
8. PRO, Cab. 45/116 (General Sir Charles Fergusson)
9. PRO, Cab. 45/116 (N. Birch)
10. OH, *France and Flanders, 1917*, I, 177–8, 541; PRO, WO 158/312, 17
11. PRO, Cab. 45/116 (Colonel C. E. Vickery)
12. Bidwell and Graham, 96
13. LHC, Edmonds III/12, 10
14. PRO, WO 95/361 (HQ Third Army), March 1917, App. D 1
15. Jones, III, 335–9
16. PRO, Cab. 45/200, I
17. PRO, WO 157/150, 17 and 21.3.17; Liddell Hart, *History of the First World War*, 411. See also Kahn, 313–14, for Allied code-breaking

18. PRO, WO 157/151, App. Summary 644 (24.4.17); after this revelation, GHQ warned all officers not to refer to Allied intercepts and code-breaking in wireless or telephone signals (WO 95/1583, App. April)
19. NLS, Haig, 2,4,5 and 17.4.17
20. NLS, Haldane, 30.3.17
21. PRO, Cab. 45/116 (General Sir Cyril Deverell)
22. PRO, Cab. 45/116 (H. Tudor)
23. PRO, Cab. 45/116 (Lieutenant-Colonel G. W. Abercromby)
24. PRO, Cab. 45/116 (Lieutenant-Colonel H. Lee)
25. OH, *France and Flanders, 1917*, I, 220–1; Repington, I, 527–8; PRO, Cab. 45/116 (Colonel C. E. Vickery)
26. PRO, WO 157/150, 5.3.17
27. PRO, WO 95/361 (HQ Third Army) April, App. A 41–2; NLS, Haldane, 8.4.17
28. PRO, Cab. 45/116 (E. R. Makins)
29. PRO, WO 95/361 (HQ Third Army) April, App. A 73
30. Dolden, 118; PRO, Cab. 45/116 (H. Braine)
31. PRO, WO 157/151, 10.5.17
32. PRO, WO 95/13 (GHQ), App. 33, 39
33. NLS, Haig, 10.4.17
34. NLS, Haldane, 10.4.17
35. PRO, WO 95/362 (HQ Third Army) April, App. A 112; OH, *France and Flanders, 1917*, II, 258–9
36. Dunn, 327
37. PRO, Cab. 45/116 (General Sir Charles Fergusson)
38. LHC, Allenby I/8, 4
39. PRO, WO 157/151, 10.4.17
40. NLS, Haig 12,13 and 14.4.17
41. NLS, Haig, 11,12,13 and 14.4.17
42. *The Fifth Battalion, The Cameronians (Scottish Rifles), 1914–1918*, 109
43. PRO, Cab. 103/113, 101–2; Edmonds, *A Short History of World War I*, 234; NLS, Haig, 14.4.17; OH, *France and Flanders, 1917*, I, 378–9, glossed over the incident to spare Allenby's embarrassment
44. NLS, Haig, 14.4.17; Haldane, 10.4.17
45. PRO, WO 158/311 (Minutes of Noyelle Vion conference, 30.4.17)
46. Repington, I, 534; PRO, WO 95/361 (HQ Third Army), App. A 279; NLS, Haldane, 28.4.17
47. PRO, WO 95/361 (HQ Third Army), App. A 30
48. PRO, WO 158/311 (Minutes of the Douellens conference, 7.5.17)
49. *Ibid.*
50. Atteridge, 220–1
51. NLS, Haig, 12.5.17

52. NLS, Haig, 22.5.16; 5.6.17
53. PRO, WO 158/311 (Minutes of Douellens conference, 5.6.17)
54. LHC, Allenby 6/VII, 56
55. LHC, Allenby 6/V, 33. Wavell, the recipient of this tale, was appalled, and noted in the margin, 'The sort of remark Haldane would make if he thought it safe, but he would kow-tow to Allenby as long as his wretched career depended on it'
56, LHC, Allenby 6/VI, 31

PART III ARMAGEDDON: JUNE 1917–NOVEMBER 1918

10 Middle East Command: June–September 1917

1. PRO, Cab. 45/80 (Field-Marshal Sir William Robertson); Robertson, *Military Correspondence*, 210
2. Robertson, *Military Correspondence*, 233
3. Elder, 341–2; PRO, WO 106/109
4. LHC, Allenby 7/1, 9
5. PRO, WO 33/935, 7561; Repington, I, 610
6. RHL, Meinertzhagen, 16 and 29.6.17; PRO, Cab. 45/80 (Brigadier-General J. T. Wigan)
7. Idriess, 306
8. Gullett, 357
9. RHL, Meinertzhagen, 15.7.17; see also Massey, 37, and Guy Powles, 122, 133, for the New Zealander's favourable reactions
10. LHC, Allenby 6/VIII, 48
11. LHC, Allenby 1/6, 12
12. LHC, Allenby 6/IX, 15
13. LHC, Allenby 6/VIII, 48; Guy Powles, 223
14. LHC, Edmonds, II, 1, Allenby to Edmonds, 25.8.20
15. LHC, Allenby 6/VIII, 43
16. Gullett, 358
17. PRO, WO 33/935, 7733; WO 106/716 and 726, 16; WO 95/4267 (EEF, GS Ops), 12.7.16
18. Jones, V, 225; 229–30
19. PRO, WO 33/905, 6558 and 5670A; Gullett, 303, 310–13
20. PRO, Cab. 45/79 (General Sir Archibald Murray); Gullett 300–1
21. PRO, WO 33/905, 7925; WO 106/612, 1.10.17; Idriess, 411
22. PRO, WO 33/935, 7827; Robertson, *Military Correspondence*, 209–10
23. PRO, WO 33/935, 7928; Robertson, *Military Correspondence*, 213–14

24. Connell, 126–7
25. PRO, WO 106/726, 4; Robertson, *Military Correspondence*, 227
26. Robertson, *Military Correspondence*, 262
27. PRO, WO 33/935, 8444; WO 33/946, 8350; Jones, V, 231
28. Jones, V, 228
29. PRO, WO 33/935, 7779A
30. LHC, Allenby 6/VIII, 63; IX/18
31. Connell, 124
32. LHC, Allenby 6/IX, 33
33. Hill, 119
34. PRO, WO 106/614,4
35. Boyle, 90
36. Macpherson, Horrocks and Beveridge, II, 226, 238
37. PRO, FO 141/466/1429, I, 9 (Report of the Cairo Purification Committee)
38. LHC, Allenby 6/VIII, 17; Barrett and Deane, 209
39. PRO, WO 33/935,7821
40. PRO, FO 141/466/1429,II,50 (enclosure)
41. Robertson, *Military Correspondence*, 214; PRO, WO 33/935, 7782
42. PRO, Cab. 45/80 (H.St J. Philby)
43. James, 148
44. *Ibid.*, 174
45. RHL, Meinertzhagen, 10 and 17.12.17
46. James, 185
47. There was ill-feeling between Lawrence and Vickery (J. Wilson, 350–1); the latter made what were scandalous allegations to Lady Scott, the explorer's widow, in 1922. When she confronted Lawrence with them, he admitted his 'proclivities' to her. I owe this revealing detail to Mrs Elspeth Huxley and Lord Kennett, Lady Scott's son
48. RHL, Meinertzhagen, 16.5.36; his recollection was confirmed by Dalmeny in a letter to Lady Allenby (Gardner, 147)
49. Gardner, 145–6
50. LHC, Allenby 6/VIII, 12, 14
51. Gardner, 147
52. *Ibid.*, 146
53. Falls, 52

11 The Fall of Jerusalem: September–December 1917

1. Von Sanders, 176
2. Von Sanders, 28–9, 190–1; Emin, 88–9; Pick, *passim*
3. Emin, 89; Wavell, *Palestine Campaigns*, 113

4. PRO, WO 33/935, 8068; WO 106/612, 10.9.17; WO 106/726, 6; Wavell, *Palestine Campaigns*, 98–9, 108–10
5. LHC, Allenby 6/VIII, 21
6. Wavell, *Palestine Campaigns*, 106–7; RHL, Meinertzhagen, 10.10.17
7. James, 204–5
8. PRO, WO 33/935, 8371
9. PRO, WO 33/935, 8317
10. PRO, WO 106/1514; Trumpener, 159–60
11. PRO, WO/935, 8350
12. Wavell, 211; Gullett, 393–4
13. RHL, Meinertzhagen, 8.11.17; PRO Cab. 45/79 (A. C. Temperley)
14. Teichman, 174
15. *Ibid*, 184–5
16. Idriess, 342
17. Jones, V, 242–4
18. PRO, WO 33/946, 8550
19. RHL, Meinertzhagen, 10.11.17; IWM, Dawnay 2; Wavell, *Palestine Campaigns*, 150
20. IWM, Dawnay 2
21. Wavell, *Palestine Campaigns*, 223
22. LHC, Allenby I/14/2, 32
23. PRO, WO 33/946, 8622
24. Wavell, *Palestine Campaigns*, 163
25. Anon., *Cavalry Journal*, (28) 51
26. Barrow, *Cavalry Journal*, 14; Barrow, 187–8
27. PRO, WO 33/946, 8583–5
28. Hill, 136n
29. PRO, WO 33/946, 8693
30. PRO, WO 33/946, 8693; Gardner, 161
31. *Hansard*, Fifth Series, C (1917), 875
32. *Guardian*, 20.12.17
33. *Morning Post*, 17.12.17
34. *Spectator*, 15.12.17
35. *Saturday Review*, 15.12.17
36. *Illustrated London News*, 19.1.18
37. *Saturday Review*, 15.12.17
38. Wavell, *Allenby, a Study in Greatness* 236–7
39. Idriess, 289–90
40. Wavell, *Allenby, a Study in Greatness* 235
41. RHL, Meinertzhagen, 16.5.36
42. Hill, 133–4

12 Marking Time: January–August 1918

1. Wasserstein, 21n.; Weizmann, 322
2. PRO, WO 33/946, 8741
3. PRO, WO33/946, 8813
4. PRO, WO 95/4369 (EEF GHQ), App. B, 2.1.28
5. PRO, WO 106/726, 6
6. Trumpener, 194
7. Von Sanders, 196; Weber, 245
8. Robertson, *Military Correspondence*, 262
9. *Ibid.*, 282
10. LHC, Allenby 6/IX, 5
11. PRO, WO 33/946, 9040, 9093; WO 106/729
12. PRO, WO 33/935, 7821
13. Robertson, *Military Correspondence*, 262
14. PRO, WO 33/946, 9142
15. LHC, Allenby 6/IX, 7
16. Pirie Gordon, 29.4.18; WO 33/946, 9358B
17. Wavell, *Palestine Campaigns*, 184–5; Preston, 244; Hill, 149
18. LHC, Allenby 6/IX, 17
19. Guy Powles, 200–1
20. Robertson, *Military Correspondence*, 263
21. Preston, 244; Gullett, 682
22. LHC, Allenby 7/4, 2; Gullett, 630–1; Hill, 146
23. PRO, WO 33/946, 8884
24. RHL, Meinertzhagen, 2.12.17
25. For instance, PRO, WO 95/4725 (Lines of Communication), Reports for March and June 1918; WO 154/164 (Anzac Mounted Division, Assistant Provost-Marshal), 5, 7, 31.10.18; Teichman, 159–60; Gullett, 359
26. PRO, WO 106/619, 59
27. PRO, Cab. 45/80 (H. Pirie Gordon)
28. Gullett, 382, 784; Guy Powles, 121
29. *Neue Orient*, 5.10.17, quoted in *Daily Review of the Enemy Press, Foreign Press Supplement* (1917–18), 406
30. PRO, WO 106/619, 36
31. Wavell, *Allenby, a Study in Greatness*, 237
32. PRO, WO 33/946, 8884; Wingate was also worried (Cab. 23/25, 24.1.18)
33. J. Wilson, 536–7
34. Boyle, 119; Guy Powles, 154–5
35. PRO, WO 33/946, 9160, 9207, 9237

36. Weizmann, 273
37. PRO, WO 33/946, 8609
38. Lawrence, *Seven Pillars of Wisdom*, 455
39. PRO, WO 33/946, 8958
40. LHC, Allenby 6/IX, 7
41. Weizmann, 274–5
42. PRO, WO 106/613, 24.5.18
43. Weizmann, 295
44. PRO, WO 95/4491 (HQ XX Corps), April 1918, App. 15
45. PRO, WO 158/621, 26.2.18, 1.7.18
46. PRO, WO 33/946, 9698, 9713, 9733
47. LHC, Allenby 6/IX, 5
48. PRO, WO 33/946, 9726
49. PRO, WO 33/946, 9783
50. PRO, WO 33/946, 9225, 9323
51. PRO, WO 33/946, 9651; LHC, Allenby 6/IX, 7
52. PRO, Cab. 45/79 (P. Gill and M. T. Hodgson)
53. PRO, WO 33/960, 9961, 9971
54. PRO, WO 95/4510 (HQ 4th Cavalry Division), Standing Orders, May 1918
55. PRO, WO 33/946, 9651, 9853
56. PRO, WO 33/946, 9877

13 Out for Blood: September–November 1918

1. PRO, WO 106/621, 27.8.18; WO 106/623, 23, 84, 90
2. PRO, WO 106/623, 84
3. LHC, Allenby 1/9,1
4. Jones, VI, 210; Preston, 267; Gullett, 686
5. Preston, 178; Macpherson, Horrocks and Beveridge, II, 215, 226
6. Pirie Gordon, 18.9.18
7. PRO, WO 106/623, 18, 84
8. Falls, *Armageddon*, 63
9. PRO, WO 106/621, 27.8.18
10. PRO, WO 106/623, 12
11. Jones, VI, 214–15
12. LHC, Allenby 1/9,1
13. Hill, 172
14. LHC, Allenby 1/9,2
15. Jones, VI, 226
16. PRO, WO 95/4371 (Warwickshire Yeomanry)
17. Massey, *Allenby's Final Triumph*, 185

18. RHL, Meinertzhagen, 5.5.37
19. Falls, *Armageddon*, 89–90, 98–9; Hill, 166
20. PRO, WO 33/960, 9000
21. PRO, WO 33/960, 10154
22. Hill, 174–5
23. J. Wilson, 549–50
24. PRO, WO 95/4371 (EEF GHQ), 1 September, Apps. M and O.
25. BL, Milner 452, 54
26. PRO, WO 95/4513 (2nd [Indian] Lancers), 28.9.18; WO 95/4510 (HQ 4th Cavalry Division), Narrative of Operations, 9–10
27. Barrow, 210–11
28. James, 254–6
29. LHC, Allenby 1/9, 12
30. PRO, Cab. 45/80 (Major G. White). White was Brigade Major for the 4th Cavalry Division and his narrative of the events of 30 September to 1 October is a useful corrective to other versions
31. PRO, WO 95/4515 (HQ 5th Cavalry Division), 1.10.18
32. PRO, Cab. 45/80 (White)
33. LHC, Allenby 7/4, 1 (where Chauvel states that Muhammad Said's brother, Abd al Qadir made the surrender to Olden); other accounts of the incident are in Pirie Gordon, 1.10.18; Gullett, Barrett and Baker, 43, 46–7; and Preston, 267. The claims for an Arab occupation are examined and dismissed in Kedourie, *The Chatham House Version*, 148–9, and Hill, 177–8
34. PRO, Cab. 45/80 (White)
35. Hill, 179–82
36. Massey, *Allenby's Final Triumph*, 261; Preston, 280; Hill, 182
37. PRO, WO 33/960, 10185
38. Hill, 184
39. LHC, Allenby 1/9, 12
40. PRO, WO 33/960, 101209
41. Hill, 184–5
42. PRO, WO 33/960, 10213
43. LHC, Allenby 1/9,12
44. BL, Milner 452, 67
45. PRO, Adm. 137/872, 568
46. PRO, Adm. 137/872, 570; WO 33/960, 10241, 10281
47. H. Wilson, *Military Correspondence*, 54
48. LHC, Allenby 1/9, 15
49. PRO, WO 33/960, 10281; H. Wilson, *Military Correspondence*, 55
50. PRO, WO 33/960, 10421; H. Wilson, *Military Correspondence*, 54
51. H. Wilson, *Military Correspondence*, 54–5

52. PRO, WO 33/960, 10316, 10334
53. OH, *Egypt and Palestine*, II, ii, 597–8
54. Lambert, 318–9
55. OH, *Egypt and Palestine*, II, ii, 642
56. *Ibid.*, 598–9

PART IV IMPERIAL PROCONSUL: NOVEMBER 1918–JUNE 1925

14 White Mutinies and Brown Mischief: November 1918–June 1919

1. H. Wilson, *Military Correspondence*, 51
2. LHC, Allenby 2/5, 9
3. PRO, WO 33/960, 10466
4. H. Wilson, *Military Correspondence*, 61
5. PRO, WO 95/4744 (Desert Mounted Corps), App. 1, 12.1.18; WO 95/4372 (EEF GHQ), 25.1.19, 21.4.19
6. PRO, WO 45/4372 (EEF, GHQ), 1.11.18; WO 95/4744 (Desert Mounted Corps), January 1919, App. D; WO 33/960, 10466, 10802
7. PRO, WO 95/4744 (Desert Mounted Corps), Narrative, February 1919, Apps. 119 and 121
8. Anon., *Cavalry Journal*, 1924, 457–8; Preston, 297; PRO, WO 33/960. 10802; WO 95/4744 (Desert Mounted Corps), Narrative, February 1919, App. GA 379
9. PRO, WO 33/960, 10788, 10560
10. PRO, WO 33/960, 10642, 10721
11. H. Wilson, *Military Correspondence*, 61
12. PRO, WO 95/4372 (EEF GHQ), November 1918, App. D, 478
13. *Papers Relating to the Foreign Relations of the United States; the Paris Peace Conference*, V, 11; Lloyd George, II, 692
14. *Ibid.*
15. PRO, WO 95/4372 (EEF GHQ), November 1918, App. B, 163
16. Darwin, 155
17. PRO, WO 33/960, 10466; Dallas and Gill, 123
18. PRO, WO 33/960, 10780
19. PRO, WO 154/164, 5.7, 31.10.18; Guy Powles, 266–7; Brugger, 80–1
20. LHC, Allenby 6/IX,7; Hill, 192
21. Hill, 192–3
22. LHC, Allenby 6/IX, 7; A. F. Naylor (Military Governor of Beersheba), letter to *The Times*, 29.5.64
23. Gullett, 790–1; Hill, 193

24. PRO, WO 95/4518 (Gloucestershire Hussars), 11–12.1.19; WO 33/ 960, 10778
25. PRO, WO 33/960, 10771, 10778, 10780
26. Dallas and Gill, 124
27. PRO, WO 95/4470 (Demobilisation Camp, al Qantara)
28. LHC, Allenby 1/10,7
29. RHL, Meinertzhage, 19.11.19
30. *Foreign Relations of the United States; the Paris Peace Conference*, V, 11; Lloyd George, II, 692
31. PRO, FO 848/2, Balfour to Wingate, 20.3.19, Curzon to Wingate, 21.3.19; FO 371/3714,m 204, 206, 290
32. Bishku, 51
33. BL, Milner 452, 87–102
34. LHC, Allenby 2/5,22
35. BL, Milner 445, 140
36. *Ibid.*, 138
37. PRO, FO 848/2, Wingate to Harding, 14.11.18
38. BL, Milner 452, 72, 79
39. Lockman, 272; Hinnebusch, 100–1
40. PRO, FO 371/3714, 53, 57, 93A
41. PRO, WO 95/4402 (Huddlestone's Force), App. 1
42. PRO, WO 95/4372 (EEF GHQ), May 1919, App. B, G66/3; Gwynn, 73; Brugger, 116
43. PRO, FO 371/3714, 196
44. PRO, WO 95/4372 (EEF GHQ), May 1919, App. B, G66/3; Gwynn, 74–5
45. PRO, Air 1/21/1/102, 65; FO 371/3714, 286
46. PRO, FO 141/825/1132, 16 (EEF Morale Report from Correspondence); WO 33/981, 11045 for Indian dislike of Egyptians; Brugger, 112
47. BL, Milner 445/1 (Reply to charges brought against British troops by Egyptian delegates during the Egyptian disturbances [August 1919]), 7
48. Gwynn, 80; Kiernan, 191, Brugger, 117–18
49. LHC, Allenby 1/10,7; PRO, FO 371/3714, 282
50. Terry, 110
51. Young, 87; Terry, 109; Bishku, 52
52. Terry, 109
53. PRO, FO 141/825/1132, 16
54. BL, Milner 446, 55; 452, 105, 112; Terry, 110–11
55. BL, Milner (MS Eng. Hist. c. 699), 109
56. PRO, WO 154/164, April 1919, App. 1
57. PRO, FO 141/825/1132, 14

58. BL, Milner (MS Eng. Hist. c. 699) 108–9
59. PRO, WO 33/995, 11865, 11887
60. H. Wilson, *Military Correspondence*, 98–9
61. PRO, WO 33/981, 11120–1, 11043; Dallas and Gill, 129
62. Quoted in Young, 242
63. PRO, WO 33/981, 11052
64. Dallas and Gill, 127
65. PRO, WO 33/981, 11052
66. PRO, WO 33/981, 11121
67. Dallas and Gill, 127
68. PRO, WO 95/4402 (Massey's Force), 9.4.19; WO 95/4470 (Army Service Corps, 493 Motor Transport Section), 15.1.19
69. H. Wilson, *Military Correspondence*, 102
70. *Documents on British Foreign Policy 1919–1939*, IV, 268–9
71. PRO, WO 33/981, 11070
72. H. Wilson, *Military Correspondence*, 202–3
73. PRO, WO 33/981, 11098
74. Khoury, 183–4
75. PRO, WO 33/981, 11173
76. PRO, WO 33/981, 11179
77. *Documents on British Foreign Policy 1919–1939*, IV, 259–60
78. *Ibid.*, 256–7; PRO, WO 33/981, 11173
79. PRO, WO 33/960, 10741; WO 95/4372 (EEF GHQ), May 1919, App. A
80. PRO, WO 33/981, 11648 (3.12.19)

15 Shifting Sands: September 1919–March 1922

1. H. Wilson, *Military Correspondence*, 61
2. BL, Milner 446, 305–6
3. *Documents on British Foreign Policy 1919–1939*, IV, 309
4. *Ibid.*, 384–5; H. Wilson, *Life and Diaries*, II, 212
5. BL, Milner 446, 305–6
6. PRO, WO 33/995, 11926
7. PRO, FO 141/819/13992, 1, 6
8. LHC, Allenby 1/10,10; Terry, 113
9. PRO, FO 141/640/9655
10. Lockman, 276
11. PRO, FO 141/505/13608 (Commandant of Police, Cairo to Allenby), 23.1.22
12. RHL, Meinertzhagen, 6.1.20
13. Wavell, *Allenby in Egypt*, 53–4

14. PRO, WO 95/4402 (GS, Upper Egypt) 15.4.19
15. PRO, FO 848/11, 1,30 (Milner to Curzon), 18.12.19
16. PRO, WO 141/657/16464, 87
17. BL, Milner 453, 45–6; Terry, 131
18. PRO, FO 141/434/10684, 1,4,14,17,20,21,25,36,47,48
19. PRO, FO 848/11 F (Milner to Curzon), 10.12.19
20. PRO, FO 371/10039 (Sudan Intelligence Report October 1923)
21. PRO, FO 848/5,44
22. PRO, FO 371/8960, 322–3
23. Bishku, 86
24. *The Times*, 20.5.21
25. PRO, FO 141/517/13333, 28
26. H. Wilson, *Military Correspondence*, 325
27. LHC, Allenby 2/5,11
28. Wavell, *Allenby in Egypt*, 45
29. H. Wilson, *Military Correspondence*, 325
30. PRO, FO 141/434/10684, 35
31. RHL, Meinertzhagen, 24.12.24
32. LHC, Allenby 2/5, 11; RHL, Meinertzhagen n.d. (Vol. 22, 122)
33. Wavell, *Allenby in Egypt*, 77

16 Death and the Nile: April 1922–June 1925

1. Wavell, *Allenby in Egypt*, 56
2. LHC, Allenby 1/10,8
3. Wavell, *Allenby in Egypt*, 56
4. Terry, 153
5. PRO, FO 371/8960, 239, 333, E 2619
6. PRO, FO 8960, 305–10
7. PRO, FO 141/657/16464, 70,78
8. Zayid, 118–19
9. BL, Milner 453, 239–40
10. PRO, FO 371/10039 (Sudan Intelligence Report, March 1924), 2
11. PRO, FO 371/10039 (Sudan Intelligence Report, July–August 1924), 9
12. PRO, FO 371/10039 (Sudan Intelligence Report, December 1924), 9–12
13. PRO, FO 371/10053, 3
14. PRO, FO 371/10053, 144; Gwynne, 156
15. For details of the Stack assassination, see LHC, Allenby 7/1, 4, 9, 15, 19; PRO, FO 141/502/17490, I, 1, 112
16. LHC, Allenby 7/1, 19
17. PRO, FO 141/502/17490,I,4

18. PRO, FO 141/502/17490, I, 3, 6, 21
19. PRO, FO 141/502/17490, I, 17
20. PRO, FO 141/502/17490, I, 5, 16
21. PRO, FO 141/502/17490, I, 34
22. *Ibid.*
23. PRO, FO 141/502/17490, I, 37
24. PRO, FO 141/502/17490, I, 23A
25. PRO, FO 141/493/17507, 199, 240A; Terry, 175
26. Terry, 172, 180
27. *Ibid.*, 172
28. LHC, Allenby 2/3, 1
29. LHC, Allenby 2/3, 7
30. LHC, Allenby 2/3, 12
31. PRO, FO 371/10883 J 306, 4.1.25
32. LHC, Allenby 2/3, 17
33. PRO, FO 371/10883 J 306 (Allenby to Foreign Office), 29.1.25
34. LHC, Allenby 2/3, 18
35. LHC, Allenby 2/3, 31
36. PRO, FO 141/493/17507, 259; Terry, 176

PART V FINAL YEARS: JULY 1925–MAY 1936

17 Final Years 1925–1936

1. *Hansard's Parliamentary Debates*, Fifth Series, House of Lords, LXXV, 530–1, 1111-13
2. *Ibid.*, LXXVI, 135–6
3. LHC, Allenby 1/14, 6; 1/10, 29
4. See PRO, FO 141/582/9214 for Allenby's financial problems in 1919–20
5. LHC, Allenby 6/IX, 17

PART VI THE MAN AND HIS TIMES

18 The Man and his Times

1. LHC, Liddell Hart, 11/1934/41
2. LHC, Allenby 2/5, 20
3. PRO, WO 33/981, 11648, 11691
4. PRO, FO 141/825, 1132, 52

5. Wasserstein, 81
6. PRO, WO 32/9614, 22
7. Weizmann, 401
8. PRO, FO 141/453/6347, 6
9. LHC, Edmonds, III, 2, 15
10. PRO, WO 106/613, 7.3.18
11. LHC, Allenby 7/4, 1
12. LHC, Allenby 7/4, 8
13. J. Wilson, 799
14. James, 191–2
15. H. Wilson, *Military Correspondence*, 295
16. PRO, FO 141/466/1415, 8, 12, 15, 17

INDEX